The Gospel of John

THE GOSPEL OF JOHN

Theological-Ecumenical Readings

Edited by
CHARLES RAITH II

CASCADE *Books* · Eugene, Oregon

THE GOSPEL OF JOHN
Theological-Ecumenical Readings

Copyright © 2017 Wipf and Stock Publishers. All rights reserved. Except for brief quotations in critical publications or reviews, no part of this book may be reproduced in any manner without prior written permission from the publisher. Write: Permissions, Wipf and Stock Publishers, 199 W. 8th Ave., Suite 3, Eugene, OR 97401.

Cascade Books
An Imprint of Wipf and Stock Publishers
199 W. 8th Ave., Suite 3
Eugene, OR 97401

www.wipfandstock.com

PAPERBACK ISBN: 978-1-5326-0126-2
HARDCOVER ISBN: 978-1-5326-0128-6
EBOOK ISBN: 978-1-5326-0127-9

Cataloguing-in-Publication data:

Names: Raith, Charles, II, editor.
Title: The Gospel of John : theological-ecumenical readings / edited by Charles Raith II.
Description: Eugene, OR: Cascade Books, 2017 | Includes bibliographical references.
Identifiers: ISBN 978-1-5326-0126-2 (paperback) | ISBN 978-1-5326-0128-6 (hardcover) | ISBN 978-1-5326-0127-9 (ebook)
Subjects: LCSH: Bible. John—Criticism, interpretation, etc. | Bible. John—Theology. | subject | subject
Classification: BS2615.2 G6 2017 (paperback) | BS2615.2 (ebook)

Manufactured in the U.S.A.   03/02/17

To Hans Boersma and Matthew Levering:
friends, mentors, and examples of drinking deeply from the
Christian *paradosis*

Contents

Preface | ix

Introduction | 1

Chapter 1 ───────────────
Knowing the Gift of God: John 4:1–26 and the Living Water | 8
   —EDITH M. HUMPHREY (ORTHODOX)
Spiritual Interpretation After Modernity: A Response
to Edith Humphrey | 28
   —JENS ZIMMERMANN (EVANGELICAL)
John 4:1–26: Response to Edith Humphrey | 36
   —DANIEL A. KEATING (CATHOLIC)
Humphrey Final Response | 43

Chapter 2 ───────────────
John 8:1–11: Revisiting the Pericope Adulterae | 50
   —DAVID L. JEFFREY (EVANGELICAL)
The Pericope Adulterae in Ecumenical Perspective: A Response
from the Eastern Edges of Catholicism | 66
   —FR. PETER GALADZA (CATHOLIC)
Response to Professor David Jeffrey | 80
   —GEORGE PARSENIOS (ORTHODOX)
Jeffrey Final Response | 88

Chapter 3 ───────────────
John 11:1–44: God Who Raises the Dead | 92
   —TIMOTHY GEORGE (EVANGELICAL)
What is Dearest to Us? A Response to Timothy George | 105
   —MICHAEL WALDSTEIN (CATHOLIC)

The Revelation of Christ's Two Natures: A Hopeful Theodicy | 126
—John Mark Reynolds (Orthodox)

George Final Response | 139

Chapter 4 ─────────────────────────────────

John 17: A Theological Reading for an Ecumenical Audience | 145
—R. R. Reno (Catholic)

Response to Dr. Reno | 158
—Richard Mouw (Evangelical)

Perichoretic Ecumenism Inspired by John 17: A Response
to Prof. R. R. Reno | 168
—Paul Gavrilyuk (Orthodox)

Reno Final Response | 173

Chapter 5 ─────────────────────────────────

John 18:28—19:16: Witnessing Truth | 177
—Fr. John Behr (Orthodox)

You Shall Judge Angels: A Response to Fr. Behr | 191
—Peter Leithart (Evangelical)

Advocacy and Justification: Christ, the Paraclete and Ecclesial
Scripture | 201
—Fr. Thomas Joseph White, OP (Catholic)

Behr Final Response | 214

Chapter 6 ─────────────────────────────────

John 21: Peter, John, and Jesus On the Beach | 218
—Michael Root (Catholic)

Response to Michael Root's John 21: Peter, John, and Jesus
on the Beach | 233
—D. H. Williams (Evangelical)

Giving Honor to Whom Honor Is Due: A Reply to Michael Root | 239
—David Bradshaw (Orthodox)

Root Final Response | 251

Bibliography | 257

Preface

IN THE FALL OF 2014, the Paradosis Center for Theology and Scripture at John Brown University held its first biennial conference. The conference, titled "Engaging the Gospel of John, Engaging One Another: Catholics, Orthodox and Evangelicals," was part of fulfilling the Paradosis Center's mission: "to bring together Christians from Catholic, Orthodox, and Evangelical backgrounds to have meaningful theological exchanges centered on Scripture and rooted in the Great Tradition, so that we might learn from one another and more fully live out in our contexts the tradition (*paradosis*) passed down from the beginning (cf. 2 Thess 2:15)." The unique structure of the conference enabled genuine theological-ecumenical engagement. The principal focus of the conference was the Gospel of John. All presenters understood themselves ultimately as providing a mutual contribution to one another's reception of the teachings contained in John's Gospel. At the same time, each session consisted of a main paper from either a Catholic, Orthodox or Evangelical scholar, with the main essay then being engaged by scholars from the other two traditions. Thanks to this format we are provided not only a textured reading of the Gospel of John but also a richer understanding of the way our theological commitments as Catholics, Orthodox and Evangelicals impact our approach to John's Gospel. We also discover how our different readings can work toward mutual enrichment, as well as ways our readings are simply at odds with one another. In the end the format enabled everyone to more deeply participate in the realities communicated to us by John.

Introduction

VETERAN ECUMENIST CARDINAL WALTER Kasper asserts, "The Bible, for both our church communities [Catholic and Protestant], is the fundamental document of our faith and I have the impression that we can make further fundamental progress by involving scripture study more fully in dogmatic questions."[1] This is the conviction underlying this volume. When Scripture is made a focal point for our theological-ecumenical engagement, the dialogue is prevented from coming unhinged from the common normative source that should consistently inform all such conversations. A loss in scriptural focus becomes a loss in appreciating how all of our theological commitments serve a common fundamental goal: "that you may come to believe that Jesus is the Messiah, the Son of God, and that through believing you may have life in his name" (John 20:31). Keeping the Gospel of John in focus keeps our theological conversation focused. It reminds everyone involved that our goal is not merely to perpetuate our ecclesial communities; rather, our communities are structured (we hope) out of the shared conviction that they facilitate genuine participation in the gospel of Jesus Christ.

Problematically, ecumenism has at times proceeded under the guise that *unity* is itself the shared ecumenical goal.[2] But identifying unity as the goal of our engagement necessarily turns our pursuit inward; that is, *we* become the focus of our ecumenical engagement. But our focus should be outward as we together pursue the fulfillment of the calling of Christ: "I press on toward the goal for the prize of the heavenly call of God in Christ Jesus" (Phil 3:14). Also, if unity is the goal, the means to obtaining it may not be theologically sound (as we have witnessed from many sectors of modern ecumenism). But by making the gospel of Jesus Christ our common focus,

---

1. Kasper, *That They Might All Be One*, 131.

2. E.g., The National Workshop on Christian Unity, whose stated goal is to "bring together all those involved in the work of Christian unity" with the hopes of "equipping those given the responsibility of seeking unity."

we avoid a reductionism that couches the sharing of "gifts" between ecclesial communities in generic concepts of generosity for the sake of an anthropocentric notion of unity. Instead, our sharing of gifts will be understood as serving the theo-centric goal of enabling one another to more deeply participate in that which Jesus Christ offers us.[3] And by allowing the shared norm of Scripture to guide our exchanges, we are forced out of a let-bygones-be-bygones (i.e., "differentiated consensus") attitude toward ecclesial identity.[4] Instead, our accountability to one other serves to further our appropriation of our common sources, all in the name of our ever-deeper participation in the love of the triune God.

At the same time, we do not proceed under the naive assumption that simply reading and interpreting the Bible using the best historical-critical tools—tools equally available to each reader explicitly apart from their ecclesial affiliation, with the tools themselves bearing the mark of no particular ecclesial context—will either yield the treasures contained in Scripture or move us forward in our Christian pursuits. In other words, we do not read Scripture despite our ecclesial commitments but rather in and through them. We have moved beyond the myth of the "neutral" interpreter and instead appreciate that a biblical text is always read from within a specific tradition and location. For this reason, the present volume makes explicit (rather than hiding) the participant's affiliation as Catholic, Orthodox, and Evangelical. Such explicit recognition of affiliation does not make the scholarship poorer, though it may run against certain academic presuppositions about "neutrality." To be sure, it does make the interaction more intense at times. But this is also what makes it more real.

We have also come some distance in appreciating how our prior philosophical and theological commitments influence our exegesis.[5] This recognition has helped undo the bifurcation of biblical exegesis and systematic theology. Thus while the majority of the contributors to this volume would be categorized by the guild as "theologians" rather than "biblical scholars," the volume proceeds under the assumption that such a bifurcation is unnecessary and in fact harmful. The volume can be thought of as an attempt to counter what Walter Moberly describes as the "severance" of biblical criticism from classical theological formulations.[6] Taking these various considerations into account, the volume proceeds on the assumption that

---

3. Hints of "receptive ecumenism" are clearly present here; see Murray, *Receptive Ecumenism*.

4. Yeago, "Spirit, the Church, and the Scriptures," 78.

5. Levering, *Participatory Biblical Exegesis*; Boersma, *Heavenly Participation*.

6. Moberly, *Bible, Theology, and Faith*, 4–5.

Scripture is most fruitfully read when it is approached from within the church's received tradition. This does not mean a simple restatement of the past (as if no room were available for creative proposals that move our understanding ever more deeply into revelation). But we should not assume that circumventing the inherited *regula fidei* is the way forward; rather a fruitful way forward must hold the working conviction that the Spirit of Christ has and will continue to guide his people into the "tradition" (*paradosis*) handed over by Christ to his apostles, and from the apostles down to us.

Yet this tradition-informed reading raises an issue of dialogic viability: our different ecclesial communities have sufficiently fundamental differences in our approaches to reading Scripture that simply placing before us the Gospel of John will not go far enough in facilitating meaningful exchange.[7] Doing so would result in our ecclesial ships simply passing in the night. Thus one ship (to stick with the metaphor) necessarily needs to take the lead to ensure a common point of navigation for the following vessels. The main essay of each chapter serves this purpose. The author of each lead essay was asked to read the Gospel of John explicitly within their ecclesial community. This approach to scriptural reading in an ecumenical setting creates the greatest potential for true gift exchange. Though the main essay leads the way, readers from within the different ecclesial communities force it out of its potential isolationist tendencies by engaging it from within their own traditions. In doing so the chapters taken as a whole provide both a richer mosaic of perspectives and a fuller reception of the Gospel of John than readings from a single theological tradition alone. Of course, the reading of the main essay might not be foreign to those of different ecclesial commitments; this is itself part of the dialogue: the recognition of genuine similarities, distinctions, and differences. And as the reader will see in what follows, the authors in this volume do not shy away from putting their scriptural and theological convictions on the table. We are all enriched as a result.

SUMMARY OF CHAPTERS

In chapter 1 Edith M. Humphrey reflects on John 4 and Jesus as the "living water." She lays out her broader theological approach right at the beginning: "God's plan is not to make us people of the written Word, but people resembling the Incarnate Word, God himself. *Theōsis* is a daunting calling." Humphrey then provides a textured reading of John 4 using the rough heuristic of

---

7. On the notion of "fundamental differences" in ecumenical dialogue, see Burgess, *In Search of Christian Unity*; Meyer, "Fundamental Difference," 247–59.

the fourfold sense of Scripture, which Humphrey has named "general" ("let any who thirst come"), "creedal" ("if you knew who it is"), "practical" ("go call your husband"), and "theotic" ("the hour is coming and is now here"). Jens Zimmermann's response targets Humphrey's underlying hermeneutic. Zimmermann seeks to clarify the kind of theological reading Humphrey practices, which is one that "by no means neglects historical-critical tools but subordinates them to a Christian, ecclesiastically-grounded reading of the scriptures." Zimmermann labels this a "Christian-humanistic reading" and unpacks the reasons why this reading will continue to challenge the "historical-critical *spirit*" prevalent in the academic guild of biblical studies. Zimmermann concludes that, "The real challenge of reading John's Gospel in a modern world, it seems to me, is to recover credibly a sacramental ontology to support the kind of reading Edith so beautifully exercised for us today." Daniel A. Keating picks up on Humphrey's fourfold reading, as well as Humphrey's use of both Western and Eastern theological sources and her reading's connection of the church to Judaism. Keating enriches Humphrey's reading by drawing on Thomas Aquinas as a later Western scholastic figure who works with the concerns and interconnections evidenced in Humphrey's paper. Keating thus reveals that Humphrey need not limit her allies only to those in the early patristic period; later Western scholastic theologians also share in her convictions.

David Jeffrey, in chapter 2, delves into into the heated debates surrounding the controversial *pericope adulterae* (John 7:53—8:11). Jeffrey does so with an eye toward explicating the underlying contexts that contributed to this pericope being excluded from (or later added to) John's Gospel. Jeffrey's analysis of these contexts sets the stage for a rich recounting of the text's liturgical and literary life in the Western church—Jeffrey notes how the pericope largely dropped out of the Eastern church—and how this life within Evangelicalism in particular since the 1960s evidences a move toward rapprochement with Catholic readings: "though they may not themselves have been fully aware of it, in moving toward classical philology, literary analysis and recovery of traditional exegesis [to address the *pericope adulterae*], they [evangelicals] were at an important turning point for modern evangelical exegesis." Fr. Peter Galadza and George Parsenios—the former an Eastern Catholic of the Byzantine Tradition, the latter Orthodox—essentially provide two types of Eastern responses. Galadza approaches Jeffrey's paper by posing three questions: one addressing the relationship between "biblical" and "ecclesial" authority—"the" supposed elephant in a room of Evangelicals, Catholics, and Orthodox—one addressing to Jeffrey's supposed totalizing of the *paradosis* to the Western tradition, and one related to hermeneutics, in particular how one reads Scripture from within a "tradition." Parsenios devotes the majority of his response to engaging the question of whether the *pericope adulterae* has a "real and natural home" in chapters 7–8 of John's Gospel, which Parsenios denies. Parsenios then addresses the life of this passage within the Orthodox church, since, as he states, "the fact that the passage is not at home in the Gospel of John does not mean that it is not at home within the life and faith of the Orthodox Church."

In chapter 3 Timothy George addresses the "remarkable account" of Jesus's raising Lazarus from the dead. For George, though the question, "Who is Jesus?" pervades the Gospel, the larger question is, "Who is the God that Jesus has come to reveal?" The Christocentric elements of John are also theocentric. The event with Lazarus reveals that Jesus has come to reveal "the God who raises the dead," which is a God "who does not fit neatly into the comfortable theodicies of our postmodern sensibility: the god of process or openness theology, a god who means well, perhaps, but who, at the end of the day, is impotent in the face of radical evil." George unpacks Jesus's revelation of this God who raises the dead through Jesus's acts of wailing, waiting, and weeping, through which the glory of God is revealed. In response Michael Waldstein seeks to "complement" George's reading by highlighting elements unaddressed by George: the Church, the Eucharist, and Mary. After refuting "Jeffersonian" Christianity that replaces gospel with law, Waldstein extends George's emphasis on "glory" to Cana (2:1–11), Golgotha (19:25–27), and Jesus's prayer to the Father (17:20–23), concluding with observations as to how to read the Gospel "wisely." John Mark Reynolds responds to George by wondering whether some "philosophical clarity" surrounding the two natures of Christ would help George's reading of John 11. Engaging the question "Can God get mad?" Reynolds wants to push George further in saying yes, if, claims Reynolds, we have a proper understanding of Jesus's two natures. For Reynolds, though God does not "get" angry (as if he received new knowledge) he does "experience" anger in the humanity of Christ. Reynolds worries that George's reading comes close to the monophysite heresy by underplaying the "cooperation" between the divine and human natures of Christ. Reynolds concludes with reflections on "God's time" versus "human time" in light of Lazarus's death to argue for the perpetual "Easter Sunday" of Christ.

In chapter 4, R. R. Reno addresses the bumper-sticker passage of modern ecumenical dialogue: John 17. But rather than following modern ecumenical trends of focusing on unity in John 17 as a thing in and of itself abstracted from its biblical-theological context, Reno draws on the ancient and medieval commentaries that read the passage as more properly addressing trinitarian and soteriological concerns, with unity situated within these concerns. For Reno, the prayer of John 17 serves "as an outline or précis for an ecclesiology organized around a central emphasis of the Gospel of John: that we can overcome the distance that separates the sinner from God by becoming at-one with Christ, and in him with the Father." Reno also points out how such at-one-ment is also a continuity of apostolic teaching, which for Reno is maintained by the Spirit through the visible magisterial apparatus. Rich Mouw agrees with Reno that the "visible unity" schemes within mainline ecumenism fail to acknowledge the "atonement grounding" offered by Reno as essential to the prayer of John 17. But if visible unity is a goal, Mouw encourages Christians, drawing on Orthodox Peter Bouteneff, to "agree to 'stop being surprised and offended' when we each state our ecclesiological starting points." While Mouw himself worries about "overdeveloped ecclesiologies," he also admits of his own Evangelical tradition, "We evangelicals need more attention to 'visible' unity." Paul Gavrilyuk responds to Reno by drawing on two of Reno's insights—the Trinitarian and the soteriological emphases of John 17—to apply them to his own Orthodox setting. Through these insights Gavrilyuk develops what he calls a "perichoretic" model of ecumenism that consists of an "exchange of gifts": "the spirit of ecumenical generosity includes an acceptance that the charisms that we find better exercised in other Christian communions, if recovered, could revitalize and heal our internal wounds."

Fr. John Behr in chapter 6 provides a rich canonical interpretation of the judgement of Jesus in John 18. Behr links the judgment of Jesus to the "Book of Consolation" of the prophet Isaiah (40–55), focusing on the "cosmic lawsuit" presented in Isaiah, in which "the Lord and his witnesses are placed on one side, and the gods of the nations and their followers are on the other side, with the Lord as both the prosecuting witness and the judge"—a lawsuit resulting in the affirmation that the Lord alone is God of the whole world, that is, "He alone *is*." Behr connects this cosmic lawsuit to John's Gospel as a whole but particularly his depiction of Jesus before Pilate, a trial in which the world is judged and Jesus is revealed as divine—the "I AM." Peter Leithart responds by engaging the cosmic lawsuit theme but with added attention to the book of Revelation. Revelation, according to Leithart, is an extension of the cosmic trial depicted in the Gospel of John: "swept up to heaven, John enters a *courtroom*." From Revelation we find that "the new creation is not fully realized until the saints come to their thrones." In his response, Fr. Thomas Joseph White addresses the judgment of Jesus but takes a different turn to consider how Jesus is "our advocate or defense lawyer, who stands before God as righteous in our stead, releasing us from condemnation and rendering us righteous before God." This leads Fr. White to reflect on a number of ecumenical hot topics: Christ's human knowledge (which, according to White, reveals a "profound continuity between christological ontology of the Eastern fathers and the progressive elaboration of Western medieval atonement theory"), the affirmation of justification as transformation by grace (which White contrasts with an imputation model of justification), the connection between Christ's mission as advocate and the Spirit's mission as advocate (by which White affirms the filioque), and the dependence of justification on the Church (which White opposes to the simple notion of the Church's dependence on justification).

Chapter 1

Knowing the Gift of God
John 4:1–26 and the Living Water

Edith Humphrey (Orthodox)

To read the fourth chapter of the gospel of John is to be embarrassed, or at least overwhelmed, by riches. In a passage such as this we see with clarity the characteristics of Scripture that led St. John Chrysostom to exult:

> Reading the Holy Scriptures is like a treasure. With a treasure, you see, anyone able to find a tiny nugget gains for himself great wealth; likewise, in the case of Sacred Scripture, you can get from a small phrase a great wealth of thought and immense riches. The Word of God is not only like a treasure, but is also like a spring gushing with overflowing waters in a mighty flood . . . great is the yield of this treasure and the flow of this spiritual fountain. Don't be surprised if we have experienced this: our forebears drank from these waters to the limit of their capacity, and those who come after us will try to do likewise, without risk of exhausting them; instead the flood will increase and the streams will be multiplied.[1]

We might be tempted to repeat the Jewish reflection for Passover—*Dayenu!* ("That would have been enough for us!") Indeed, we might think it more than enough to drink deeply of the waters of the Scripture. Yet the waters of John 4 do not signify merely Scripture, but the gift of God himself, to

---

1. Chrysostom, "Homily 3.1," 34–50.

which Scriptures point: the construction "gift *of God*" is clearly meant, in this passage, to be the objective genitive, that gift *who is God*, not merely a gift divinely given. If reading Scripture is like trying to drink from a fire hose, how much more exhilarating is the reception of the very Spirit of God? God's plan is not to make us people of the written Word, but people resembling the Incarnate Word, God himself. *Theōsis* is a daunting calling, but not beyond the purview of the One who calls into existence the things that are not, and who says, "Be holy, as I am holy!" We find in this passage a luminous narrative that shows how delicately God brings us to the water and nourishes us: "The Gospel leads its readers and hearers progressively into a greater understanding . . . by initiating them step by step . . ."[2] As Jesus gently leads the Samaritan woman—known to us in the Eastern church as St. Photini, the illumined one—so the Holy Spirit leads his people in a characteristic way. So the blessed Augustine advises us: "In that woman, then, let us hear ourselves, and in her acknowledge ourselves and in her give thanks to God . . ."[3]

If I were to follow the usual pastoral method of the fathers in commenting upon this passage, I would allow its narrative to unfold sequentially. However, only certain branches of the tree can be followed in such a procedure, and I assume that this audience knows the story well, so I will structure our discussion in a different manner, following the cue of St. John Cassian[4] and the blessed Augustine,[5] with a little modification. We will first consider the passage in terms of what we can call a "general reading"—that is, a reading that is patent to any careful inquirer, and that attends to the literary and historical context of the passage. Then, we will move on to a "creedal reading," considering the Christological and Trinitarian aspects. This will be followed by a "practical reading," in which we will see the moral and ethical implications, the guide for Christian living offered here. Finally, we will engage in what I will call a "theotic reading," looking for the transforming, illumining qualities of the narrative and its interconnection with the sacramental and spiritual life to which St. Photini (and we!) are called. The astute will have realized that these four approaches roughly correspond to the literal, allegorical, tropological and anagogic senses employed from the time of St. John Cassian on, but which he argues were known even by the NT authors. I present these as heuristic and intertwined categories, not as a rigid schema and, true to my Antiochian context, will insist that the first

---

2. Bauckham, *Testimony of the Beloved Disciple*, 120.
3. Augustine, *Tractates* 15.10, 101–2.
4. Cassian, *Conferences* 14.10, 164–65.
5. Augustine, *Literal Meaning Genesis*, 1.1.

strategy of reading is not expendable, nor must it be suppressed by the three others. I see the first general reading as an opening up of the conversation to any welcome hearer of the Scriptures, the second creedal reading as what makes the engagement Christian (for in the passage we discern the *regula fidei* or the canon of truth), the third practical reading as receiving the passage in its incarnational and ecclesial power, and the fourth theotic reading as fulfilling all those other approaches, bringing the general, creedal and practical to the end that God has designed. All four approaches are important in understanding and receiving "the gift of God" to which Jesus refers.

GENERAL READING: "LET ANY WHO THIRST COME!"

Attention to the historical and literary context of the passage brings us immediately into conflict with many commentators who have reduced the Lord's conversation with Photini to a pretext for timeless truths. Ernest Renan is the most blatant in his promulgation of this reductionism:

> Le jour où il prononça cetter parole, il fut vraiment fils de Dieu. Il dit pour la première fois l'édifice sur lequel reposersa la religion éternelle. Il fonda le culte pur, sans date, sans patrie, celui qui pratiqueront toutes les âmes élevées jusqu' à la fin des temps. Non seuelment sa religion fut ce jour-là bonne religion de l'humanité, mais, ce fut la religion absolue. Et si d'utres planets ont des habitant doués de raison et de moralité, leur religion ne peut être different de celle que Jésus a proclamé près du puits de Jacob.[6]

The "saying" to which Renan refers is, of course, that word found in verse 24: "God is Spirit and those who worship him must worship in Spirit and in Truth." Renan is not so much wrong about what he affirms but about what he denies—though, of course, to say that Jesus "became" the Son of God by uttering these words is damning the Almighty with faint praise. His modernist idea of religious developmentalism is further complicated by his concentration upon Jesus's "religion" as "eternal," "pure," "timeless," "without nationality," and "absolute." This is such an odd conclusion to draw from

---

6. Renan, *Vie de Jésus*, 94. (My translation: "The day that he pronounced this saying, he became truly the son of God. He declared for the first time the foundation upon which the everlasting religion will rest. He founded the pure cult, without date, without nationality, that which all elevated souls will practice until the end of time. Not only did his religion become that day the excellent religion of humanity, but it became the absolute religion. And if on other planets the inhabitants are endowed with reason and morality, then their religion can be none other than the one that Jesus proclaimed at Jacob's well.")

a passage that focusses upon history (Jacob's well), upon the distinction between Samaritans and Jews made by both Photini and Jesus (4:9; 4:20; 4:22), upon the historical coming of Messiah (4:25), and upon the patrimony of Israel: "salvation is from the Jews" (4:22)! Of course, some readers both ancient and contemporary have done their best to soften Jesus's unequivocal statement about the origin of salvation, with the most egregious examples occurring during the Nazi terror, when two German churches actually expunged Jesus's offensive statement from Bibles.[7] *Mutatis matandis,* under the specter of "supersessionism," the passage continues to be snubbed by those engaged in ecumenical dialogue. As Richard Neuhaus puts it, "our passage has not been treated kindly by Christian commentators."[8]

Faithful and perspicuous readers have not, however, banished the historical from this passage, nor seen the eschatological light of true worship as rendering the temporal dimensions irrelevant. Renan's move from history to the abstract is not God's story of salvation, but a human construct, what C. S. Lewis calls "one of those sensible synthetic religions which are so strongly recommended today."[9] Instead, the historical details of the earlier chapters of the story are key, and preparatory for what N. T. Wright has aptly called "the climax of the covenant"—one covenant, in reality, though in two parts! The particularity of the earlier chapters of that divine narrative and their continuing significance are drawn out by St. John Chrysostom, the blessed Augustine, St. Cyril of Alexandria, and St. Caesarea of Arles, to name a few. Some may be astonished at the care with which the Golden-Mouthed depicts the context of John 4, explaining the psychology of Jesus's departure from Judaea (not to reject but to soften his enemies), the history of Northern Israel and the Samaritans, and the origin of Jacob's well.[10] The well of Old Testament wisdom is, indeed, "deep," as Origen remarks, associating this well with the OT Scriptures.[11] St. Cyril of Alexandria also points out the ongoing significance of this ancient wisdom, declaring that our Lord, in turning to the Samaritans (who typify those Gentiles who will join God's people), continues to show reverence for the OT patriarchs, "embracing" them "again and again," "preserving to them the pristine unfading grace."[12]

---

7. Marchadour, *Les personnages dans l'évangile de* Jean, describes on page 89 the actions in 1936 of the Lutheran Church of Germany and in 1939 of the Church of Baden.

8. On possible reasons for the verse's suppression in contemporary discussion, see Neuhaus, "Salvation is from the Jews."

9. Lewis, "Introduction."

10. Chrysostom, *Hom. John* 31.2 (108–9).

11. Origen, *Commentary on the Gospel of John*, 13.37–39.

12. St. Cyril of Alexandria, *Commentary on the Gospel of John*, 2.4 (203).

And so it is that the story is shot through with references to the temporal and the spatial—Jacob, Joseph, the fathers, the sixth hour, Jacob's sons; Pharisees, Judea, Galilee, Samaria, Sychar, the city, the well, the pot, the mountain, Jerusalem, the cultic distance between Jewish men and Samaritan women. John's ideal reader is one who knows the Scriptures, and who is aware of the usual goings-on at wells—the meeting of a man and his future bride, including (possibly) some flirtation (Genesis 24, 29, Exod 2:15–22, cf. Prov 5:15). With such expectations in place, the evangelist sets us up to be redirected, along with the adulterous Samaritan: we are disturbed by the woman's too-familiar "tone," but before long we will see how the light shines clearly at noon where it did not quite penetrate Nicodemus's midnight. Though Jesus draws the woman's attention away from the well to mysterious "living water," and away from the dispute between Samaritans and Judaeans, he also ratifies the Jewish meta-narrative and his part in it. Jesus does not here completely relativize Judaism and Samaritan schismatic teaching: "we worship what we know." As he announces this in-breaking era, he does not imply that the Jerusalem temple was simply a mistake or that the narrative surrounding it was mistaken, for "salvation is *from* the Jews," though not *in* Judaism! In leading her towards spiritual mystery, Jesus never suggests that the physical is irrelevant. Part of his awakening of her spiritual imagination involves a focus upon Photini's very enfleshed condition: "Go and call your husband!"

Indeed, the entire conversation is prefaced by that intriguing narratival comment, "He *had to* go through Samaria." Though some have considered this is a reference to the short distance of the Samaritan route for the hurried traveler, the circumstances of the narrative (Jesus displays no haste), the customary Johannine use *dei* for the unfolding of the divine plan, and the reference to God's harvesting at the end of the story (4:34–35) suggest otherwise. The trip through Samaria is a serendipitous by-product of Jesus's ministry, for his purview is with the Jews: some ancient commentators see this "by-work" action of Jesus[13] as a means by which the inclusion of the Gentiles is foreshadowed. What happens in space and time matters! For both evangelist and many of the fathers, the actual details of the story are so important that they are labored over—John corrects the report to the Pharisees that Jesus baptized (4:2); the blessed Augustine speculates that he only literally baptized the apostles;[14] the Golden-Mouthed suggests that the report was deliberately false so as to arouse the Pharisees' envy![15]

---

13. Chrysostom, *Hom. John* 31.2 (107).
14. Augustine, *Letter* 265.5
15. Chrysostom, *Hom. John*, 31.1–2 (107).

Just as Jesus must deal with the strangeness of the Samaritan woman, so we must acknowledge the strangeness of that day as we read the gospel: not to do this renders us susceptible to the imaginative leap made by many scholars of the so-called "historical" Jesus, who peer into the well of history, and imagine Jesus in the reflection of their own faces.[16] The comments of Neuhaus are apt: "Christianity is not defined by an essence but by the man of the cross, a permanently suspect character, forever a stranger of that strange people, the Jews. Through Jesus the Jew, we Christians are anchored in history, defined not by an abstract essence but by a most particular story."[17] Neuhaus's comments match that of St. Cyril of Alexandria, who suggests, "Jesus implies that his own sojourn in the world with a body is the time and season for a change of such customs."[18] "Timeful," rather than timeless, describes the assumption of humanity and God the Son's deep entrance into our world. Though the text leads us into mystery, its point of departure is the world of women, wells, Samaritans, Jews, and conflict: such matters are patent to any interested reader, and will direct the astute reader to deeper issues.

As St. Ephrem of Syria noted long ago, the historical givenness of the situation is the context for St. Photini's growth in understanding: "she first saw [Jesus] as someone thirsting; then as a Jew; then as a prophet; and after that as God."[19] John's gospel, though replete with mystery, and though coopted by Gnostics in the second century, does not adopt the Gnostic strategy of mystification: rather, it calls out, like Wisdom, to any who will hear, "If anyone thirsts, let him [or her!] come" (John 7:37). Mystery comes into the space-and-time world, and beckons. This universal call is memorialized in song by Charles Coller, an ordinary nineteenth-century Christian, not distinguished by any specialized education or tradition, but active in the Salvation Army as an lay musician:

> From the heart of Jesus flowing cometh Heaven's peace to me,
> Ever deeper, richer growing through the Cross of Calvary.
> Passing mortal understanding, yet to seeking ones made known,
> And for all the race expanding, gift of God unto his own.[20]

---

16. Tyrrell, *Christianity at the Crossroads*, 44.
17. Neuhaus, "Salvation is From the Jews," n.p.
18. Cyril of Alexandria, *Commentary on the Gospel of John* 2.4 (211).
19. Ephrem, *Commentary on Tatian's Diatessaron* 12.18 (199).
20. *Song Book of the Salvation Army*, "From the Heart of Jesus Flowing," 490.

CREEDAL READING: "IF YOU KNEW WHO IT IS"

However, the focus of this passage, consonant with the rest of the fourth gospel, is not upon the progress of fallen humanity, the "if you knew," but upon the gift itself, upon the identity of Jesus ("who it is who speaks"), and his communion with the Father (and the Spirit). The periscope chosen for this conference, verses 1 through 26, begins with a reference to Jesus's ministry as more significant than that of the Baptist, and ends with Jesus's self-identification as "I AM." If we were to continue until the entire story of the Samaritan concludes, that is, to verse 46, we are similarly offered an identification, this time by the Samaritan people: "this is the Savior of the world." Jesus's identity as Messiah and Savior links him with humanity, while the reference to Father, his allusion to the Spirit, and his use of the Tetragrammaton, mark him as the divine Son. Though we do not hear clearly about the Holy Spirit in this passage, Jesus's conversation with the Samaritan woman is illumined several chapters later in 7:37–39, as typical of the gospel's progressive explication of its symbolic world:[21]

> On the last day of the feast, the great day, Jesus stood up and proclaimed, "If any one thirst, let him come to me and drink. He who believes in me, as the scripture has said, 'Out of his heart shall flow rivers of living water.'" Now this he said about the Spirit, which those who believed in him were to receive; for as yet the Spirit had not been given, because Jesus was not yet glorified.[22]

Chapter 7, then, moves faithful readers, in their turn, forward in understanding, just as the Lord inducts St. Photini into mystery at the well. What, then, does this chapter itself teach us of the twin mysteries of the Incarnation and Trinity?

We are struck by what seem to be two polar opposites—Jesus's utter humanity, and his sovereign Lordship. We run the gamut, seeing him exhausted from his trip, hearing him aptly hailed as *Kyrios*. (What a shame that contemporary English no longer uses "Lord" in multiple ways, so that our translators cannot replicate the evangelist's ironic polyvalence, must decide if the term should be rendered "Sir" in the light of the Samaritan's

---

21. On this strategy, see Bauckham, 120. Especially helpful here is his remark concerning the fecundity of holy symbols, a comment that may be considered a contemporary equivalent to St. John Chrysostom's words on the fountain of Scripture: "[S]ymbolism is not just a code that can be translated into an adequate description.... The realities to which symbols refer are transcendent realities that escape linguistic capture. That is why the symbols proliferate through the Gospel without redundancy. "

22. All Scripture references are to the RSV, unless I offer my own translation.

ignorance, or "Lord" in the *sensus plenior!*) This balance between humanity and divinity is apparent throughout the story. It is helpful to remember, too, that in our contemporary division into chapters we may forget the luminous words that preface our story: "He whom God has sent utters the words of God, for he gives the Spirit without measure. The Father loves the Son and has given all things into his hand. Whoever believes in the Son has eternal life; whoever does not obey the Son shall not see life, but the wrath of God remains on him" (3:34–5).

These words about the One who is "above all," but who has been sent by the Father and received power (3:32–33) introduce a story in which we will see God-in-action-as-Man. As man, he is misinterpreted as being in competition with John; as man he avoids confrontation, and is compelled to travel; as man he must be in Judaea, Galilee, or Samaria; as man he sends his disciples to buy food, and is weary; as man, he asks for a drink, and confounds the woman by breaking protocol; as man, he uses the first person plural and refers to himself as Jewish; as man, he receives the title "Messiah," though he is not merely a human anointed one. As God, he does not himself baptize with water but will baptize with the Spirit; as God, he humbles himself in the human arena; as God, he makes an overture to the "woman" (cf. Genesis 3); as God, he lures her by speaking of the "gift of God" and inculcating in her a thirst for more than she now imagines; as God, he knows not only the history of Jacob's well, but the woman's own intimate life (just as he did with Nathanael); as God, he reveals worship of the Father (cf. John 1:18) and announces a new era; as God, he utters the holy Name, "I AM."

Yet the moment we make such divisions, we miss the wonder of our Lord, in which the natures are not mingled, but are truly united. As St. Hilary of Poitiers put it "If we do not understand the mystery of his tears, hunger and thirst, let us remember . . . that he who thirsted gave from himself rivers of living water."[23] In such paradoxes, the kontakion of St. Romanos, whose feast-day is nigh upon us, serves us even better:

> The Source of the breath of life for all, when He was
> Weary from a journey, sat down near a spring of Samaria.
> And it was the season of burning heat.
> It was the sixth hour, as the Scripture says,
> It was the middle of the day when the Messiah came
>   to illumine those in darkness.
> The Spring came upon the spring, not to drink but to cleanse.
> The fountain of immortality was near the streams of the wretched woman

---

23. Hilary of Poitiers, *On The Trinity* 10.24 (188).

> as though it were in need.
> He is tired from walking, He who tirelessly walked on the sea,
> He who furnishes exceeding great joy and redemption.[24]

The union of the divine and human natures is not simply a paradox, but indeed, the means by which God embraces us. As St. Ambrose concisely remarks, "Jesus is wearied by his journey, that he may refresh the weary."[25]

I find it interesting to notice what the evangelist does and does not do with his symbolism: and this can be extended to the Christian tradition in general, I think. Jesus is the bread, the vine, the door, the Shepherd. He is not however, associated with any of the four elements, and so he is not himself "the water of life." Rather, he gives gifts that are associated with such elements. Could it be that the Son is more aptly depicted by symbols associated with humanity—human figures, mixed and baked bread, cultivated vines, constructed doors, spoken Word, and so on. The one exception to this is, of course, the primal Light, a symbol that goes far beyond the four elements, and upon which humanity depends. Here is the exception that proves the rule, for our Lord is human, but also the source of all creation. It seems, however, that at least three of the elements (not earth!) are appropriately associated with the Holy Spirit, who "is present everywhere and fills all things." For John, *moving* air (*pneuma*) and *moving* water are indicative of the Spirit: and this is not his own typology, but seen also in the prophetic literature of Ezekiel and Zechariah (The synoptics, of course associate the Spirit with fire, both in speaking about the baptism from Jesus and at Pentecost, with precedents in the Exodus pillar of fire, and in the purification envisaged in Malachi 3–4). The Christological symbols, then, find their context in the human domain, whereas the Pneumatological symbols are, so to speak, "wilder" and less approachable.

And yet the Spirit will be given to drink, becoming a spring within those who receive him, and not a source of destructive inundation. Some commentators have exegeted the living water differently, such as the historian Eusebius, who associates the water with the gospel,[26] or Origen, who implies that it is "teaching that is internal and lasts forever" over against the "introductory" well of the OT or ephemeral human ideas.[27] Most, however, have followed the lead of Jesus, who speaks particularly about *the* gift of God (4:10) and then the evangelist, who discloses the mystery at 7:39, in speaking of "the Holy Spirit," not yet given to the Church (in fullness), but

---

24. Melodus, "Kontakion on the woman of Samaria" 9.4 (88–89).
25. St. Ambrose, *On the Christian Faith* 5.4.53 (291).
26. St. Eusebius of Caesarea, *Proof of Gospel* 6.18.48–49
27. Origen, *Commentary Gospel of John* 13.13–39 (71–76).

promised. Jesus's words to the Samaritan woman are not as transparent as his conversation with Nicodemus concerning the Spirit and the birth from above, but in them she eventually discerns (as do we!) not only the mystery of Christ, but the mystery of God who is both Spirit and Truth, as well as the Father: "The Father seeks those . . . who will worship Him in Spirit and in Truth."

Classical theologians have discerned the fecundity of Jesus's gnomic statement to her, focusing upon how it illuminates the Trinitarian mystery, rather than yielding an abstract religion à la Renan and the late nineteenth-century liberals. Consider, for example, the fuller context of that beloved word of St. Evagrius:

> If you wish to pray, you have need of God, who gives prayer to him who prays. Invoke him, then, saying "Hallowed be thy name, thy kingdom come," that is, the Holy Spirit, and your only begotten Son. For this is what he taught us, saying "Worship the Father in Spirit and in Truth." He who prays in the Spirit and in truth is no longer dependent upon created things when honoring the Creator, but praises him for and in himself. If you are a theologian, you will pray truly; And if you pray truly, you are a theologian[28]

St. Evagrius implies, then, that Jesus indicated the particular Holy Spirit when he spoke of worshipping *en pneumati* (the article is not grammatically essential for this meaning) and of Jesus when he spoke of worshipping "in Truth." Similarly, St. Ambrose moves towards a Trinitarian reading when he remarks, "When God is said to be worshiped in truth (by the proper meaning of the word itself often expressed after the same manner), it ought to be understood that the Son too is worshiped. So, in the same way, the Spirit is also worshiped because God is worshiped in Spirit. Therefore the Father is worshiped both with the Son and with the Spirit, because the Trinity is worshiped."[29] Commenting on this passage, St. Basil puts it succinctly, "The Holy Spirit cannot be divided from the Father and the Son in worship."[30] However, to discern Trinitarian teaching in the statement is not to restrict its meaning so that Jesus's words are made to speak only of the divine mystery and not of the worshipper's truthful adoration, as well. As one contemporary exegete reminds us, there is in the fourth gospel *une puissance symbolique* that allows for a both/and rather than an either/or interpretive

---

28. Evagrius of Pontus, *Chapters on Prayer* 59–61, 62.
29. Ambrose, *On the Holy Spirit* 3.11.85 (147).
30. Basil, *On the Holy Spirit* 26.64 (97).

strategy. Thus we are wisely advised by Fr. Rodney Whitacre, who supplements an anthropological focus with a Trinitarian insight:

> To worship *in spirit and truth* means to worship as one who is spiritually alive. . . . Worshipping in spirit is connected to the fact that *God is spirit* (4:24). And worshiping in truth is connected with Jesus, the Messiah who explains everything (4:25–26). This picture of Jesus will be developed more when it is said that his words are spirit and truth (6:633) and he himself the truth (14:6). So worshiping in s*pirit and truth* is related to the very character of God and the identity of Christ. It is to worship in union with the Father, who is spirit, and according to the revelation of the Son, who is the truth. Indeed, it is to be taken into union with God through the Spirit (chaps. 14–17).[31]

Several questions emerge from these explorations. The first is to note that this passage in no way solves the debate concerning the *filioque*, since Eastern and Western Christians are united in agreeing that the Son *sends* the Spirit: the controversy is over the eternal procession of the Spirit, not the economic matter in history. The second is to discern what it means to call the Father "spirit," and whether we stumbled over pre-Chalcedonian confusion in the fourth gospel (*me genoito!*), such as some have charged Paul with regards to the Second Adam and the S/spirit (cf. 1 Cor 15:45). The challenge of calling the Father "a spirit" while distinguishing the persons of the Trinity is articulated as early as St. Hilary of Poitiers. Carefully, he explained it thus:

> . . . Therefore he said that they are the true worshippers who shall worship in the Spirit and in Truth. And these who are to worship God the Spirit in the Spirit shall have the One for the means, the Other for the object, of their reverence. For each of the two stand in a different relation to the worshiper. . . . The words "God is spirit" do not alter the fact that the Holy Spirit has a name of his own and that he is the gift to us."[32]

In other words, we worship the Father, who has no body and is not to be rendered in pictures: he is the object of our worship. Paradoxically, we also worship *by means of* the Holy Spirit, whose coming and deep immanence in the Church came about because of the Incarnation and exaltation of the Son. Though this may sound at first like the splitting of theological hairs, an abstruse differentiation of the persons of the Triune God, C. S. Lewis helps us to see the wonder of the divine mystery. When we are instructed of Jesus

---

31. Whitacre, *John*, 106–7.
32. Hilary, *On the Trinity* 2.31 (60–61).

concerning the nature of God, when we pray to God by means of God interceding and dwelling within, we are no longer merely servants, but friends:

> You may ask, "if we cannot imagine a three-personal Being, what is the good of talking about Him?" Well, there isn't any good talking about Him. The thing that matters is being actually drawn into that three-personal life, and that may begin any time—to-night, if you like.
>
> What I mean is this. An ordinary simple Christian kneels down to say his prayers. He is trying to get into touch with God. But if he is a Christian he knows that what is prompting him to pray is also God: God, so to speak, inside him. But he also knows that all his real knowledge of God comes through Christ, the Man who was God—that Christ is standing beside him, helping him to pray, praying for him. You see what is happening. God is the thing to which he is praying, the goal he is trying to reach. God is also the thing inside him which is pushing him on—the motive power. God is also the road or bridge along which he is being pushed to that goal. So that the whole threefold life of the three-personal Being is actually going on in that ordinary little bedroom where an ordinary man is saying his prayers. The man is being caught up into the higher kinds of life—what I called Zoe or spiritual life: he is being pulled into God, by God, while still remaining himself.[33]

If *that* is the result of the gift of God, then we must cry out with St. Ambrose, "Who will give this fountain to my breast? Let it spring up in me, let what gives eternal life flow on me. Let that fountain overflow on us and not flow away. . ."[34] Any may come who thirsts, and in coming they will be accosted by *Jésus, maître de désir*,[35] who, by means of the intimation "if you knew," will lead us into theological wonders beyond our imagination, but not irrelevant to our space and time existence. This movement from the "common reading" to the "creedal" leads inevitably to the "practical," for our Lord is the Second Adam, the One who became flesh for us.

PRACTICAL READING: "GO, CALL YOUR HUSBAND!"

If the creedal reading is what makes our understanding of Scripture specifically Christian, announcing the twin mysteries of the God-Man and

---

33. Lewis, *Mere Christianity*, 161.
34. Ambrose, *On the Holy Spirit* 1.16.180–81 (114).
35. Marchadour, *Les personnages dans l'évangile de Jean*, 84.

the Trinity, then the practical reading is necessary to fulfil James's dictum "faith without works is dead," and to exemplify the first step in St. Gregory Nazianzen's vision that the Word becomes "thick."[36] Jesus, in meeting the woman in the locale of the well, also meets her at the point of her moral degradation, and calls her attention to it, though with some delicacy. His insistence upon accuracy in this situation leads St. Photini, perhaps like Peter the rock, to receive Jesus as a prophet by divine *theoria* (4:19): after all, what is the role of the prophet if not to bring what is hidden to light? Impressively, the correction of her allocution before His divine tribunal does not shut the woman down, but moves her to ask questions even deeper than those begged by her own ethical poverty. Some have seen her theological debate as a means of deflection, but even if there is a hint of avoidance in the dialogue, it does not become the woman's permanent state. When she leaves her pot to go and speak to the townspeople, it is the marvel that this One knows "all I ever did" (4:29) that leads her to entertain the teaching of Jesus—specifically his self-identification as Messiah! Jesus saw Nathanael at prayer under the fig-tree, and amazed him with the revelation; Jesus sees the woman in her adulterous life, and this is the catalyst for her faith.

The fathers have seen other indications in our passage of teaching on the practical level, as have our contemporaries. For St. John Chrysostom, Jesus's pattern of travel is traced as a model: his departure from Judea is taken as a prefiguration of the early Church, directed by the Spirit from Jerusalem to Samaria, to the Gentiles.[37] The blessed Augustine makes a similar connection, but emphasizes the suffering and martyrdom to which the Church was subjected, the unhappy occasion of her missionary diaspora:

> Certainly, if the Pharisees' knowledge that our Lord was making more disciples and baptizing more than John had been such as to lead them wholeheartedly to follow him and desire baptism by him, he would not have left Judea; rather, he would have remained for their sake. But seeing as he did that this knowledge about him was coupled with envy, making them persecutors instead of followers, he left. He also could have stayed among them, if he had wanted to, and escaped their hands. . . . But he wanted to provide himself as an example for believers in time to come, that it was no sin for a servant of God to seek refuge from the fury of persecutors. . . . He did it like a good teacher, not out of fear for himself but for our instruction.[38]

---

36. Gregory Nazianzen, *Oration* 38.2. The concept is also famously discussed by St. Maximos in his *Ambiguum* 33.

37. Chrysostom, *Hom. Gospel of John* 31.2.

38. Augustine, *Tractates on the Gospel of John* 15.2 (99–100).

St. Caesarius of Arles draws out from the encounter the characteristic hospitality of God, and contrasts this with the tendency of some in his own day to delay baptism, the human reception of God's gift:

> The good Lord spontaneously offers himself to her, even though she did not ask for it, in order to fulfill that prophecy, "I appeared openly to those who sought me not, I was found by those who asked me not . . . ." Not everyone knows the gift of God, because not all desire the living water, for if they did desire it they would never postpone the sacrament of baptism . . . . Do not delay the remedies of your salvation because you do not know when your soul may be demanded of you.[39]

The clemency and transparency of God is thus strikingly contrasted against the squeamishness of those who will not receive and respond to Him: typically for the homilies of St. Caesarius, the practical aspect of the Christian life takes center-stage.

St. Cyril trains our eyes on another matter that spins centrifugally away from the narrative. In his competent hands, the interchange becomes the occasion for teaching concerning holy matrimony: Jesus is described as "helpfully affirming" (!) St. Photini's comment that she has no husband, since it is "the approval of the law and the bond of pure love that makes marriage blameless."[40] His literal treatment of the woman's situation contrasts with many of the fathers, who move on from the woman' actual status to allegorize the five (or six) men, rendering them the books of the law (Augustine) or pagan gods (St. Romanus Melodus), and intimating that Jesus is the true husband to which humankind should be wed. Like the Golden-Mouthed, St. Cyril dwells upon the human situation and uses it as a bridge to his congregation or readership, affirming Christian teaching on blameless marriage and God's will for a holy people. Though the passage does not directly lend itself to this kind of discussion, in contrast to the narratives of the blind man and the adulterous woman (cf. 5:14; 8:11), sexual morality is one of those questions that will naturally intrude, given the notice of St. Photini's lifestyle. If the woman is rebuked (however gently) by Jesus on the grounds of an illicit marriage, then, the reader or congregation may well ask, what is the Lord's teaching on marriage that is holy? St. Cyril's pastoral recognition of this point is a potent reminder of the interconnected nature of truth, and how it is impossible to extricate a spiritual kernel from a passage while ignoring its bordering practical matters.

---

39. Caesarius of Arles, *Sermon* 170.3–4 (419–21).
40. Cyril, *Comm. Gospel of John* 2.4 (210).

The theme of human witness is more central to the passage: Jesus declares "what we know," the woman leaves the discussion to involve others, these others come to Jesus to hear and see for themselves, and Jesus closes the entire episode with a reference to the waiting harvest. St. Cyril provides a welcome word to our contemporary context, insisting "let him that teaches in the church follow this pattern and not refuse to help women. For in all things one must not follow one's own will but the service of preaching."[41] He continues to uphold the role of proclamation in pointing to Jesus's example of selfless service, pointing out that Jesus did not stop to eat, though weary, but was concerned "for the salvation of those called"; thus, "he encourages the teaches in the churches and persuades them to disregard all fatigue and be more zealous for those who are being saved than caring for their own bodies."[42] The blessed Origen and St. John Chrysostom also stress the theme of testimony, but seize upon the woman as a model, since she is used "as an apostle, as it were" (so Origen),[43] and like the Apostles who left their nets, abandoned her jar to fulfill this role "by calling not one or two people, as Andrew or Philip did, but a whole city" (so Chrysostom).[44]

The two figures of the Lord and the woman have proved fertile ground for preachers through the ages who are intent on stirring up their congregations to be salt and light in the world. Speaking anecdotally, I have noticed that, in my youth, I was instructed by preachers who tended to concentrate upon the model of Jesus, offering it as a pattern for apologetics and evangelism—a daunting task, actually, considering that most of us lack the divine insight of the One "who knew what is in man" (2:25)! More recently, however, with the increased concern for women's ministry in the church, St. Photini has become a kind of poster-child for the cause. This latter move, though tempting due to her position alongside St. Marry Magdalene and St. Thecla as "equal-to-the-apostles," risks obscuring the illumined one's own witness, which, like that of the Baptist, was to point to Jesus, and not to herself or to the status of women (3:29–30). When the practical becomes an end in itself, and not a rung on the ladder provided, we face not only the peril of a stall, but indeed of a fall from the upward calling. The general reading, the creedal reading, and the practical reading are meant to find their fulfillment in the theotic, to which we now turn.

---

41. Cyril, *Comm. Gospel John* 2.5 (221).
42. Ibid., 224.
43. Origen, *Comm. Gospel John* 13.169 (104).
44. Chrysostom, *Hom. Gospel John* 34.1 (118).

THE THEOTIC READING: "THE HOUR IS COMING AND IS NOW HERE"

A striking feature of Johannine narrative is that it remarkably unites the personal and with the symbolic or the luminous. As many readers have noted, the living quality of its narrative and characterization is its poignant symbolism and continuing vitality beyond the original context. Thus we see alongside the common characterization of the fourth gospel as "spiritual," the forceful judgment of C. S. Lewis concerning the particularity of the gospel and its probative connection with historical.

> Read the dialogues: that with the Samaritan woman at the well, or that which follows the healing of the man born blind. Look at its pictures.... I have been reading poems, romances, vision-literature, legends, myths all my life. I know what they are like. I know that not one of them is like this. . . . The reader who doesn't see this has simply not learned to read. I would recommend him to read Auerbach.[45]

The reader remarks upon the anonymous Samaritan woman, Jesus's archetypal designation of her as "woman," the pregnant symbolism of the well, and the possible meanings of the five "men"; she or he also notes the bracing verisimilitude of the dialogue, the forthrightness of St. Photini, and the psychological appropriateness of her concourse with the town's people. St. Photini may stand as an emblem for the illumined outsider; simultaneously she retains a life of her own. The image of the well may bespeak the Old Testament writings or human wisdom; it also remains firmly attached to its context in Sychar, and brings to our minds the world-savvy character of the patriarch Jacob!

To us it may seem a tour de force that the evangelist so incorporates the personal with the luminous. But what if this is part and parcel of reality? What if our personhood is inextricably caught up with the iconic, as we are by nature image-bearers; what if our subjectivity is exegeted precisely at those points where we are inter-connected with others? Perhaps this coalescence of the personal with the symbolic is not a Johannine literary feature (or at least not simply this) but a pointer to the reality in which we live, where we are each unique yet defined by communion. If the Word is himself "towards" the Father (John 1:1), surely it must come as no surprise

---

45. Lewis, "Fernseed and Elephants." (Lewis here refers to Auerbach's book *Mimesis: The Representation of Reality in Western Literature*). Lewis's trenchant address is available *in Christian Reflections* (1981), *Fern-seed and Elephants (1998)* and online at http://orthodox-web.tripod.com/papers/fern_seed.html

that we, too, are ourselves in relation to God and to each other. And so we lament the "dry and barren"[46] human being who is seen in St. Photini prior to her rendezvous at the well; we exult in the suggestiveness of the image of one who will be illumined and watered, along with the depth of her salty personality. With St. Cyril, we rejoice: "Now human nature runs back to its pristine beauty, and drinking in that which is life-giving, it is made beautiful with a variety of good things and, budding into a virtuous life, it sends out healthy shoots towards God."[47]

But it is not simply *internal* human nature that is vivified by the time that is coming and now is, by the gift of God who is the "treasury of blessings and giver of life." No, the advent of God the Son into our world, and the gift of the Holy Spirit made available to us through his conquest of death by death, his pioneering resurrection and representative glorification means more than a renewal of nature in general, or the spiritual. It is the bringing to culmination of all that we are—body, soul, and spirit—to a state beyond that enjoyed by even our first-parents. St. John Chrysostom brings his sermon on the Samaritan woman to a conclusion that speaks of practical emulation as well as total glorification in the beatific vision, that accounts for the "even now" as well as the wonders that lie before us:

> Let us then imitate this woman of Samaria; let us commune with Christ. *For even now He stands in the midst of us*, speaking to us by the Prophets and Disciples; let us hear and obey. How long shall we live uselessly and in vain? Because, not to do what is well-pleasing to God is to live uselessly, or rather not merely uselessly, but to our own hurt; for when we have spent the time which has been given us on no good purpose, we shall depart this life to suffer severest punishment for our unseasonable extravagance. . . . *It was not for this that God brought us into this present life, and breathed into us a soul, that we should make use of the present time only*, but that we should do all our business with a regard to the life which is to come. Things irrational only are useful for the present life; but we have an immortal soul, that we may use every means to prepare ourselves for that other life. For if one enquire the use of horses and asses and oxen, and other such-like animals, we shall tell him that it is nothing else but only to minister to the present life; but this cannot be said of us; our best condition is that which follows on our departure hence; and *we must do all that we may shine there, that we may join the choir of Angels, and stand before the King continually,*

---

46. Cyril of Alexandria, *Comm. Gospel of John* 2.4 (207).
47. Ibid.

through endless ages. And therefore the soul is immortal, and the body shall be immortal too, that we may enjoy the never-ending blessings.[48]

Despite the spiritual trajectory of this passage, St. John never loses touch with the body; despite the paucity of the material world when divorced from the source of all blessings, it is not derided, but caught up in that time of never-ending blessings. The vision of *Theōsis* is not one that treats the material world and the body as refuse, but one that honors God as the creator of all that is, and that is realized by means of created elements, especially the body of the Son, by which God reconciles us with himself. "Even now he stands among us"—but what joy awaits us when all is said and done!

After all, we have it on the very best authority that the Father seeks worshippers, and we see this search in progress as Jesus speaks with St. Photini concerning the life-giving Holy Spirit. We see embodied the promise of the spring within, as she goes to speak to her own people, and then again when they remark, having themselves welcomed Jesus's own teaching, "It is no longer because of your words that we believe, for we have heard for ourselves, and we know that this is indeed the Savior of the world" 4:42). And this paradox, too, is a characteristic of the theotic life—each of us is to become a conduit of life and meant to be "taught of God" without slavish reliance on others (John 6:45; 1 Thess 4.9 cf. Isa 54:13; Jer 31:34), all the while being enriched and helped by those with whom we are joined. Mediation and confluence take their places alongside the immediate presence of the Lord to each member. What is true of the Holy Trinity—the integrity of each person conjoined with the unity of the Godhead—is to be, it seems, mirrored in the redeemed and glorified Body of Christ. And so it is that the Lord seeks out St. Photini herself, while the Father seeks "worshippers" (plural). The "we" factor continues into our final home, as is made so clear to us both by the elder's letter, and by the Apocalypse of Jesus to John:

> That which was from the beginning, which we have heard, which we have seen with our eyes, which we have looked upon and touched with our hands, concerning the word of life—the life was made manifest, and we saw it, and testify to it, and proclaim to you the eternal life which was with the Father and was made manifest to us— that which we have seen and heard we proclaim also to you, so that you may have fellowship with us; and our fellowship is with the Father and with his Son Jesus Christ. And we are writing this that our joy may be complete. (1 John 1:1–4)

---

48. Chrysostom, *Hom. John* 31.5 (112). The emphasis is mine.

> Then he showed me the river of the water of life, bright as crystal, flowing from the throne of God and of the Lamb through the middle of the street of the city; also, on either side of the river, *the tree of life with its twelve kinds of fruit, yielding its fruit each month; and the leaves of the tree were for the healing of the nations.* There shall no more be anything accursed, but the throne of God and of the Lamb shall be in it, and *his servants* shall worship him; they shall see his face, and his name shall be on *their* foreheads. And night shall be no more; they need no light of lamp or sun, for the Lord God will be their light, and *they shall reign for ever and ever.* (Rev 22:1–5)

This fellowship includes mediation: the completion of joy as apostles are joined by others, the healing of the nations, the twelve crops that mediate life. Yet the light comes directly from God and the Lamb, so that mediation is in no way at enmity with the immediate presence of the Godhead. In the end, all becomes prayer and praise—worship—as the historical, the doctrinal, and the practical are brought into that final communion with our Triune God. There we will no longer need the lessons of history open to anyone with a general attention. Where there is prophecy, it will pass away (for the Word himself will be present); where there is ascesis, it will no longer be necessary; but worship will last forever.

Until we gaze with open faces upon the One who is the Word, though, we have the evangelist's words, we have the father's commentaries, and we have St. Photini, who was met by the Lord at the well, who became equal-to-the-apostles, and who—if the legend tells us truly—glorified Him like the prophet Jeremiah, by being cast into a well, where she gave the ultimate witness at the end of her earthly life. Continual meditation upon this "happenstance" meeting at the well will yield more spiritual life than we can imagine, as we continue to dwell upon its general, creedal, practical and theotic elements. "Let the one who thirsts come": let the one who comes consider Who it is Who is speaking; let us hear the Master as He challenges us on practical matters; and may we welcome and be drawn into the hour that now is and is to come! So shall we know the Gift of God and drink from the spring that never runs dry. We close with sage advice from St. John Cassian concerning our reading of Scriptures, not as a series of strategies, but as a consistent way of life akin to the praying of the Jesus Prayer:

> If you wish to achieve true knowledge of Scripture you must hurry to achieve unshakable humility of heart.... Then, having banished all worldly concerns and thoughts, strive in every way to devote yourself constantly to the sacred reading so that continuous meditation will seep into your soul, as it were, will shape

it to its image. Somehow it will form that "ark" of the Scriptures (cf. Heb 9:4–5) and will contain the two stone tablets, that is, the perpetual strength of the two testaments. There will be the golden urn which is a pure and unstained memory and which will preserve firmly within itself that everlasting manna, that is, the eternal, heavenly sweetness of spiritual meanings and of that bread which belongs to the angels....

Therefore the sequences of holy Scripture must be committed to memory and they must be pondered ceaselessly. Such meditation will profit us in two ways. First, when the thrust of the mind is occupied by the study and perusal of the readings it will, of necessity, avoid being taken over by the snares of dangerous thoughts. Second, as we strive with constant repetition to commit these readings to memory, we have not the time to understand them because our minds have been occupied. But later when we are free from the attractions of all that we do and see and, especially, when we are quietly meditating during the hours of darkness, we think them over and we understand them more closely. And so it happens that when we are at ease and when, as it were, we are plunged into the dullness of sleep, the hidden meanings, of which we were utterly unaware during our waking hours, and the sense of them are bared to our minds.

As our mind is increasingly renewed by this study, Scripture begins to take on a new face. A mysteriously deeper sense of it comes to us and somehow the beauty of it stands out more and more as we get farther into it. Scripture shapes itself to human capacity.[49]

---

49. John Cassian, *Conferences* 14.10 (164–65).

Spiritual Interpretation After Modernity
A Response to Edith Humphrey

JENS ZIMMERMANN (EVANGELICAL)

INTRODUCTION

I AM HONORED AND genuinely humbled by the task to respond to such a thoughtful, beautiful, and edifying reading of John's gospel. According to the arrangement of this volume, I am to offer a response from an evangelical perspective to Edith Humphrey's interpretation of the Johannine text. What, however, should an evangelical response look like? It may be worth pausing for a moment to think about the assumed expectations of such an attempt. What evangelical tradition do we have in mind? Are we talking about the gospel-centered faith arising from Luther, Calvin, and English Puritans generally summed up under the term Protestantism? Or do we mean North American evangelical*ism* which combines well-meant social activism with the rather thin ecclesiology of its roots in Anabaptist theologies of the Radical Reformation, adding to this heritage its narrow literalism, destructive individualism, and its generally modernist, non-sacramental outlook? Such distinctions matter, I believe, even at the level of sophisticated, scholarly biblical exegesis. On the one hand, the guild of biblical studies remains divided among those who read the Bible merely as a cultural artifact of tremendous historical value and those who read it as the Word of God, addressed to his people. Among the latter group of consciously Christian interpreters, which includes Protestant, Catholic, and

Orthodox scholars, many have produced impressive, even leading work in the field and have earned the respect of their non-believing peers. Even among such intentionally Christian interpreters, however, there is a division between two kinds of theological interpretations. The set of interpreters, which includes Edith Humphrey along with the other scholars in this volume, practice the kind of theological interpretation that implements Stephen Fowl's advice of "keeping theological concerns and ends primary to all others."[1] This kind of exegesis by no means neglects historical-critical tools but subordinates them to a Christian, ecclesiastically-grounded reading of the scriptures. Such spiritual interpretation has traditionally been a Christological hermeneutic with the goal of transformation into Christ-likeness, or what Edith Humphrey calls *"theotic"* reading. Given that the contributors to this volume and many other Christian interpreters will agree with such spiritual interpretation that Professor Humphrey has presented in this volume with such great skill, I cannot really offer a *critical* response; the best I can do is to describe in my own terms her interpretive approach to the text and to reflect briefly on why I think reading the way she does may continue to be a challenge, not only to some evangelicals but also to those in the academic guild of biblical studies who still suffer from the lingering effects of ingesting the historical-critical spirit with their training. Let me hasten to add the rejoinder, surely unnecessary in present company, that grammatical-historical methods have been used in textual criticism from antiquity, ever since people have gathered, preserved, handed down, and commented on authoritative texts. When I mention the effects of the historical-critical *spirit*, I mean the kind of hermeneutic that rejects theological or spiritual interpretation in the name of objective historical criticism, only to substitute its own individualistic, modern framework in the name of critical exegesis.

CHRISTIAN HUMANIST (INCARNATIONAL) HERMENEUTICS

I begin, then, by taking Edith's reading into my own frame of reference, not in order to co-opt her excellent work for my purposes, but to see to what extent she recognizes her own hermeneutic in this restatement. Edith has presented to us what I would call a Christian-humanist reading, or, which I take to be the same thing, an incarnational interpretation of the scriptures. By Christian humanism, I mean the Christological outlook that determined the exegesis of the church fathers, an outlook Henri de Lubac fittingly

1. Fowl, *Theological Interpretation of Scripture*, 39.

described as an "all-embracing humanism." The essence of this Christian humanism is—to use Athanaeus's pithy formula—that God became human so that we could become godlike. In Christ, to speak with Irenaeus, all humanity is recapitulated and put back on track to become formed into the image of him who is the true form of the father according to which man had been shaped from the beginning.[2] Becoming godlike—or, to allay Protestant fears, becoming "Christlike"—is therefore the goal of the Christian life. Perhaps we can convince fellow Protestants to embrace *theōsis* more readily by appealing to one of the more Protestant saints (aside from C. S. Lewis, of course). In his *Homilies on the Gospel of John*, St. Augustine comments that, in Jesus, God became "visible as human, so as to make visible human beings into gods; the Son of God became the Son of Man, so as to make the sons of men into sons of Gods." For the fathers, the goal of Christianity, including the interpretation of the scriptures, was education or *paideia* into Christlikeness. Among the evangels, the gospel of John states most clearly the purpose of the Christian life: the purpose of Christianity is to be drawn into the divine life, the attainment of our full humanity in union with God and one another. In short, as Edith clearly shows, a Christian humanist reading of the Bible aims at *theōsis* or deification.

A *theotic* reading, however, is by definition incarnational and therefore irrevocably enfleshed in the particularities of time and place. As Humphrey demonstrates in her beautiful representation of fourfold exegesis, our knowledge of God obtained through the scriptures must necessarily follow God's own pattern of self-revelation through history. In my own experience, the greatest objection to theological exegesis in biblical studies departments is that spiritual interpretation does not take history seriously. Yet the incarnational pattern of God's self-revelation makes non-historical fundamentalism theologically impossible. Ignoring history is impossible because God revealed himself as a concrete historical human being. Another important result of God's becoming human is that our knowledge of God is by nature interpretive and requires a Christological hermeneutic. Indeed, our particular text for this conference points out not just the historicity of God's self-revelation but also the epistemological consequence that knowledge about God is never immediate but accessible only through interpretation. In John 1:18 we read that "no one has ever seen God; the only son who is in the bosom of the father interpreted "ἐξηγήσατο" God the Father. In the Greek, Jesus is the "exegete" of God.[3] Given the possible meanings of *exegeomai*, Jesus "explained," "interpreted" or "revealed" the Father by "setting him forth in

---

2. Heb 1:3; Col 1:15; John 1:18, etc.

3. I am indebted for this insight to Moloney, *Gospel of John*, 95.

language," by "narrating him." Jesus, as Hans Urs von Balthasar put it, is the perfect interpretation of God which we have to interpret in turn. We only know God through the incarnate Christ and Christ only through our interpretations of him, which themselves are always in the "flesh" of history. The incarnational pattern of God's self-revelation presents us with the double hermeneutical challenge which the philosopher Hans-Georg Gadamer has identified as the "fusion of horizons." Not only do we have to reconstruct God's own self-interpretation *within* a particular culture and history, but we also do so governed by our own historically determined preconceptions and concerns.[4]

Reformation theology, even if it may have prepared the facile and highly problematic individualistic modern understanding of *sola scriptura*, has nonetheless contributed an important emphasis on historical-critical exegesis. Through its marriage of Christology with the historical consciousness of Renaissance humanism, Protestant exegesis has greatly contributed to the recovery of the incarnational, historical dimension of biblical hermeneutics.

HISTORICAL CONSCIOUSNESS AND FUSION OF HORIZONS

With the rise of a truly historical consciousness that understands the genuine distance that exists between ancient and modern cultural horizons, the question arises how a universal message of salvation, enshrined in an ancient cultural outlook and cosmology, can be translated into our modern world. How can past and present horizons be fused to ensure the continuing relevance of the gospel? It remains the fascinating and paradoxical legacy of modern Protestant theologians to have fully grasped the hermeneutical challenge posed by the incarnation as a unique historical event only to solve this challenge by escaping from history. Take Rudolf Bultmann's famous idea of demythologization, for example. Hardly anyone has more clearly articulated the problem of translating the gospel from its ancient context for a modern consciousness than Bultmann, only to proceed by reducing the gospel to a timeless existential-gnostic message of authentic selfhood.[5] In order to preserve the timeless kernel of the gospel, he strips the Christ event of its supposed historical, and therefore also Jewish, husk (the Christ

---

4. Augustine already realizes something like this when he writes that "so whatever much then we understand and however much we see, even when we have been *put on a level with the angels* (Luke 20:36), we shall not see as the Son sees" (*Homilies of John*, Homily 21, 374).

5. Bultmann, "New Testament and Mythology," 3.

event's "objective, mythical form"[6]) and translates the new humanity inaugurated by Christ into the liberation of the inner man's faith toward "self-commitment, capable of faith and love, of his authentic life."[7] Bultmann's intentions are rather laudable. He believes that the mythological language in which the historical events of cross and resurrection are described try to convey the permanent meaning, the timeless redemptive significance of Christ's redemptive work. Yet the best intentions cannot avoid the inevitable distortions that follow when, in fusing past and present horizons, the past horizon becomes fully assimilated to and thus distorted by Bultmann's own interpretive framework. Severed from its native historical narrative of God with Israel, the gospel is easily transformed into a modern philosophy that "opens up for men the possibility of authentic life."[8]

The separation of Christ from history is not merely a theoretical violation of hermeneutics but often has disturbing practical consequences, as was vividly illustrated by Protestant exegesis in Germany during Hitler's regime, when Nazi theologians gladly drew on scholarship that allowed the separation of the Christian gospel from its Jewish roots. German anti-Semitism, when on rare occasions ascending to such intellectual heights, fed on the supersessionism suggested by Bultmann's or Harnack's gnostic gospel. When Christianity boils down to an existential message, the Jewish scriptures are no longer needed, and the Jews are no longer intrinsically part of God's redemptive plan. Supersessionist theology thus encouraged anti-Semitism.

It took incarnational theologians such as Bonhoeffer to point out that Christian theology remains forever dependent on God's history with Israel. Bonhoeffer did not deny, of course, that Jesus himself consciously takes up and transforms Israel's story by presenting himself as the fulfillment of God's messianic promises to his people. But Bonhoeffer did deny that a reader can take this transformation for granted, can accept it second hand, as a settled truth. Rather, each reader has to work through, re-experience, and appropriate for himself this history to understand the full weight of Jesus's own affirmation that "salvation is from the Jews." This is also what I take Professor Humphrey to say with her admonition that a *theotic* reading always incorporates Jesus's "ratification of Israel's metanarrative." Bonhoeffer put the same matter more urgently: "Whoever wishes to be and perceive too quickly and too directly in New Testament ways is to my mind no Christian. One must not speak the ultimate word before the penultimate." Not by

---

6. Ibid., 35.
7. Ibid., 33.
8. Ibid., 39.

leaving the Old Testament behind but by staying within this story of which Christ is the culmination will we understand who Jesus is, and who God is. Bonhoeffer notes, "Only when one knows that the name of God may not be uttered may one sometimes utter the name of Jesus Christ [. . .]. Only when one accepts the law as binding may one perhaps sometimes speak of grace."[9] For Bonhoeffer, past and present horizons are fused in a way that the whole of the past horizon constantly stands before us in its difference to elucidate our present understanding of God. As Bonhoeffer put it, it is only by staying with Jesus within the Jewish narrative that we can ever grasp who Jesus really is.

The notion of grasping the true identity of Jesus is, of course, the whole point of our text. The literary structure of John makes clear the educational or *theotic* purpose of this book, namely to take readers who already know or have heard about Christ up into the better knowledge that he is indeed the *Logos* through whom and for whom all things were made, that he is son of man and of God, that he is life itself and the gift of God who takes us into the divine communion. The first eighteen verses of John are the hermeneutical key in light of which the whole book is to be read. Every recounted scene, including the encounter at the well, shows us people who either grasp or do not grasp Jesus's true identity. What St. Ephrem notes about the woman's growth in understanding is what this text intends for every reader. To quote Edith quoting Ephrem: the woman at the well "first saw [Jesus] as someone thirsting; then as a Jew; then as a prophet; and after that as God." The purpose of John's gospel is to draw the reader into Jesus's interpretation of himself as the promised messiah who is the light that illumines every human being, revealing our supernatural destiny of union with God and one another.

READING THE GOSPEL AFTER MODERNITY

I want to end by pointing out what I consider to be the hermeneutical problem that may prevent certain evangelicals and biblical scholars from accepting the kind of incarnational, *theotic* reading Edith has offered and, I suspect, many of us resonate with. You see, I don't think that our challenge is really confessional, since a great number of evangelicals, Reformed, Orthodox, and Catholic Christians already agree on the need for spiritual interpretation. I think the real challenge lies in the difficulty of overcoming the limitations posed by a typically modern ontology which experiences reality as non-sacramental. The premodern universe, whether Christian or

---

9. DBWE 8, 213.

pagan, was *intrinsically* symbolic, because all things were meaningfully connected through their participation in some divine reality. Whether gnostic, stoic, Jewish, or Christian, the premodern universe was an intelligible, symbolic universe, governed by an inherent rationality in which the human mind shared and to which it had to conform in knowledge. For many pagan, Christian, and Jewish readers of Scripture, the Word or *Logos* was the central hub for the holistic, interconnected totality of meaning relations for which the intellectual historian Louis Dupré coined the term "onto-theological synthesis." Based on this synthesis, history and language are porous media for accessing transcendent realities. In the modern universe, by contrast, language no longer shares in such realities and thus takes on a merely instrumental character. Within modernist ontology, history now becomes an object that we hold up to our eyes, trying to see what was really there in a time-bound historical context. Modernity traps us, to use Charles Taylor's terms, in a buffered self, confronted by a self-contained object that we then somehow connect to our own horizon of meaning.

What I am getting at is this: the reason that church fathers read the woman at the well in John's gospel as a prefiguration of the Christian church and did *not* regard such reading as arbitrary allegorical *imposition* is because their worldview rendered plausible the notion that in his actions, Jesus writes with a divine finger on the very pages of history, giving events their ultimate spiritual meaning within the folds of history. This, surely, is Augustine's view when he interprets the woman at the well as a type of the church:

> It is part of this symbolism of this episode that this woman, who was a type of the Church, came from a foreign people. In fact, the Church, a foreigner to the Jewish people, was going to come from the nations. So then, let us listen to ourselves in her and recognize ourselves in her, and in her give thanks to God for ourselves. She, after all, was a figure, not the true reality, and because she prefigured the reality, that is what she became. *For she came to believe in the one who proposed her to us as a figure.*[10]

Jesus, in other words, turned the woman into a symbol because as the head of the church his actions made it so. For a premodern exegete such as Augustine, this encounter is orchestrated in its very historicity as a symbol by God so that we can take part in its meaning.

Now I submit to you that this hermeneutical presupposition of a sacramental universe remains hard to swallow for many because they are thoroughly modernist in their training and outlook. When I read Edith Humphrey's discussion of historical issues, her conception of history and

---

10. Augustine, *Homilies on the Gospel of John*, 280–81.

the supporting ontology on which the integrity of her beautiful hermeneutic depends struck me as more Augustinian than modern. And this is a good thing, because clearly the recovery and practice of fourfold exegesis and *theotic* reading require a sacramental universe. But can we really just take up where Augustine left off as if modernity never happened? Can we just jump right back into the fundamentally different understanding of temporality and of history that governed the premodern interpreters? Humphrey's reading of John speaks out of a tradition that lived in a sacramental universe. There is a great desire among young evangelicals to reconnect with that tradition, but can we just ignore how deeply modernity, with its separation of the natural and supernatural, has shaped our outlook? Don't we have to do the hard theoretical work of recovering a sacramental reality and of explaining to those Christians still in the grip of a modernist epistemology why such a recovery is plausible? In my view, New Testament exegetes have not done enough of this theoretical hermeneutical work, and this negligence explains the continuing failure of any real dialogue between those scholars who read theologically and those who claim to do merely historical-critical work. Among biblical scholars, have we really progressed much beyond the standoff between Barth and Bultmann? Have we got much further than the two sides, with Barth simply asserting the power of God's word to transcend history without providing any hermeneutic justification (what Bonhoeffer called Barth's "positivism of revelation"), and with Bultmann as the other extreme of supposedly respecting the historical gulf between past and present, while smuggling his Heideggerian message of self-authentication across the historical chasm? The real challenge of reading John's gospel in a modern world, it seems to me, is to recover credibly a sacramental ontology to support the kind of reading Edith so beautifully exercised for us today. The real challenge for the reading of Scripture after modernity is the intellectual effort to render plausible the claim that Christ "is the true light who illumines every human being."[11] The response to this challenge cannot come from unreflective historical exegesis, but requires philosophical and, above all, theological work.

---

11. John 1:9.

John 4:1–26
Response to Edith Humphrey

DANIEL A. KEATING (CATHOLIC)

INTRODUCTION

As I READ THROUGH Edith Humphrey's commentary on John 4, I experienced delight and admiration, both because of the mastery of the subject displayed and the exegetical proficiency in evidence. Humphrey moves skillfully back and forth between ancient and contemporary modes of commentary, without apology, embarrassment, or awkwardness. This is a fine piece of theological commentary.

What I wish to do in this brief response is to comment on four of the many excellent insights that Humphrey has offered and develop them with an eye especially to the relationship between eastern and western theological traditions and the church's ongoing relationship to Judaism. En route, I will make occasional reference to St. Thomas Aquinas's commentary on these verses, as a formative voice in the western tradition who integrates with particular aptitude a variety of Greek and Latin writers who preceded him.

THE USE OF EASTERN AND WESTERN FATHERS

My first topic is how Humphrey has seamlessly woven together the testimony of the Eastern and Western Fathers, employing them to illuminate her own commentary and at the same time bringing their testimony into the light as guides to shape own understanding of the text. References to

John Chrysostom, Origen, Basil, Cyril of Alexandria, Ephrem and other Fathers from the East are gracefully intertwined with citations of Hilary, Ambrose, Augustine, John Cassian, Caesarius of Arles and other Fathers from the West. This is clearly not, however, just an eclectic or random selection of texts strung together to demonstrate an equitable use of eastern and western sources. Rather, the citations serve the flow of the commentary and provide a kind of spine for its development. This is a genuinely *theological* commentary drawing richly on the varied voices of the Fathers.

Let me add two perspectives on the use of the Fathers from the East and the West. First, as I myself read through a selection of patristic commentaries, I was unable to detect an "eastern" reading in contrast to a "western" one. While each commentator has his own particular views and orientations, there do not seem to be two streams that diverge in any noteworthy ways. Instead, we find a richly varied but harmonious commentary across the Greek and Latin Fathers. This itself is a noteworthy finding, even if it covers only a very small range of commentary in the Gospel of John.

Second, I found in Thomas Aquinas a remarkable synthesis of eastern and western sources, woven together to shape his own impressive commentary on these verses. In the *Catena Aurea* for John 4:1–26, Thomas gathers together thirty-three selections from Latin authors and forty-eight from Greek authors, St. John Chrysostom being cited most frequently. In his *Commentary on John*, Aquinas cites St. Augustine just slightly more frequently that Chrysostom, but still we find a predominance of explicit citations from Greek writers overall. This is a surprising find: this most western of theologians draws heavily on the Greek tradition as well as the Latin, not slavishly but respectfully and critically. At one point, for example, he sets side-by-side the respective explanations by Chrysostom and Augustine of the text, "but Jesus himself did not baptize" (John 4:2). Aquinas concludes that in this case Augustine's reading is better because his account more closely follows what we read in the Scripture. But on another occasion, when explaining the phrase "salvation is from the Jews" (John 4:22), Thomas ignores Augustine's narrow reading and adopts an interpretation much more in line with Chrysostom. More on this in a moment.

READING THE TEXT ACCORDING TO THE FOUR-FOLD SENSE

My second topic is how Humphrey commendably shapes her commentary according to the ancient four senses. In our contemporary climate for biblical exegesis, this is a brave act and she accomplishes it with considerable skill. The senses are well-handled, not as comprising a rigid schema by which we manufacture meanings—like pushing meat through a sausage grinder—but as intertwined readings of the text by which the skillful and faith-filled reader can perceive the multiple truths that the text conveys. I found particularly helpful Humphrey's insight that this fourfold reading of the Scripture is not just a "series of strategies," but also a kind of exegesis of our lives before the word of God, so that we become more and more akin to Christ himself.

When launching the "general" or "literal" reading of the text, Humphrey refers to her own "Antiochian context" and says that "the first strategy of reading is not expendable, nor must it be suppressed by the three others." Let me offer two comments on this Antiochian context in an ecumenical perspective. First, attention to this first, basic level of reading is underlined famously by Thomas Aquinas at the start of the *Summa*, where he places great emphasis upon it and sees it as the foundational sense of Scripture. And of course this first sense is the one largely employed by the Reformers. Second, as we are talking about Antioch, let me add a word in appreciation for the biblical exegesis of that eminent *Alexandrian*, Cyril of Alexandria. It still remains common in both scholarly works and standard textbooks to distinguish sharply between the Antiochene concern for the historical and literal on the one hand and the Alexandrian orientation toward allegory and the spiritual senses on the other. While there is certainly some ground for this distinction, I believe it is usually exaggerated and often does not fit the actual biblical exposition of the Fathers.

Cyril is a case in point. An Alexandrian who is eager to develop a spiritual sense of a passage, Cyril normally gives a great deal of attention to what we would call the literary and historical context, especially when commenting on the prophets of the Old Testament. Manlio Simonetti, for one, acknowledges that in Cyril "the literal interpretation is highly developed, much more so than in any other Alexandrian exegete," but he then estimates the overall result as "desultory" because, he claims, it tries to combine the two approaches in an eclectic manner.[1] I respectfully disagree—at least in most instances. While there may be flaws and deficiencies in Cyril's exegesis, he combines an attention to the literal-historical with a profound movement to the spiritual senses in an impressive manner, and in my judgment produced the most fruitful commentary on the fourth gospel in the patristic era. In Cyril's biblical commentaries, the characteristic marks of Antioch and Alexandria join hands in a fruitful union.

---

1. Simonetti, *Biblical Interpretation*, 81.

THE GIFT GIVEN IS GOD HIMSELF

My third topic takes up a point made by Humphrey on the opening page of her paper. She writes:

> Yet the waters of John 4 do not signify merely Scripture, but the gift of God himself, to which Scriptures point: the construction "gift *of God*" is clearly meant, in this passage, to be the objective genitive, that gift *who is God*, not merely a gift divinely given. If reading Scripture is like trying to drink from a fire hose, how much more exhilarating is the reception of the very Spirit of God?

This is a crucial exegetical point. Jesus is offering the woman the gift of living water, the Holy Spirit in person, who will live within her and be an unending source of divine life from within. This in fact is just the point that Aquinas underlines in his commentary on these verses. He writes:

> Now water is of two kinds: living and non-living. Non-living water is water which is not connected or united with the source from which it springs, but is collected from the rain or in other ways into ponds and cisterns, and there it stands, separated from its source. But living water is connected with its source and flows from it. So according to this understanding, the grace of the Holy Spirit is correctly called living water, because the grace of the Holy Spirit is given to man in such a way that the source itself of the grace is also given, that is, the Holy Spirit. Indeed, grace is given by the Holy Spirit: "The love of God is poured out into our hearts by the Holy Spirit, who has been given to us" (Rom 5:5). For the Holy Spirit is the unfailing fountain from whom all gifts of grace flow: "One and the same Spirit does all these things" (1 Cor 12:11). And so, if anyone has a gift of the Holy Spirit without having the Spirit, the water is not united with its source, and so is not living but dead.[2]

Thomas is sometimes criticized for placing so much emphasis on the created effects of grace that he effectively denies the gift of God himself to the believer. He is charged with keeping God at one remove from his redeemed creature, with "grace" being the medium that connects them.[3] But here we

---

2. Aquinas, *Commentary on John*, 4:10–26, lecture 2 (577), 215.

3. For this critique of Aquinas in some contemporary Orthodox writers, see Plested, *Orthodox Readings of Aquinas*, 205–6. Lossky, *Vision of God*, 166, regards the division in Western Scholasticism between grace as God's presence within us and grace as a created *habitus* as "a distinction which can only be a separation." Williams, *Ground of Union*, 87–89, defends Aquinas against the critique that he overly emphasizes the created quality of grace in the soul.

see in the clearest terms that for Aquinas the gift of the Spirit himself must be given to the believer if genuine spiritual life is to be received. It is the Spirit given who is the constant and unending source of grace and life.

While I am on the subject of Aquinas's commentary on verse 10, let me draw attention to another striking and surprising feature that immediately follows—and it is a feature that I did not find in any of his patristic sources. Aquinas notices that in his text for verse 10 the word "perhaps" appears: "If you knew the gift of God, and realized who it is who says to you, 'Give me a drink,' you *perhaps* would have asked him that he give you living water." The word here in Latin is *forsitan*, and it is used to translate the particle, "*an*" in the Greek text. The use of "*an*" with the aorist indicates possibility rather than certainty—and the Latin translator chose to insert the word "perhaps" to indicate this uncertainty. Aquinas notices this sense of possibility and brings to our attention the need for free will in choosing for the living water that God is offering. He states it thus:

> For grace is not given to anyone without their asking and desiring it. Thus we say that in the justification of a sinner an act of free will is necessary to detest sin and to desire grace. . . . Thus it is significant that he says, "you perhaps would have asked him." He says "perhaps" on account of free will, with which a person sometimes desires and asks for grace, and sometimes does not.[4]

This specific attention to the requirement of free choice—of desiring and asking for grace or refusing to ask—sounds like something that would more readily come from the pen of an Eastern writer—from Basil or from Cyril. Here we find it in a commentator in the Augustinian tradition in a text that only hints at the role of free will.

SALVATION IS FROM THE JEWS

My final point arises from Humphrey's commentary on the text, "salvation is from the Jews" (John 4:22). I heartily endorse her observations on how this passage has been ignored by many Christians who are wed to a supersessionist reading of the relationship between Israel and the Church. But I wish to comment on her summary statement that "'salvation is *from* the Jews,' though not *in* Judaism!" I think I know what she means by this, and agree with what I understand her intended meaning to be, namely, that salvation was not to be found *in the reality and practice of Judaism as it was then conducted*. Or to say this differently: salvation was not to be found in

---

4. Aquinas, *Commentary on John*, 4:10–26, lecture 2 (578), 215.

the dispensation of the Law, nor was full access to the living God available through Solomon's Temple (and its successor). But I would argue that *in a certain manner* salvation is still "in Judaism," both in the sense that Christ is and remains a Jew, the Jewish Messiah, and salvation is "in him"; and also in the sense that the Church is engrafted into Israel, but Israel now brought to completion in the Messiah (Rom 11:17–24).

What do the Fathers have to say on this text? As noted above, Augustine has an especially narrow reading, limiting "the Jews" only to those Jewish disciples of Jesus who followed him and became the foundation of the church. He makes no allowance for "the Jews" more generally as a reference to Israel throughout salvation history. This is not Augustine at his best.[5] Chrysostom and Cyril both allow a wider and more generous reading, acknowledging the gift of God to Israel throughout history as the root from which Christ and the church have sprung[6]—and this is a reading much more in accord with the Evangelist's intent here. Aquinas not only takes this generous reading, but offers extended commentary to fill out how this occurred, identifying the varied gifts of grace that God gave to Israel.[7]

But as far as I can tell, the entire patristic tradition, both East and West, views this text, "salvation from the Jews," as a point of departure—a place from which the church has set out and left Israel entirely behind. In other words, they take a supersessionist view of Israel in the sense that they see the church displacing Israel as the people of God, and view Israel "according to the flesh" (*kata sarka*; Rom 9:5) as no longer under grace in any positive sense, but in fact under a kind of curse because of unbelief. In his commentary on verse 22, Cyril strikingly speaks of "the total loss of grace" that the Jews suffered because of their rejection of Christ.[8] The language could hardly be stronger and is fully in accord with his wider reading of Israel's place in the divine economy after the coming of Christ.[9]

The Fathers are marvelous when describing what is new in Christ, when expounding on all the riches that our nature and our persons have received through the Incarnation, Passion and resurrection of the Son of God;

---

5. Aquinas, *Tractates on John*, 15.26.

6. Chrysostom, *Homilies on John*, 33.1; Cyril of Alexandria, *Commentary on the Gospel of John*, Book II, chapter 5 (on John 4:22).

7. Aquinas, *Commentary on John*, 4:10–26, lecture 2 (604–6), 224. For Aquinas, salvation comes from the Jews in three ways: in their teaching of the truth, in their spiritual and prophetic gifts, and in the coming of Christ from their midst.

8. Cyril of Alexandria, *Commentary on John*, Book II, chapter 4 (on John 4:4–5).

9. The full phrase is "as enduring the total loss of grace" (ōs holoklēron ēdē tēs charitos hypomenousa zēmian). For an account of Cyril's approach to Israel and the church, see Keating, "Supersessionism in Cyril of Alexandria," 119–24.

when displaying, in other words, the glory of deification, of *theōsis* But for the most part their theological understanding of the relationship between Israel and the church was one-sided. On the one hand, they applied Jesus's judgment against the Jewish leaders of his day to *all* Jews and to *all* Israel through time; on the other hand, they left underdeveloped Paul's nuanced teaching in Romans 9–11 on the situation of unbelieving Israel that remains "beloved for the sake of their forefathers" (Rom 11:28, RSV).

Humphrey helpfully draws our attention to what Fr. Richard John Neuhaus wrote on this text and the question of supersessionism. His treatment offers what I consider to be a more adequate way of understanding that "salvation is from the Jews." For Neuhaus, the phrase, "salvation is from the Jews," in not "a point of departure" but instead "remains until the end of time our point of arrival." He adds that this does not mean that we are in full agreement but that we, Christians and Jews, are locked together in argument until God brings his kingdom fully: "The end of supersessionism, however, cannot and must not mean the end of the argument between Christians and Jews. We cannot settle into the comfortable interreligious politesse of mutual respect for positions deemed to be equally true. Christ and his Church do not supersede Judaism but they do continue and fulfill the story of which we are both part."[10]

With this I will conclude and express my gratitude to Humphrey for so skillfully and so inspiringly displaying the theological and pastoral riches of this encounter between Jesus and Photini at Jacob's well so long ago.

---

10. "Salvation is from the Jews." The Second Vatican Council set the Catholic Church on a new course in relationship to the Jewish people, expressed in the following declaration: "As Holy Scripture testifies, Jerusalem did not recognize the time of her visitation, nor did the Jews in large number, accept the Gospel; indeed not a few opposed its spreading. Nevertheless, God holds the Jews most dear for the sake of their Fathers; He does not repent of the gifts He makes or of the calls He issues-such is the witness of the Apostle. . . . True, the Jewish authorities and those who followed their lead pressed for the death of Christ; (13) still, what happened in His passion cannot be charged against all the Jews, without distinction, then alive, nor against the Jews of today. Although the Church is the new people of God, the Jews should not be presented as rejected or accursed by God, as if this followed from the Holy Scriptures" (*Nostra Aetate*, 4).

Humphrey Final Response

I AM VERY GRATEFUL to my colleagues for their generous responses to my paper, an exercise in wading in where biblical scholars (angelic or otherwise) fear to tread. As a supplement to this, my first foray into an ancient way of reading Scripture, I want to affirm my continued appreciation of the historical-critical approach, when used judiciously and not to mask a hermeneutic of suspicion or to avoid the challenges that the Scriptures direct to us. Indeed, last year, as President of the Canadian Society of Biblical Studies, I offered an address[1] in which I (partially) lamented the lost goal of objectivity in scholarly discussion of the Scriptures. In that paper, I likened modernist methods to the game of chess, in which the moves of the game matter, but not the disposition of the players: in that scenario, those of different backgrounds find a level field on which to mount their arguments and offer their analyses, and also to evaluate the work of others. Our more engaged "postmodern" perspective removes the pretense of neutral-free scholarship, but also renders the players more vulnerable to dismissive attitudes by those who share other convictions: thus, it is more like the contemporary game of "scruples,"[2] which can be entertaining, or marginalizing, depending on the civility of the players! Besides this, the new approach, unhampered by a strategy of fostering (even in its aims) objective thinking, can lead to wild and improbable hypotheses, or to an ideological eisegesis of Scripture.

There is a place for engagement in scholarship; there is also value in agreeing as to certain procedures, and observing what happens when these are followed, catalyzed by various questions and various concerns.

---

1. "From Chess to Scruples: Changing Paradigms in Biblical Scholarship and the Games We Play," *Canadian Society of Biblical Studies/Société Canadienne des Études Bibliques Bulletin* 73 (2013–2013), 1–25.

2. Scruples is a game that presents moral dilemmas to be answered by each player, invented by Henry Makow in 1984, that has profited from high exposure on American television, both in *Carson's Tonight Show* and the first season of *Everybody Loves Raymond*.

Assessing the strengths and weaknesses of both approaches, I find myself both delighted by an engaged, in-house reading of the Scriptures among those who believe, while also welcoming a widened discussion with those outside the faith—in the latter case, the "neutral" approach associated with the historical-critical methods seems to be the most fruitful. Of course, I left myself vulnerable in my paper on John 4, since in the Paradosis conference, we tackled the gospel of John together as family. And I am pleased to hear the suggestions and expansions of my brothers, Jens Zimmermann and Daniel Keating.

I begin with the questions asked by my evangelical colleague. Jens asserts that there is a good deal of work to be done in rehabilitating the sacramental perspective for those who have been formed by a modernist epistemology, a system that presents each of us as a "buffered self" without direct access to historical events, let alone each other. I am no philosopher, so I cannot enter thoroughly into the task here set forth for us. I will say, however, that there may be aid for the philosophically-minded in Jean-Luc Marion's notion of the "saturated phenomenon," which begins with experience in this world and suggests that there is more to some perceptions than meet the eye—indeed, they can overflow the container! To this I would add that it is misguided for us in this day and age, nor was it ever sufficient, to speak in terms of "timelessness" over against historical specificity, as though a sacrament were the participation of earthly things in a timeless reality. Consider as a cautionary tale the mid-twentieth century hymn of Brian Wren, who assumed that Christians should rejoice along the following docetic lines:

> Christ is alive! Let Christians sing.
> His cross stands empty to the sky.
> Let streets and homes with praises ring.
> His love in death shall never die.
> Christ is alive! No longer bound
> to distant years in Palestine,
> he comes to claim the here and now
> and conquer every place and time....
> Christ is alive! His Spirit burns
> through this and every future age,
> till all creation lives and learns
> his joy, his justice, love, and praise.[3]

Clearly this twentieth-century hymnodist is still breathing the air of anti-materialism, assuming that Jesus had to be set free from the body in order to

---

3. Wren, *Poems of Grace*, 145.

meet human need. This is almost the polar opposite of the patristic understanding that "what is not assumed is not healed." This brings me, then, to the nature of sacramentalism. It is, I think, a mistake to anchor the patristic sacramental consciousness too firmly in a general ancient mindset of animism and/or Logos philosophy, as Jens appears to do:

> Whether gnostic, stoic, Jewish or Christian, the premodern universe was an intelligible, symbolic universe, governed by an inherent rationality in which the human mind shared and to which it had to conform in knowledge . . . [in this schema,] history and language are porous media for accessing transcendent realities. . . . Their worldview rendered plausible the notion that in his actions, Jesus writes with a divine finger on the very pages of history . . .

It seems to me that the specific genius of the Christian story is that it took unlikely root in a matured Jewish mindset that, though probably originally henotheistic, was insisting by the second temple period upon an ontological divide between the divine and the created order: "Who has known the mind of the Lord?" For apologetic purposes, of course, Christians had recourse to Stoic and neo-Platonic ideas, but always the apophatic impulse and the eschewal of idolatry chastened these avenues: at times more successfully than others! Holding together the truth concerning a God *totaliter aliter* who was at the same time "the lover of humankind" and creation rendered (and should render) Christian ideas of sacramentality quite different than the high-flown philosophy of the Stoics, the formal imagination of the Platonists, or the folksy enchantment of the animist. In all this, however, I would insist that the Christian mind, perceived in its tradition and its Scriptures, fosters a concept of timefulness rather than timelessness. The Incarnation forbids any other approach to the particular.

This is interconnected, too, with what we mean when we speak of *theōsis*. Chastened and grounded by the revelation of a truly creating (and non-pantheistic) God, many fathers (including St. Athanasius and the blessed Augustine)[4] could outrageously declare that "God became man that man

---

4 Αὐτὸς γὰρ ἐνηνθρώπησεν, ἵνα ἡμεῖς θεοποιηθῶμεν, Athanasius, *De Incarnatione Verbi* 54.3. (Note that the verbs are "humanized" and "made god"—not "made godlike"). *Deus factus est homo ut homo deus fieret*, in Migne *Sermones Ad Populum Classes II De Tempore CXCI*, "God became man so that man might become God," Augustine, Sermon 191 (27). The quote from Augustine is not found in all manuscripts, and is sometimes ascribed to a disciple, but even if this is the case, it shows the entrenchment of *theōsis* among Latin fathers and students, as well as in the East. See also Irenaeus, *Adv. Haer.* V, preface; Gregory Nazianzen, *Poema dogmatica* 10, 5–9; Gregory Nyssa *Oratio catechetica magna* 25.

might become god." The miracle of participatory transformation was predicated on the distinction between Creator and creation, including humankind. But ancients actually meant what they said, and did not use *theōsis* metaphorically to speak about mere Christ-likeness, as Jens glosses. The transformation goes far beyond our being "put back on track": it is our promised inheritance of the divine glory and our actual growth into the likeness of the One after whose image we are created. *Theōsis* then, is the corresponding and responsive miracle to the Incarnation, and is bound up with the Ascension of the One who has made us siblings and friends, and no longer slaves.

Here, then, is the place where the fusion of horizons must be located—in God's creational and re-creational actions, not only *upon* but *in* our world. A fourfold interpretation that begins with the "general" reading rightly emerges from the space-time *cosmos* in which God is invested—a divine investment that values both the historical flow (*chronos*) and the particular moment *(kairos)*, and that promises to rejuvenate the material world declared to be "very good!" This is the necessary departure point that remains in view as we perceive openings in the text for deeper (and more exalted!) meanings. Throughout this repeated reading, the original intent of the first human author does not exert a stranglehold, but is recognized amidst the inherent polyvalence afforded the Scriptures by the Lord in his "many-colored wisdom" (3:10). In Him is life, and in Him is the light that shows up colors not only in our world, but also in the written word. Here, then, are the points of contact with postmodern ears that seek for multiplicity, and with contemporary readers who affirm the importance of the physical. These moments of connection may be stressed, alongside the philosophical overtures suggested by Jens. That they might be heard seems less implausible now than formerly, especially considering the warm welcome that Richard Hays's newest book, *Reading Backwards*,[5] has received in some circles. From the New Testament itself, he has recovered the apostolic procedure of reading according to the canon of truth, and thus he demonstrates its promise to a readership once chained by authorial intent and sandwiched by epistemological buffers.

My second interlocutor, Daniel Keating, is happy to notice that we see these themes in the Western Church as well as in the Eastern fathers, and goes so far as to say that he is unable to detect an "eastern" reading in my interpretations. This delights me, in some ways, for I also find many convergences across the traditions; it is clear that our approach to the family library of Scriptures should be C/catholic as well as O/orthodox (both words in upper and lower case). As might be expected, he wants to bring the

---

5. Hays, *Reading Backwards*.

masterful Thomas Aquinas into the mix—something that I did not do, since I was intent mostly to investigate fathers who wrote decidedly before the unhappy schism. (Speaking about putative divisions, thank you to Daniel for reminding us that the interpretive differences of Antioch and Alexandria have been over-blown, as Frances Young[6] has so ably demonstrated! Though this dichotomy has been exaggerated, we can discern, St. Cyril notwithstanding, a demonstrable *tendency* of more Antiochian interpreters to stress the literal as a *sine qua non* for the other meanings; this I will celebrate and to this I will cling!)

As for the learned Thomas, his weighted readings of the fathers who comment on the evangelist John provide much food for thought. Especially welcome is his insistence that God gives himself, and not simply a substance known as "grace." The problem is, of course, that the Thomistic language is so grace-laden, that is, shot through with the word *gratia*, that we tend to forget his direct reference to the Spirit. Instead, his constant use of the noun leads us (perhaps wrongly) to visualize grace as separate from the Giver, as something that can be meted out, enumerated, and interconnected with merits. Consider these phrases and statements: he speaks about "this grace of spiritual regeneration . . . this grace to the Gentiles . . . the salutary grace . . . dispensed in two ways" (249); he goes on to assert, "for a man to merit receiving what he asks, he should ask for things which are not in opposition to the will of the giver, and also ask for them in a way which is acceptable to the giver" (614); he asks why Jesus received good things from others, and answers, "so that those who give him these things might acquire merit" (637).[7] It is difficult for those steeped in the Eastern tradition to hear such kind of particular and enumerated descriptions and immediately recognize them as having to do with the Spirit who is the treasury of blessings and fills all things. Perhaps it is only a matter of vocabulary, but I think it is also a matter of approach –the one more transactional, the other more sacramental. And it is this that gets us to the heart of the matter.

Daniel is quite taken with the revered Thomas's emphasis on free will in his reading of John 4:10: "If you knew the gift of God, and who it is that is saying to you, 'Give me a drink,' you would have asked him, and he would have given you living water," or, according to the Latin in play, "you *perhaps* would have asked him . . ." The Latin, then, adds to the apodosis the word *forsitan* ("perhaps"), which Daniel approves as an appropriate rendering of the Greek particle *an*. (This little particle routinely accompanies verbs in unreal or hypothetical situations.) He says, correctly, that "the use of '*an*'

---

6. Young, *Biblical Exegesis*.
7. Thomas Aquinas, *Commentary on the Gospel of John*.

indicates possibility." More precisely, its use in the main clause signals that this is an action that is dependent upon a condition specified in the subordinate clause. ("*If* such-and-such, *then* [*an*] this would have been, or would be the case.") As my colleague Robert Gagnon puts it, "As an invariable by-product of the condition, if the condition had been fulfilled, then the action would have followed!"[8] To add "perhaps" is to add a further condition within the main clause—a move not indicated by the grammar. Consider the interchange between Jesus and St. Photini. The problem is that she did not know the one who is questioning her: but as soon as she does, she responds! Our text, then, is not emphasizing the debated issue of free will (though this is a doctrine that I would not dispute). Rather, the One who sees what is in the heart of each of us is reaching into St. Photini, and beginning to illumine her. This woman who has been made to show forth his likeness is being called into the light and she *will* respond—that is the wonder of Jesus words and the living water! The Creator is at it again, educing the potential of the one whom he has made, and calling her into life. Sadly, the Latin text redirected our medieval theologian away from this wonder, and into a discussion of the necessity of human action. As a result, the spotlight is trained away from the main Actor in this divine drama, and onto more technical questions of merit and dispensed grace.

All this said, I am grateful for being reminded of the thoroughness and frequent insight of Thomas. Indeed, I have been delighted by much of what I have read in his commentary on the fourth gospel. Especially intriguing is his notation concerning the report that Jesus himself did not baptize: he takes this as a practical pattern for prelates that they should distribute responsibility (section 554). Especially congenial is his insistence upon the historical richness of the narrative: "The Evangelist is so careful to record all these matters [concerning Jacob and the well] in order to show us that all the things which happened to the patriarchs were leading up to Christ, and that they pointed to Christ, and that he descended from them according to the flesh" (560).[9] Clearly, this incomparable Western theologian has a firm grasp of the great metanarrative, and the importance of history in understanding Jesus's actions on our behalf. This emphasis is essential, indeed, to the strategy of reading that I have followed.

Finally, we turn to the inestimable Fr. Neuhaus and the tortured question of supersessionism. I think, in concert with my paper, Fr. Neuhaus would insist that salvation does not come through an "ism." Instead, Jesus's

---

8. I would add that there seems to be a confusion here with the grammatical use of *kai ean*, which often *is* used in a purpose clause to indicate a "perhaps" or a "mayhap" possibility.

9 Thomas Aquinas, *Commentary on the Gospel of John*.

words are pointed when he tells St. Photini that salvation comes "from *the Jews*." Jesus, after all, is not from Juda*ism*, but from the Jewish people: he himself is the true Israel, just as he is the New Adam. Certainly, as Daniel speculates, I meant to say that salvation is not found in the reality and practice of Judaism at that time—or at our time, either, for that matter. But I meant more to say more than that, for our faith is is personal, from beginning to end. The Church is engrafted into Abraham and the patriarchs, personal roots, whose foundation is the living God, that God who calls those who are not into existence, and who resurrects the dead. But Judaism, in the sense of a religion centering upon the Temple (Sadducees) or the Torah (Pharisees/rabbinic Judaism) was mistaken, as St. Paul so painfully points out. Similarly misconstrued is a Christian faith centered on the Bible rather than on the Incarnate Word! We are engrafted into a people, and the foundational root of that vine turns out to be the One who is also its fruit—Jesus himself, who in the Johannine thesaurus is the vine, the ladder, the way, the life, the Alpha, the Omega. The glory of Torah, we are told, is meant to be put aside, along with that of the Temple (2 Cor 3:7:11; John 4:21): their purpose was penultimate only, and the One who fulfills them has now come.

This means not only that Christians and Jews today must remain "in argument,"[10] but that we must not pretend "out of a desire to be polite"[11] (so Neuhaus) that Jews are not called to respond to Christ, just like every other people group. When Fr. Neuhaus says, then, that "Christ and his Church do not supersede Judaism"[12] this is not his last word, but he goes on to clarify what he means. He means, that *true* Judaism, centering upon the Lord, must go on to the completion of the story, to acknowledge the Savior, the One who was baptized with his people, as well as into the elements of the world, for the sake of all. What we mean by "Judaism" is, of course, a matter of definition. But our faith is, from first to last, personal, because it is in a (truly) living Human[13] that the glory of God is seen. If we place our faith in systems—or for that matter, in methods of interpretation—we will find ourselves, at the end, bankrupt, or only talking to ourselves.

Instead, of course, we are meant to meet the One who is the Word in the written Word. As in the encounter with St. Photini, he will initiate the conversation, and tell us everything we ever did. Since it is by means of the Church that he often speaks to us in the present age, I want to thank my brothers for helping me to see what I have done, and for encouraging me to do it better!

10. Neuhaus, "Salvation is from the Jews."
11. Ibid.
12. Ibid.
13. The allusion is to Irenaeus : *Gloria Dei est vivens homo, Adv. Haer.* 4.20

CHAPTER 2

John 8:1–11
Revisiting the Pericope Adulterae

DAVID L. JEFFREY (EVANGELICAL)

JOHN 7:53—8:11 HAS BEEN long a disputed and sometimes divisive text. My reflection on it is divided into three parts. In the first I shall attempt to deal in cursory fashion with the extensive body of scholarship which has been devoted, especially over the last half-century, to the place and propriety of the *pericope adulterae* in the Johannine corpus.[1] This text-question has had two concerns, namely the issue, first, of whether the narrative was in fact written by the author of John's Gospel, and second, the less contested issue of whether it is a genuine Jesus story and therefore worthy of inclusion in the Gospel canon, Johannine or not. My review on these points is directed toward an issue arising from them, namely possible reasons for the pericope's exclusion from (or later addition to) John's text. This will require, in the second part of the paper a consideration of various historical views which have reflected discomfort with the action of Jesus represented in this narrative, not excluding the context in Second Temple Judaism for the dilemma to which Jesus is put. In the third part of this paper I shall move through what is for me more familiar territory, namely liturgical and literary ramifications as they appear in later iterations of this famous story, for these tell us much about how the Western Church in all its branches has

---

1. Keith, "Recent and Previous Research," in *Pericope Adulterae*, 307–404, offers the best brief survey of the literature.

understood it, toward one possible reading of the text in which evangelical and Catholic contributions can be seen as mutually reinforcing. I shall observe that what seems to have made this passage initially discomfiting to some early Christians more than others remains oddly reflected in the issues that divide opinion in its reception history generally. Finally, I will observe that in evangelical contexts since the 1960s there has been a notable shift away from a concern to defend Johannine authorship of the *pericope adulterae* toward an appreciation of the passage in the light of its use in two millennia of the tradition—effectively a move toward rapprochement with Catholic readings.

IS JOHN THE AUTHOR?

This is a question which, for practical purposes, has been in dispute since the early second century. In our era it has been decided in the negative more often than not, but for the most part the negative opinion has been treated for canonical purposes as not excluding an intrinsic claim of the pericope on historical validity. As an attributed "Jesus story," as Frederick A. Schilling puts it, "the story has an altogether authentic quality," and the economy of its narration, in Rudolf Schnackenberg's locution, evidences "a perfection of skill: not a word too few or too many."[2] That said, the question of its place (or not) in the text of John's Gospel has occasioned the spilling of so much ink that we may reasonably ask the question, "why has this issue mattered so much?"

The textual arguments and witness of manuscripts for the pericope is of evident text-critical interest. None of the earliest four Greek MSS have it,[3] and the total number of later Greek MSS known to omit it comes to something like one hundred.[4] *P66* and *P75* are the oldest extant texts of John, dating from the early third century. Both are of Egyptian provenance, as are the fourth-century witness to John, *Aleph* (Sinaiticus) and *B* (Vaticanus), both also of Egyptian provenance. Hodges notes close affinities among these four such as suggest a common prototype from an earlier date.[5] After

---

2. Shilling, "Story of Jesus and the Adulteress," 95; Schnackenberg, *Commentary on the Gospel of John*, 2:167.

3. Metzger, *A Textual Commentary*, 219–20. All of these manuscripts, P66, P75, Codex Sinaiticus, and Vaticanus lack the pericope.

4. An impressive inventory, still almost complete, of known manuscripts is available in von Soden, *Die Schriften des Neuen Testaments*, 735–36.

5. Hodges, "Woman Taken in Adultery," 323. Cf. Fee, "Codex Sinaiticus," 44, who takes the view that Sinaiticus among Greek examples represents the Western MS tradition.

these early Egyptian texts, however, the record becomes more complex. The pericope is referred to in the *Didascalia Apostolorum* (Syria, third century),[6] and the fragments of Papias identified by Eusebius suggest that this second-century bishop of Hierapolis—author of the five-volume *Expositions of the Sayings of the Lord*, a man who knew the apostle John and flourished early in the second century—certainly knew this particular Jesus story or one so like it as to suggest a common source event.[7] In the East, nevertheless, this pericope eventually vanishes, or seems to, since it does not make it into the Orthodox lectionary and accordingly receives no comment by such figures as Origen, John Chrysostom, Cyril, or Theodoret.[8] Meanwhile, it appears frequently enough in second and third-century Old Latin versions, as well as in Greek MSS known to Jerome, that the story is included in his Vulgate and also in *D*, the early fifth-century Codex Bezae, the earliest major bilingual text of the Gospel. Both *D* and Jerome include the narrative as part of John's Gospel.[9] Moreover, Augustine, Gregory the Great, Cassiodorus in a brief note on Psalm 56 (ACW 52:42), Ambrose, and Didymus the Blind all treat this passage as authentic in one way or another.

On the other hand, we should acknowledge that the list of biblical scholars of the last century who argue against the *pericope adulterae* being authentically Johannine is long and impressively credentialed, comprising too extensive a bibliography to be thoroughly summarized in my paper (even my notes are selective); the "nays" include such venerable authorities as R. H. Lightfoot, Frederick Schilling, Rudolf Bultmann, C. K. Barrett, Vincent Taylor, Ulrich Becker, Bruce Metzger, Rudolf Schnackenberg, Raymond Brown, Chris Keith, Earle McMillan, Fausto Salvoni, Wieland Willker, and Bart Ehrman.[10] All except Brown are mainline Protestant or

---

6. Quasten, *Patrology*, 2.147–52.

7. See Holmes, *Apostolic Fathers*, 725–26. Bart Ehrman thinks that the text as we now have it is a conflation of two such stories, "Jesus and the Adulteress," 24–44.

8. Metzger's observation that "no Greek Father prior to Euthymius Zigabenus (twelfth century) comments on the passage" (*A Textual Commentary*, 220) is misleading to the degree that Greek commentators are bound to be silent on a passage that doesn't occur in the approved lectionary. All except Chrysostom of these commentators, notably, were Egyptian. See Burgon, *Causes of the Corruption*, 256–57. As for Chrysostom, whilst he passes over the pericope in his regular homilies, it seems he knew the text; see his *Opus imperfectum*, Homily 42 (PG 86:867), cited by Bonaventure in his *Commentary* at 8:4, in which Chrysostom remarks of the accusers, "They call him teacher and truthful ... for this is the primary power of hypocrites: fake praise."

9. Seventeen of the twenty-three Old Latin manuscripts of John 7–8 contain at least part of the pericope.

10. A recent survey of the scholarship on this side of the question may be seen in Keith, *Pericope Adulterae*. Keith makes a strong argument for the view that the pericope is a later interpolation, motivated by a desire to show that Jesus was literate—i.e., could write as well as read.

secular scholars. Most of these think the story a later addition. Some speculate that it might be displaced Lukan narrative (e.g., Kyle R. Hughes, Fausto Salvoni), though this view seems not to have been convincing to a majority of commentators (and it is not so to me, though my reasons are literary rather than documentary).[11]

The scholars who have supported Johannine authorship are a much smaller group; they share in one way of the earlier opinion of Hermann Freiherr von Soden. All are evangelicals (some might even be described as 'fundamentalists,' yet I want to suggest that they are not on that account deserving of dismissal): Alan F. Johnson, Zane C. Hodges, Edward F. Hills, Alison Trites, and J. Duncan M. Derrett among others, all addressing the canonical placement issue in the 1960s and 70s, raised points of fact and cautionary notes worthy to be considered. Let me instance a few of these. First, regarding Bruce Metzger's opinion that the *pericope adulterae* "is obviously a piece of floating tradition which circulated in certain parts of the Western Church" and was "subsequently inserted in various manuscripts at various places," Hills is surely right to insist that Von Soden long ago showed accurately that when the pericope is found in early New Testament texts, the preponderant position is its current location in John.[12] "Floating" misleads. Alan Johnson's suggestion that "internal evidence of linguistics and context . . . should demand a more careful consideration of the internal character of the *pericope adulterae*"[13] is hardly unreasonable, and his caution that statistical method as a means of deciding authorship of a smallish text is unscientific is roundly supported by textual scholars in Classics.[14] Zane Hodges takes on the critical consensus on different grounds, arguing in two connected articles that the "appearance or non-appearance after John 7:52" of our pericope "is in no way accidental but is in fact a deliberate act of textual emendation."[15] He makes a reasonable observation that the four earliest extant Greek copies of John, all of which, as we have seen, exclude it, are not a proof that it was a later addition, since all four may well "be derived from a single parental example which lies far back in the stream of transmission" (323). While this last point is speculative, his insistence that we

---

11. Chris Keith comes to the same conclusion, finding "suggestions of Lukan authenticity implausible"; *Pericope Adulterae*, 384.

12. von Soden, *Die Schriften*, Teil 1, 1Abt. 500.

13. Johnson, "Stylistic Trait," 92.

14. Yule, *Statistical Study of Literary Vocabulary* is cited both by Johnson and by Metzger to make the same caution—Metzger in his *The Text of the New Testament*, 178–79. Yule shows that it takes a sample of at least ten thousand words to make a rational statistical case for assigning authorship.

15. Hodges, "Woman Taken in Adultery," 321.

not forget that all four of these earliest and interdependent copies in Greek are Egyptian directs our attention beyond documentary issues per se to a context with implications for the subject matter of this narrative. Further, while the Syriac Peshitta also omits it, it would appear that altogether more than four hundred Greek MSS of John have in fact included it.[16] Hodges is one of those who note a pattern, namely that while Syriac and Coptic copies tend not to have it, many others, both Greek and Latin, do.

A few words about Alison Trites's approach, and then we can move on to the question which piqued the interest of Hodges. Trites performs a literary analysis of the entire Gospel, in which he sees the text as a literary unity, and narratively organized much as one would if marshaling arguments to present a case in court. What John does everywhere, says Trites, is to "present witnesses and offer evidence to substantiate the Messiahship and divine Sonship of Jesus."[17] Emphasizing the forensic elements in early chapters, he contextualizes the debate between Jesus and Jewish officials as, by chapters 7 and 8, increasingly like a process in a court of law, in which the moral qualification of witnesses (141) as well as claims and evidence are contested. In John 1–12 inclusively he sees a pattern in which legal terms and narrated conflicts frame up "a juridical situation in which the woman is the accused, the scribes and Pharisees are her accusers, and Jesus is placed in the role of judge" (144). He notes the author's attention to the Jewish requirement that at least two witnesses testify, and that there are Talmudic analogues to the forensic requirements adduced, as well as a Second Temple analogue to some aspects of the confrontation, namely the apocryphal narrative of Susannah and the Elders from Daniel 13. These contextual elements, he wants to say, make a reasonable case for inclusion of the pericope right where today we find it in Western Bibles.[18] Here context and literary analysis are mutually reinforcing.

None of the North American evangelical contributions I have instanced from the pro-Johannine side strike me as conclusive regarding the canonical question, yet each seems to support the probability that the pericope is indeed an authentic Jesus story. Taken together, they serve to remind us that text-criticism alone, absent other elements of historical context and literary analysis, was proving to be insufficient in some evangelical quarters,

---

16. Hodges, "Woman Taken in Adultery," 325. As Metzger (1971) notes, however, in a number of these witnesses "the passage is marked with asterisks or obeli" (221), likely an indication that the scribes recognized the passage as in some dispute.

17. Trites, "Woman Taken in Adultery," 139.

18. Again, Keith concurs: "PA not only fits its context . . . but continues and heightens the issues addressed in the preceding context, regarding Jesus's authority as a teacher in John 7 and the theme of judgment in John 7 and 8"; *Pericope Adulterae*, 381.

even for attempts to resolve questions of authorship and placement.[19] I suggest that we can perceive here the tentative beginnings of a shift away from preoccupation with resisting textual criticism when construed as undermining the authority of Scripture, and toward another basis for assessing authority. That is, though they may not themselves have been fully aware of it, in moving toward classical philology, literary analysis and recovery of traditional exegesis, they were at an important turning point for modern evangelical exegesis.

For anyone who takes John's remark in 20:30 seriously—namely that "Jesus did many other miraculous signs and in the presence of his disciples, which are not recorded in this book"—the matter of narratorial intention with regard to selection invites speculation, whether we construe such intention as Trites does, as a matter of literary design on the part of the original narrator, or whether we consider it from the point of view of later scribes, editors, or lectionary makers (here with reference to its inclusion or exclusion) as reflexes of intention at some later level of redaction. What is now more interesting than the text-critical arguments of these evangelical essays is the way they reveal a perceptible opening up to new perspectives on textual questions. One of these openings is a willingness to engage the early commentators—patristic especially, but also medieval—with greater care. In what follows I shall join company with those who have tried to extend their enquiries a little further.

WAS THE PERICOPE ADULTERAE ADDED —OR SUBTRACTED?

Some reasonable clues as to how we may imagine the divergence between Coptic, Syriac, and some Greek MSS on the one hand, and different Greek MSS and Old Latin MSS on the other is provided by commentary or mention of the pericope in those Fathers who do speak of it. Among them, as I have noted, is the author of the third-century Syrian Greek text, known in the West as *Didascalia Apostolorum*, which quotes it, speaking of what Jesus

> ... did with her that sinned, whom the elders set before him, and leaving the judgment in his hands, departed. But He, the searcher of hearts, asked her and said to her, "Have the elders

---

19. Schnackenberg remarks pertinently, "Possibly our schematic form-critical categories are too rigid for this type of material in the Gospel tradition" (*Commentary on the Gospel of John*, 2.169); a review of the life of the *pericope adulterae* in the ecumenical *paradosis* amply warrants his view, and suggests why he makes the remark just at this juncture—the conclusion of his remarks on the passage.

condemned thee, my daughter?" She said to Him, "Nay, Lord." And he said unto her, "Go thy way: neither do I condemn thee."[20]

The point at issue in the *Didascalica* is that a failure to receive a repentant sinner is itself a sin against the Lord's example.

Whether, as R. H. Connolly supposed, the version given here came from the apocryphal *Gospel According to the Hebrews* or another non-canonical source cited in the *Didascalia*,[21] the narrative clearly was well enough known in the third century to be adduced as a reliable Jesus story. Papias, active during the first half of the second century, knew of a narrative very like our pericope, probably in the form later found in the *Didascalia*, although his citations have led Bart Ehrman to conjecture that he conflated two narratives or versions of this narrative in his account.[22] As Michael Holmes has noted in his critical text of the *Apostolic Fathers*, a version of our story which may have been found in the lost *Gospel According to the Hebrews* was known to Didymus the Blind, the fourth-century Alexandrian biblical exegete; Holmes also sees the pericope as a warning against judgment invalidated by culpability in the accusers.[23]

It seems to have been generally recognized by early commentators that the presenting issue was in some cultural settings highly sensitive. Ambrose, in a reference to John, seems to have been aware that the question of just judgment with respect to adultery could readily make some people shy away from this story because, as he puts it carefully, "of extraordinary anxiety in the inexperienced."[24] Yet he insists that Christ "could not err," and hence dubiety about the issue should abate. Augustine is likewise aware of the squeamishness of some of his contemporaries concerning this text, largely because of the severity of their views about the sin of adultery:

> ... certain persons of little faith, or rather enemies of the true faith, fearing, I suppose, lest their wives should be given impunity in sinning, removed from their manuscripts the Lord's acts of forgiveness toward the adulteress, as if He who said, "sin no more" had granted permission to sin.[25]

20. *Didascalia Apostolorum*, 76; Funk, ed. *Didascalica et Constitutiones Apostolorum*, 1.92.

21. Hills, *King James Version Defended*.

22. See n. 6 above.

23. Didymus, *Commentary on Ecclesiastes* 223.7–13; quoted by Holmes, *The Apostolic Fathers*, 725.

24. *Apologia David et altera* 11.3, 359–60.

25. Augustine makes his comment precisely in the context of addressing the problem of "Adulterous Marriages" (27) in *St. Augustine, Treatises on Marriage*, 27.107; also 108–9.

That Augustine the pastor might have been familiar with typical North African sentiments on this issue is not to be doubted; his denunciation of the "double standard" for adulterous men is uncompromising (*On Adulterous Marriages* 2.8.7). He may also have known, as Willker suggests, Tertullian's opposition to any forgiveness of the sins of adultery and fornication. On Tertullian's view, expressed in his *De Pudicitia* ("On Modesty"), such sins should never be forgiven.[26] Cyprian, another North African, confirms that there were bishops in his time who would not provide absolution for such sins.[27] That there were cultural grounds for misconstruing the purport of this pericope is thus evident, though one wonders how such early interpreters could see Jesus's forgiveness of this adulterous woman as problematic in such a way as to distinguish it from his responses to the "professional" women of Luke 7 and John 4.[28]

We can conclude on the evidence, I think, that the *pericope adulterae* was known from very early times, but that, as Augustine suggests, it was a passage in dispute because the debate about forgiveness for such sins was hotly contested in the second and third centuries, and perhaps most intensely in North African and Palestinian environments. (Of related cultural interest, in Roman law a case of proven adultery was not susceptible of judgment as a capital offense until the third century.[29]) Augustine thus gives us reason to suspect that the narrative may have more often been subtracted from John's Gospel before the fourth century than added to it afterward. Context, rather than text, if he is right, would have been the determining factor.

We might ask if there are any similar factors in Jesus's own culture, the culture of Second Temple Judaism, to adumbrate, if not warrant, Augustine's view of the likely reasons for such intense discomfort with the *pericope*

---

26. Tertullian, *De Pudicitia* 1; 6. Tertullian was angry at the edict of Bishop Calixtus of Rome, offering the possibility of repentance for the sin of unchastity.

27. Cyprian, Epistle 51.21, 26.

28. That there was a different standard for courtesans and prostitutes than for married women is clear on much cultural evidence; that there was a classic double-standard between men and women accordingly, and that Jesus was disapproving of it, is part of the purport of this narrative. It is evident, as F. F. Bruce noted, that Jesus was aware "that the law dealt more severely with women than with men. For a betrothed or married woman to have sexual relations with a man other than her bridegroom or husband was a capital offense; for a married man to have such relations with another woman than his wife was relatively venial, provided the woman was not betrothed or married to another man. . . . Jesus's ruling therefore came as a challenge to the conscience of each man who heard him"; Bruce, *Gospel of John*, 416.

29. Derrett, "Law in the New Testament," 1-26, notes pertinently that in Roman law adultery did not become a capital offense until the third century (11n1).

adulterae. It appears that these exist. The scholar who devoted most extensive attention to the Jewish legal background was J. Duncan M. Derrett, the celebrated Professor of Oriental Laws at the University of London and frequent contributor to the *Evangelical Quarterly*. Unlike the other evangelicals I have adduced, however, Derrett makes no effort to prove that the narrative is by John. Rather, he contends that first-century Jewish Christians put it in its current position on what are substantially Trites's literary reasons—namely, that's where it fits.[30] Derrett likewise thinks that Middle Eastern sensibilities were likely to take offense at what can only appear as leniency on Jesus's part of a sort they themselves might not approve. He stresses the critical requirement in a Sanhedrin case of two witnesses who independently agree on several details of a scene where the woman was observed in the act, and notes that, as in Islamic countries, witnesses who fail this test are themselves subject to the death penalty. Derrett's is an exquisitely detailed analysis of pertinent Talmudic and Mishnaic legal considerations, and it is further informed by texts from the Second Temple period that serve as corroboration. One of these he mentions in passing, much like Hodges and Trites, is the apocryphal story of Susanna (Daniel 13).

As it happens, this Second Temple text, written about 80 BCE, is one to which I gave some attention myself almost two decades ago.[31] Though at the time I was unaware of Derrett's essay, my own close study of the Mishnaic context of Susanna took me eventually in the direction of the *pericope adulterae*. I would like very briefly to retrace those steps here, as I think that they may assist us further with our question of context and sensitivity. This will lead me to offer a commensurable and, I hope, creditable reading of the text proximate to the readings of recent evangelical voices but perhaps more conspicuously grounded in the Catholic tradition.

The story of Susanna and the Elders, as it is usually called, was not approved at Jamnia, is not found in Tanakh, nor is it referred to in early Jewish commentary. Though it may possibly have been in the first LXX, it is only in the reworking by Theodotion (about 150 CE) that the present text, included as Daniel 13 in Catholic and Orthodox Bibles, takes its present form. Protestant Bibles now exclude it, though it was still printed as an apocryphal addendum in the KJV in the seventeenth century, and permitted as non-canonical "virtuous" literature by the Thirty-Nine Articles.

---

30. Derrett supports Guilding, *Fourth Gospel and Jewish Worship*, 110–12; 214n1, in this view (Derrett, "Law in the New Testament," n. 3).

31. Jeffrey, "False Witness," 57–71. On the dating, Rabbi Brull attributes the composition of Susanna to the times of Simon Ben Shetach, president of the Sanhedrin about 100 BCE, a judge who is known to have advocated the rigid cross-examination of witnesses (*Pirke Aboth* 1.9–10).

"Susanna" is thus a marginal text of Second Temple Judaism that has largely disappeared from view for evangelicals, much as the *pericope adulterae* has from the Orthodox tradition.

Parallels between our pericope and the Susanna story are apparent, although there are also crucial differences. In Susanna, an entirely innocent young woman is trapped by two witnesses, slandered and condemned to death by stoning according to the Law of Moses (e.g., Deut 19:15-19; Lev 20:10; Num 5:11-31; Lev 24:14). In the other story a presumably guilty woman is entrapped and condemned. In both narratives the claim of the false witnesses is to have caught their victim *in flagrante dilicto*, though without presenting empirical evidence. In both stories the co-perpetrator is conveniently missing. In the first story the purpose of the accusers is revenge upon a victim who had refused their sexual advances; in the *pericope adulterae* the entrapment of the woman serves an ulterior motive, the design for further entrapment of Jesus himself by two groups (scribes and Pharisees), who wish to show that Jesus misconstrues the Law. Resolution in both cases comes about by a virtuous judge who discerns abuse of the letter of the law by false witnesses who are themselves guilty by the same law. The "Young Daniel come to Judgment," as Shakespeare's Shylock unwittingly refers to Portia in *Merchant of Venice*,[32] anticipates Jesus in our story in his exposé of legalistic corruption of the Law itself, and in both cases the self-incrimination of the accusers is accomplished by one unexpectedly more attuned to the intent, or spirit of the law, than are the professionals. John Lightfoot, the great seventeenth-century Cambridge talmudic and rabbinical scholar, suggests that in the *pericope adulterae* Jesus was making inferential use of a rabbinic caveat on the provisions of Num 5:31 to the effect that the adulterous woman shall be punished only if the "husband" or accuser be guiltless (Sanhedrin 51.2; cf. Maimonides on Sotah 2-3), and possibly invoking with his finger in the dust another principle like unto it, from the Bemidbar Rabba, "If you follow whoring yourselves, the bitter waters will not try your wives."[33] Whatever we make of the mysterious markings on the ground made by the finger of the Lord (*egraphen*, 8:8 could possibly mean "draw" as well as "write"), the image projected from this gesture immediately recalls Exodus, God there writing the law on stone with his finger (Exod 31:18). Ominously, for readers of Daniel, it might recall a third such biblical incident, namely that in Daniel 5, in which the divine hand scares the excrement right out of the regal bowels as it inscribes on Belshazzar's

---

32. Shakespeare, *Merchant of Venice*, Act 4, Scene 1, 223-24.

33. Lightfoot, *Commentary on the New Testament*, 3.325-32. See Sotah 28a (Soncino 137-38); 47b (Soncino 251-52).

palace walls a definitive judgment against his profanation. In all these narratives, it is clear that a greater authority than those who think themselves in charge has been revealed. Here in our text, the Son of God who fulfills the Law establishes an authority with respect to the Law which vastly exceeds the authority of the scribes and the Pharisees (cf. Matt 7:29). It is from his demonstration of greater authority that Jesus abrogates the penalty which might conceivably have been enacted. Surprisingly, perhaps, the woman in our story is not explicitly represented as repentant.[34] In a parallel to some of the healing narratives, she is simply rescued from her predicament and, in another echo of those miracles, Jesus says to her, "Go, and sin no more" (8:11). The omission verbally of the element of repentance suggests that, as in the Susanna story, the narrative is primarily about just judgment in respect of the law—which is to say, it is primarily about the authority of Jesus. Strikingly, Jesus establishes his authority in ways that quite precisely correspond to what the prophet Isaiah says of the coming Messiah, that "he shall not judge by what his eyes see, or decide disputes by what his ears hear, but with righteousness he shall judge the poor and decide with equity the meek of the earth" (Isa 11:3–4 ESV).

HOW DOES THE PARADOSIS / TRADITIO ASSIST AN EVANGELICAL READING TODAY?

It is notable that the history of the Roman missal suggests a pairing of the *pericope adulterae* with the Susanna story in the lections for Saturday before the third Sunday in Lent, going back as far as the sixth century; the pairing is likewise present in both the Old Sarum and new Roman rite.[35] Here the Epistle (Daniel 13) sets up the Gospel (John 8) to highlight the way in which, with Jesus as with Paul, the diagnostic afforded by the Law shows that "all have sinned and come short of the glory of God" (Rom 3:23). Paul's treatment of this theme likewise seems to echo our passage, when he says:

> Therefore are you inexcusable, o man, whoever you are who judge, for in whatever you judge another you condemn yourself, for you who judge practice the same things. (Rom 2:1)

---

34. For Rudolf Schnackenberg, "penitential discipline lurks, at most, in the background"; *Commentary on the Gospel of John*, 2. 169; cf. Frederick Dale Brunner, for whom her repentance is implicit but present in the narrative: ". . . he does say, in so many words, 'I forgive your sins,'" and he argues that "there is an almost perceptible repentance in her muted *oudeis, kyrie*, 'no one, sir,'" *A Commentary on the Gospel of John*, 507; 509.

35. See Jeffrey, "False Witness," 60; cf. Schilling, "Story of Jesus," 105.

This passage goes on to add, "You who say 'Do not commit adultery', do you commit adultery?" (Rom 2:22).

But the textual context in John's Gospel, if indeed the matter of the Law and authority to judge from it is the main issue, prepares us equally well for the conventional placement of this story. Jesus's challenge to his adversaries right before this incident in John is "Did not Moses give you the law, and yet none of you keeps the law?" (John 7:19), and again "Judge not according to the appearances, but judge with a righteous judgment" (7:24), an echo of Isa 11:3-4. Righteous judgment, in contrast with that of his accusers, is a standard which he himself is about to exemplify. Nicodemus's question in the Sanhedrin then following, seems perfectly to bridge to our pericope: "Doth our law judge any man before it hears him out, and come to know what he does?" (John 7:51). The response of his colleagues seeks to contradict the authority of Jesus, since to them he seems to violate the saying, "out of Galilee there arises no prophet" (7:52). The issue here again is Jesus's authority to judge concerning the Law. The Gospel reading in the Roman and Old Sarum lectionaries for Saturday of the third week in Lent, following Susanna as the epistle, highlights clearly the disqualification of witnesses who do not themselves keep the law, warning that a judgment based upon mere appearances is not just judgment (cf. Isa 11:3). This puts wise Daniel, the paragon of Old Testament obedience and just judgment, and the wisdom and just judgment of Jesus on the same page, so to speak. But the question of adultery, actual or falsely accused, is now merely the painful occasion for exposing a far deeper adultery, namely that adultery against God, perpetrated by those who, in the phrase of Moses, "go whoring after alien gods" (Lev 17:7); in the thundering denunciations of Ezekiel and Hosea, disobedient Israel is characterized in precisely such terms (Ezek 23:20; Hosea 4:12; 9:1; cf. Isa 56:1; 57:3). In this light, the woman's adultery is the presenting symptom of a more fundamental spiritual disorder, and it is this general disorder which Jesus, like the prophets before him, puts under righteous judgment.

When we consult Western medieval exegetes on the *pericope adulterae* we can be sure that the lectionary provides at least part of their context for their reading of the text. Here the theme of authority and the law, not dispute over the forgivability of adultery, is foregrounded. A reasonable conspectus may be found in the *Catena Aurea* of Thomas Aquinas.[36] Aquinas cites Bede

---

36. *Catena Aurea: St. Thomas Aquinas*, 4.280-83. Bonaventure's commentary draws on many of the same sources, but the Franciscan doctor notes the canonical placement controversy and likens it to another: "they have said it was inserted into the Gospel of John just as the story of Susannah was inserted into Daniel," *Commentary of the Gospel of John*, 8.3 (455). Bonaventure clearly thinks that the *pericope adulterae* has greater

(*Homilies on the Gospels*, 1.25): "His writing with his finger in the ground perhaps showed that it was He who had written the Ten Commandments of the Law on stone." The bulk of the citations Aquinas includes follow Augustine's reading, namely that "he who judges not himself first cannot know how to judge correctly in the case of another," and that Jesus, who alone has right standing before the Law, has "smitten" his opponents "with the voice of justice, as with a weapon; they examine themselves, find themselves guilty, and one by one retire" (qu. *Tractatus in Joannem* 33.5). The point here echoes Matt 7:1-2: "Judge not that ye be not judged," and makes apparent the dependence of all who are "adulterers," literally or figuratively, on the mercy of God. "So then," concludes Augustine, "our Lord condemned sin, but not the sinner."[37]

The concern over abuse of the Law by those for whom such abuse is an instrument of power forms a consistent theme in fourteenth-century English homiletics, particularly among the followers of John Wyclif, who were sensitive on this point (Susanna occurs frequently in their lists of saintly women).[38] In the biblical *Ludus Coventriae* or "N-town" English play of the late fourteenth century on this pericope, a "fifth-business" character is added to the text of our periscope, called Juvenis, "young man." When apprehended with the woman, he threatens his captors, "Scribus" and "Phariseus," and because they fear him, they let him go.[39] This addition is clearly a borrowing, or conflation, from Daniel 13 and one which underscores the practice of a double standard (where is her partner?). In all such adaptations and homilies, unjust judgment, abuse of the law, and the theme of Jesus as righteous judge are paramount. The concern is not to focus on the sin of adultery itself, but to show that in the Gospel, as in the Old Testament, we are to understand, as John Wyclif put it, *legem Moysii, lex Dei*, and *lex Dei, lex Christ est*.[40]

If neither the canonical question nor the issue of adultery *per se* are the primary focus for Aquinas, any more than for the Wycliffite exegetes and authors of vernacular enactments, the same can still be said for

---

authority for its placement, but his connection of the two narratives doubtless owes to their joint placement in the Sarum lectionary.

37. Aquinas and Bonaventure both cite this line from Augustine, found in his *Tractates on John's Gospel*, 33.6 (*Fathers of the Church*, 57).

38. Jeffrey, "False Witness."

39. Block, *Ludus Coventriae*, 200-9.

40. Jeffrey, "False Witness." For a fuller treatment, see my "John Wyclif and the Hermeneutics of Reader Response," 272-87. The formulation by Bonaventure on this point is "the Lord did not act against the Law, since he was above the Law." *Commentary on the Gospel of John*, 8.16 (Karris, 459-60).

post-Tridentine Catholic commentators. A representative example of the latter is the seventeenth-century Jesuit, Cornelius Lapide. On the matter of canonical placement Lapide simply cites the Council of Trent, session 4, which ruled the story canonical and Johannine. He notes also the parallel with Susanna, and apropos the severity of the death penalty prescribed in Lev 20:10, observes that such penalties were common amongst "Romans, Saxons, Persians, Egyptians, Arabs, Parthians, Turks . . . and other heathen nations."[41] Yet the bulk of his commentary falls on the injustice of false accusation and the need for self-examination on the part of anyone who would invoke the law in judgment on another person.

Not so with John Calvin. Calvin returns to the early question of whether the text belongs to John at all, not resolving it, but he concludes, on the basis of both Latin and Greek manuscript evidence, with the majority: "there is no reason why we should not make use of it."[42] In characteristic fashion, Calvin claims to hew only to what he thinks the bare words of the text will yield him, yet here as elsewhere, his ostensibly *sola scriptura* stance doesn't get in the way of speculation or personal opinion:

> Those who suppose that He wrote something or other are mistaken, in my opinion. Nor do I approve the ingenuity of Augustine, who thinks that in this way the distinction between the Law and the Gospel are indicated, in that Christ wrote, not on tables of stone but on man who is dust and earth. Rather, Christ intended, by doing nothing, to show that they were not worth listening to.[43]

He goes on to say that one effect of Jesus's dismissive response to the woman's accusers is to demand "perfect innocence from the witnesses," but he reverts sharply from his predecessors by foregrounding the issue of her alleged adultery:

> Those who deduce from this that adultery should not be punishable by death must, on the same reasoning, admit that inheritances should not be divided, since Christ refused to arbitrate between two brothers. Indeed, every crime will be exempt from the penalties of the law if the punishment of adultery is remitted, for the door will then be thrown open to any kind of treachery . . .[44]

---

41. Cornelius, *Great Commentary*, 310.
42. Calvin, *Calvin's New Testament*, 4.206.
43. Ibid., 4:207.
44. Ibid., 4:209.

He then has some unpleasant things to say about "Popish theology," in which he claims that softness on adultery and abuse of "the law of grace" is in practice a cover for miscreance, and a result of that "diabolical celibacy, that those who are not allowed to have a lawful wife may fornicate indiscriminately."[45] Clearly, Calvin has here come full circle against the Catholics; we can imagine him and Tertullian happily smoking a cigar or two together in mutual congratulation over their superior rectitude on the issue.[46]

Theodore de Beze follows his mentor Calvin quite closely on this point,[47] but later shapers of the evangelical tradition decline somewhat in rigor. Matthew Poole (1635) focuses on the hypocrisy of the scribes and Pharisees in what he calls "an Age of very great Corruption as to mens Lives, as well as to Doctrine, and corruption of Worship; and as other Enormities of Life were very common and ordinary, among them, so it is probable were Adulteries,"[48] thus blurring by a general dismissal issues that might better be kept somewhat distinct. Matthew Henry (1721), though he regards adultery as "an exceedingly sinful sin," marks the turn of evangelical interpretation toward a justification by appeal to the rationality of Enlightenment liberalism, stressing the need for the virtue of "toleration" borne of recognition of one's own sinful nature and propensities: "*Aut sumus, aut fuimus, vel possimus esse quod hic est*—we either are, or have been, or may be what he is. Let this retrain us from throwing stones at our brethren and proclaiming their faults."[49] Once we have arrived at the point of reducing the power of the *pericope adulterae* to the platitude that folks who live in glass houses shouldn't throw stones, we have come, alas, to the brink of evangelical modernity on the issues in this text, and perhaps to other modernities more or less indistinguishable as to effect. Pace the venerable Matthew Henry, it is hard to imagine our biblical narrator in this passage as thinking of the Lord as here authorizing a policy of "Don't ask; don't tell."

---

45. Ibid.

46. A criticism from the Catholic side of the Puritan tendency to invert the order of severity of the Seven Deadly Sins (pride, envy, wrath, covetousness, sloth, gluttony, lechery), fixating on adultery whilst overlooking pride, is reflected in Shakespeare's play, *Measure for Measure*, in which the Susanna and John stories feature, along with Romans 2, in the background. Readers of American literature will be familiar with a similar excursus in Nathaniel Hawthorne's *The Scarlet Letter* (1850).

47. de Beze, *Jesu Christi Domini*, 258.

48. Poole, *Annotations upon the Holy Bible, being a Continuation of Mr. Pool's Work by Certain Judicious and Learned Divines*, 2.sup. John VIII.

49. Henry, *Matthew Henry's Commentary on the Whole Bible: Vol. 5, Matthew To John*, 982.

CONCLUSION

In reviewing what evangelical scholars of the last half-century have contributed to our understanding of the *pericope adulterae,* I hope to have shown that their efforts illustrate something of a critical turn in evangelical biblical scholarship more generally. From attempting to defend the authority of Scripture from what evangelicals sometimes took to be text-critical challenges, in the 1960s and 1970s a number of evangelical scholars would seem to have been led by considerations of canon and placement to consider the value of philologically grounded literary analysis and recovery of context from two millennia of tradition, especially commentary and liturgical use. This turn marks the beginning of a new era in evangelical biblical scholarship, best exemplified at the time by Derrett among those I have mentioned, leading some in the direction of a better establishment of their understanding of New Testament texts in the light of Jewish backgrounds, and others toward recovering the interpretation of the *paradosis/tradition* in the teaching of the universal Church down through the ages. In ways only gradually evident to the community of scholars at large, the efforts of evangelicals to engage text-critical scholars were, *inter alia,* leading them toward securing their faith in the authority of Scripture by a parallel appeal to the authority of the Tradition. The more recent phase of evangelical scholarship, whether in the guise of "New Perspectives" or historical theological conversation with patristic and medieval readings, has had already far-reaching positive effect for the opening up of substantive dialogue among our three traditions, and at a high common denominator theological pitch in which text-critical tools are instrumental goods, not the ultimate subject. Of course, not all Protestants are evangelical, and not all academic evangelicals have followed these paths. Those who have, however, have become increasingly grateful for dialogue with Catholic and Orthodox believers, especially with fellow Christians who do not abstract their study of the Bible from the living Word preached *ex corde ecclesiae.*

The Pericope Adulterae in Ecumenical Perspective
A Response from the Eastern Edges of Catholicism

Fr. Peter Galadza

It is an honor to have been invited to respond to such a fine paper. But if Professor Jeffrey, a superb biblical scholar, considers the analysis of a scriptural passage to be alien territory, what am I, a liturgist—and a Byzantine liturgist at that—to do in such terrain? Let me then fall back on the old tourist's ploy: the posing of questions. And while in some instances the questions near the conclusion of my paper may seem too broad in their focus, I hope ultimately to elucidate their specific significance for our deliberations today.

To give a sense of where I am headed, here are the questions that I will be posing.[1]

1. Is it possible that Professor Jeffrey's (albeit nuanced and tentative) preference for the "subtraction" (or "suppression") hypothesis regarding the *Pericope Adulterae* (PA) is guided by a view of biblical authority that underrates the role of ecclesial authority in transmitting Revelation?

2. Is it not the case that Professor Jeffrey has nearly totalized the *Western* Christian Paradosis/Traditio, and thus inadvertently overlooked some

---

1. Prof. Jeffrey began with a creative allusion to Caesar's *Gallic Wars*. I am happy to continue with the tri-partite theme, and am particularly grateful to him for removing some of the gall by supplying such a fine bibliography for my own foray.

troubling questions about Tradition and the PA that emerge when one includes a fuller review of the *Eastern Paradosis*?

And finally, speaking of "Tradition":

3. What, in fact, is the Tradition that I have been asked to represent, and what is the significance of any "confessional" Tradition in an exercise such as ours?

PRESUPPOSITIONS REGARDING BIBLICAL "VS." ECCLESIAL AUTHORITY

My first question, regarding biblical "vs." ecclesial authority, draws attention to *an* "elephant in the room"—if not *the* elephant. At a gathering that includes Evangelicals on the one hand, and Catholics and Orthodox on the other, the elephant's scent is bound to intrude. (Though note that I have placed the word "vs." in quotation marks. More on that below.)

As regards the thrust of my question, I am wondering whether the apparent anxiety about the PA's "canonical authenticity" (and note the quotation marks here as well) derives from a variant of *sola scriptura*. Prof. Jeffrey admits, for example, that "[t]he scholars who have supported Johannine authorship . . . [a]ll are evangelicals, some even 'fundamentalists . . .'" And while I naturally agree with Prof. Jeffrey that this should not cause one to dismiss their views, in this instance their confessional background is not insignificant. Certainly their approach to authority vis-à-vis the Church would compel them to reject the antinomy of "Church-under-Scripture" and "Scripture-under-Church" in favor of the antinomy's former pole alone.

I suspect then that it is this factor that may have prompted Professor Jeffrey to avoid giving greater attention and credence to the work of Chris Keith (whom he does, nonetheless, cite in passing).[2] The latter's superb works are unquestionably the most comprehensive recent scholarship on the PA, and along with so many other reputable scholars Keith argues very convincingly for an "interpolationist" approach to the passage.

Of course, as a non-specialist I am hardly competent to dismiss Prof. Jeffrey's approach in favor of Prof. Keith's. However, I do have the right to ask what would happen to a particular view of biblical authority were one to admit that subsequent to—and possibly even two centuries after—the production of the Johannine autograph, someone did indeed insert the PA into

---

2. Keith, *Pericope Adulterae*. But Keith has also produced the best summary of the PA's history of interpretation, which Professor Jeffrey does not cite: Keith, "Recent and Previous Research on the *Pericope Adulterae* (John 7.53 8.11)," 377–403.

John's gospel? Sympathizers of the Chicago Statement of 1978, for example, would no doubt feel uncomfortable with such an admission.³

Intriguingly, Professor Jeffrey has written: "The evasion of biblical authority occasioned by our narrow fixation on such issues as text-critical placement [in the case of the PA] is not the only modern injury to the authority of Scripture." I am not sure exactly what Prof. Jeffrey means here by "the evasion of scriptural authority," but if he is contending that a preoccupation with critical questions all too often quashes the actual message and power of the scriptures, then I fully agree. However, if he is suggesting that Scripture becomes less "authoritative" when we study—and acknowledge—the extent to which humans (guided by God, of course) have been determinative in its composition, and that this "determination" is evidenced in complex—nay frustrating—historical processes, then I cannot agree. I am especially convinced of this in the case of the PA because Chris Keith's book-length study, which applies all the methods of modern critical analysis in the most rigorous fashion, is nonetheless a stellar work of faith-affirming edification. And it edifies while plausibly hypothesizing that the PA may have been interpolated as late as the mid-fourth century (though circulating as a story "*at least* from the early second century").⁴

Moreover, because some scholars might indeed believe that an interpolationist approach is injurious to biblical authority one can ask what would lead them to such a conclusion? Would it be the fact that acceptance of the interpolationist position requires one—though *antinomically*, as I have said—to affirm an authority of the Church over scripture? Of course, my qualifier "antinomically" is vital—and without it Protestants have every right to fear "papolatry" or at least "ecclesiolatry."

In his most recent book, N. T. Wright pithily evokes something of this antinomy—without, however, dwelling on the dynamics of the paradox, and, alas, without stretching it sufficiently—when he writes: "I develop [my view of biblical authority] in conscious dialogue with the conservative position, which seems to me to go like this: it's either the Bible or the pope, so it must be the Bible; so we have to stand by every letter of Scripture or Catholicism will swallow us up." Several sentences later he writes: "The phrase

---

3. Article 10 of the Chicago Statement reads: "We affirm that inspiration, strictly speaking, applies only to the autographic text of Scripture, which in the providence of God can be ascertained from available manuscripts with great accuracy. We further affirm that copies and translations of Scripture are the Word of God to the extent that they faithfully represent the original," *The Chicago Statement on Biblical Inerrancy* (Topic No. 1).

4. Keith, *Pericope Adulterae,* 213 (emphasis in the original). He actually suggests the mid-third century as the most likely period when the interpolation began to be made.

authority of scripture can only, at its best, be a shorthand for *the authority of God in Jesus, mediated through scripture* [emphasis in the original]."[5]

As noted, however, I believe that Wright has not sufficiently stretched the paradox. By this I mean that after the phrase "mediated by scripture" he should have added: "which itself is mediated by the Church." And while I fully realize that this short phrase could be debated here far longer than the duration of our entire conference, my intention is simply to note that without it I see no way to accept the findings of critical scholarship regarding the PA on the one hand, while on the other approaching the pericope with the reverence due the Word of God.

Having mentioned Catholicism and the pope, let us see whether the Catholic Church's most recent dogmatic pronouncement on Revelation is of any help. Paragraph 19 of Vatican II's *Dei Verbum* reads:

> [I]nspired writers composed the four gospels, *by various processes* [emphasis added]. They selected some things from the abundant material handed down, orally or in writing. Other things they synthesized, or explained with a view to the needs of the churches. They preserved the preaching style, but worked throughout so as to communicate to us a true and sincere account of Jesus; for whether they wrote from their own memory and recollections, or from the evidence of "those who from the beginning were eyewitnesses and ministers of the word," their intention was that we might know "the truth" concerning the things of which we have been informed (see Luke 1: 2–4)[6]

While I have not been able to locate any Catholic commentary on this part of the Vatican II dogmatic constitution that would confirm my impression, I hope I am correct in my hunch that this formulation allows one to admit an interpolationist approach to PA without jeopardizing the pericope's status as Word of God. Of course, this requires one to think of

---

5. Wright, *Surprised by Scripture*, 27–28. I should note, however, that Wright's prime concern in the section of his book from which I have taken these quotations is issues such as the literalist interpretation of the creation accounts.

6. *Decrees of the Ecumenical Councils*, 978. However, the Vatican website has a far more literal translation, which may not provide as many possibilities for what I am hoping to cull from the text: "The sacred authors wrote the four Gospels, selecting some things from the many which had been handed on by word of mouth or in writing, reducing some of them to a synthesis, explaining some things in view of the situation of their churches and preserving the form of proclamation but always in such fashion that they told us the honest truth about Jesus."

"writers" as extending beyond "the four evangelists," and "composition" as a process extending beyond the completion of the autographs.[7]

But this brings us to another issue: our understanding of "canonical authenticity." Is a text canonical because biblical scholars (influencing Bible publishers) have decided that it can be traced to the autographs, or is it canonical because the Church has proclaimed it to be so? Again, we are confronted with another part of the "elephant."

Returning, however, from the elephantine to a more compact focus on the PA, there are two more issues that should be treated before we move on to the second of my three questions. Referring to Cornelius Lapide's views, Professor Jeffrey writes: "On the matter of canonical placement, Lapide cites the Council of Trent, session 4, which rules the story canonical and Johannine." While this is correct as regards what can be inferred about Trent's view of PA's canonicity, the question of PA's status as "Johannine," is another matter. And while one can debate the meaning of Trent's own reference to "authenticity"—and whether it actually requires one to accept the PA as Johannine—Pius XII, in *Divino afflante Spiritu* made a significant pronouncement about the nature and status of the Vulgate that would militate against such acceptance. In the aforementioned Encyclical of 1943, after insisting that modern biblical criticism "is not only necessary for the right understanding of the divinely-given writings, but also is urgently demanded [. . .]," the pope writes the following about the Vulgate.

> [I]f the Tridentine Synod wished "that all should use as authentic" the Vulgate Latin version, *this, as all know, applies only to the Latin Church* and to the public use of the same Scriptures; *nor does it, doubtless, in any way diminish the authority and value of the original texts.* For there was no question then [at the time of Trent] of these texts, but of the Latin versions, which were in circulation at that time, and of these the same Council rightly declared to be preferable that which "had been approved by its

---

7. Anyone surprised by such an approach should know that some Orthodox actually go much further, and propose what can only be considered an "open canon." The following assertion by the Greek Orthodox biblicist, Savvas Agouridis, is quoted approvingly by the noted Romanian Orthodox scripture scholar, Eugen Pentiuc: "If for instance an archaeological pickaxe were to uncover an authentic epistle of Paul the Apostle, no one would imagine excluding it from the canon. . . . Through such a new possession our knowledge and spiritual experience would simply be enriched in a truly authentic and genuine way." Cited in Pentiuc, *Old Testament in Eastern Orthodox Tradition*, 130. This, of course, is not the Catholic approach. Thus, even if St. Paul's (lost) third epistle to the Corinthians were to be discovered, it would not be included in the scriptures for the basic reason that since the apostolic period it has not fed any part of the Body of Christ.

long-continued use for so many centuries in the Church." Hence this special authority or as they say, authenticity of the Vulgate, *was not affirmed by the Council particularly for critical reasons, but rather because of its legitimate use in the Churches throughout so many centuries;* by which use indeed the same is shown, in the sense in which the Church has understood and understands it, to be free from any error whatsoever in matters of faith and morals; so that, as the Church herself testifies and affirms, it may be quoted safely and without fear of error in disputations, in lectures and in preaching; *and so its authenticity is not specified primarily as critical, but rather as juridical* [emphasis added].[8]

I have not been able to research scholarly reflection concerning this curious distinction between "critical" and "juridical," but it seems obvious that Pius is correctly voicing the conviction that the Scriptures have enlivened the Church in myriad ways—long before the rise of modern historical consciousness—and that this vivification of the Church dare not be dismissed, even when historical consciousness might incline us to do so.

WHY TRADITIO AND PARADOSIS ARE MORE DIFFERENT THAN JUST LATIN AND GREEK—AND WHY TRADITIO IS NOT ALL OF TRADITION

Let me now turn to my second question, which is far more rhetorical than the first. In asking whether Professor Jeffrey has nearly totalized the Western Christian tradition, the answer that I expect, of course, is "yes." Professor Jeffrey himself suggests—though understandably without delving into the problem—that the Paradosis represented by Byzantine (or Orthodox) worship, to name just one Eastern tradition, is different from the Latin. He notes that the PA "eventually vanishes, or seems to, and because it does not make it into the Orthodox lectionary, receives no comments by such figures as Origen, John Chrysostom, Cyril, or Theodoret." Moreover, as regards a Paradosis, we have just seen in the lengthy quotation from *Divino Afflante Spiritu,* that the status of the Vulgate, whose influence is so crucial in disseminating the PA, applies only to the Latin Church. (Pius even adds: "as all know," even though most don't know, because they equate "Catholic" with "Roman Rite Catholic.") Of course, Pius was compelled to state that the Vulgate's status applies to the Latin Church alone, as millions of his own Eastern Catholic subjects (and "subjects" they were) relied on a variety of other versions—from the Greek to the Peshitta. Let me then reiterate: the

---

8. Pius XII, *Divino Afflante Spiritu,* 70.

relativization of the Vulgate is significant in our context because of the way that Latin texts—beginning with Jerome's pronouncements—have figured in the acceptance of the PA.

Before returning to the historical dimension of this question, allow me to make a marginal note about Professor Jeffrey's use of the term "Paradosis," and then briefly outline the present status of the PA in the Byzantine Catholic lectionary (and thus the Orthodox lectionary as well).

As regards the marginal note: certainly the interaction of the PA with Western liturgy, and the commentary that it has garnered among Latin Fathers, as well as the subsequent reflection on its message in later writings—all of this makes it *a* tradition. But this is not the same as "*the* Paradosis" which *materially* comprises something far greater, and *formally* "does not comprise anything at all," being rather "the very ὑπόθεσις of the sacred books—their fundamental coherence due to the living breath passing through them, transforming their letter into a 'unique body of truth.'"[9] Fortunately, however, as I shall note below, Professor Jeffrey's thinking certainly conforms to the formal dimension of the Paradosis, even if materially he is tapping *a* tradition rather than *the* Tradition.

This material dimension becomes clearer if we turn to the present status of the PA in Byzantine worship. Unlike the Latin tradition, where the PA has had the liturgical visibility described by Professor Jeffrey, the PA's status within the Byzantine tradition is marginal to the point of invisibility. For the pericope to be heard, a Byzantine Rite cleric (whether Catholic or Orthodox) would have to specifically choose to celebrate a Eucharist on several of the minor commemorations of holy women,[10] and then actually read the PA rather than (or, theoretically, along with) the gospel that is appointed in the Byzantine *lectio continua*. In other words, the PA is not part of the Byzantine *lectio continua* in spite of the fact that the Byzantine Rite sequentially apportions as readings essentially the entirety of the four gospels throughout the whole year. Consequently, even someone attending a daily celebration of the Byzantine Eucharist could easily never hear this passage. (This is particularly significant for a tradition that considers the liturgy to

---

9. Lossky, "Tradition and Traditions," 142.

10. The following lectionaries typically represent the present-day Byzantine Catholic and Eastern Orthodox ordo: ΘΕΙΟΝ ΚΑΙ ΙΕΡΟΝ ΕΥΑΓΓΕΛΙΟΝ. Page 50 is where the PA would appear if it were part of the *lectio continua*. But it is not. In the following lectionary, the PA does not appear at all—even in a category designated "For Holy Women": *The Divine and Holy Gospel*. The "generic" category of "holy women" (with the PA as its appointed reading), is far more typical of the Slav tradition than the Greek. See *The Holy Gospels of Our Lord, God and Savior Jesus Christ*, 310.

be the privileged locus of scriptural interpretation.[11] I shall not, however, delve into the even more significant—and tragic—fact that eighty percent of the *Old* Testament does not figure in the Byzantine lectionary at all.)

Just as important in some ways is the fact that the PA's themes are also absent from Byzantine (and thus Orthodox) hymnography. While Greek hymnography mentions other sinful women, even the lengthy and scripturally inspired Penitential Canon of Andrew of Crete makes no allusions to the PA.[12] This is significant because this composition of almost 300 stanzas consistently refers to OT persons and passages that do not figure in the Byzantine lectionary. The Cretan's hymnographic canon was composed before AD 740, the year of his death. Our earliest extant Greek lectionary containing the PA also dates from the eighth century. However, one may presume that Andrew had no knowledge of it—at least as Scripture.

This brings us back to the details of the PA's position within the Byzantine lectionary. Not surprisingly, it is Evangelical scholars who have studied the latter extensively in order to argue for the PA's hypothetical presence in earlier, but no longer extant, Greek codices. Maurice Robinson and William Pierpont have done the Eastern Churches a great service by meticulously researching and presenting the Byzantine text type.[13] However, Robinson's bias in favor of the omission hypothesis leads him to misread liturgical history in significant ways. For example, in an attempt to suggest that a very early lectionary system caused the displacement of the PA's verses from the Pentecost lection, and that this would have supposedly influenced subsequent codices—even those with the full gospel text—he hypothesizes that "the lectionary lessons for (at least) the major feasts and Sundays may have had a mid-second-century origin." This, he continues, "would be of great significance in regard to those early witnesses which omit the PA."[14] Unfortunately, however, we have no way of establishing a pericope order for any of the Greek speaking Churches before the fifth century, and it is highly unlikely that one could have existed in the mid-second century. (Incidentally, what we know about homilies in the fourth century also does not enable us to establish an actual order of pericopes for the liturgical year at that time.) When we arrive at the period straddling the fifth to eighth centuries, we do

---

11. The following remark by the Orthodox scholar, John Breck, is illustrative: "As Orthodox, our responsibility is to insist upon the fact that the true place of the Word—its exegesis as well as its proclamation—is within the liturgical, sacramental community of the Church." Breck, *Power of the Word*, 45.

12. For the text of this composition see Mother Mary and Kallistos Ware, trans., *The Lenten Triodion*, 378–415; and Mathewes-Green, *First Fruits of Prayer*.

13. See, for example, their volume, *The New Testament in the Original Greek*.

14. Robinson, "Preliminary Observations," 43.

have the Georgian Lectionary with its list of daily readings, but again the PA is entirely absent.[15] Granted, the Georgian Lectionary does not provide the kind of *lectio continua* that would satisfy anyone skeptical of the argument from silence, but the absence remains telling. This is especially so as the Georgian Lectionary provides many readings for saints, and—as we shall see below—when the PA eventually does enter the Greek liturgical tradition, it is as a reading for holy women.

When we finally do find a Greek lectionary that has continuous readings of John (for the period following Easter) the PA is still absent from the *lectio continua*—just as today. That lectionary is manuscript *l* 627, Mount Athos Dionysios 90 (*olim* 1) from the eighth century. On fol. 28r of this *aprakos* Gospel manuscript, we find John 7:14-30 for the Wednesday of the Fourth week of Pascha. The text then proceeds to John 8:12-20—for the Thursday of the Fourth week of Pascha.[16] As noted, this is identical to the order of the present-day Byzantine lectionary, where PA is not part of the *lectio continua*.

Robinson makes a great deal of the fact that the PA does appear in the eighth-century manuscript 047, listed since 1942 as Princeton University Library (Library Med. and Ren. Mss, Garrett 1).[17] The codex is the first extant Greek lectionary to contain the PA, and the manuscript is a continuous-text lectionary, not an *aprakos*. The PA is found on fol. 137v-138r. Robinson asserts that the Princeton manuscript is a witness to the presence of the PA in the Menologion. He makes this assertion in the context of his reference to the PA as a reading for women saints such as Theodora, Pelagia, and Mary of Egypt.[18] However, a look at the codex reveals the following: On 137r at 7:52 there is an indication for the beginning of a pericope, presumably related to the marginal note at the top of fol. 137r: τη αγια ν ("For Holy Pentecost").

---

15. Tarchnischvili, ed., *Le grand lectionnaire de l'Église de Jérusalem—Ve-VIIIe siècle*.

16. Gregory, *Textkritik des Neuen Testamentes*, 437; Aland, ed., *Kurzgefaßte Liste der griechischen Handschriften des Neuen Testaments*, 257.

17. Previously located at the Monastery of St. Andrew on Mount Athos. Incidentally, in the Georgian tradition, the PA begins to appear in lectionaries in the tenth century.

18. Robinson, "Preliminary Observations," 44. Note, however, that the reference to the commemoration of Mary of Egypt is for the Menaion commemoration, rather than the commemoration on the Fifth Sunday of Lent (in the Triodion). As mentioned above, a cleric would have to choose to celebrate a Eucharist on April 1 (which actually usually falls during Great Lent, thus preventing a full Eucharistic celebration in the Byzantine Tradition), and he would have to read the PA instead of (or added to) the pericope found in the *lectio continua*. Incidentally, the gospel pericope appointed for the commemoration of Mary of Egypt on the Fifth Sunday of Lent—and thus actually heard by the worshipping community—is Luke 7:36-50.

On 137v, however, there are no marginal notes indicating the subject of the reading and we find no markings at all. And while fol. 124v provides us with a table listing several commemorations and their pericopes from John, we find no reference to any saint. Thus, it is not clear why Robinson considers the Princeton manuscript a witness to the PA in the Menologion—or for that matter a liturgical commemoration of any kind. Thus, references in lectionaries to the PA as a reading for women saints actually appear only later.

The preceding discussion of lectionaries and hymnography has simply been intended to reiterate how the PA has remained virtually absent from the Byzantine Church's consciousness.[19] In one of the footnotes to his paper, Professor Jeffrey remarks on Bruce Metzger's observation that "no Greek Father prior to Euthymius Zigabenus (twelfth century) comments on the passage." He states that Metzger's pronouncement "is misleading to the degree that Greek commentators are bound to be silent on a passage that doesn't occur in the approved lectionary." However, the fact that the PA doesn't occur in the approved lectionary—except *eventually* in the very marginal way noted above—is precisely the point. In other words, speaking of the PA in the (Greek) Paradosis is not the same as discussing its status within the (Latin) Traditio. And the fact that other Evangelical scholars have misread Greek liturgical history in the interests of finding the PA there, indicates how easy it is for conviction to overlook fact.

However, this problem is not only a frustration for Evangelicals. It is frustrating for Eastern Christians as well. Imagine the following. In the case of the longer ending of Mark, Byzantine Christians rightly insist on maintaining it prominently in their bibles because it comprises the third reading of the Sunday Matins cycle.[20] They do so in spite of the opinions of text critics. And then there is another text-critical case, the phrase "and fasting" in Mark 9:29. The putative "addition" is always defended by Byzantine Christians as it is read precisely during the Great Fast (Lent). Besides, it is found in their hymnography.[21] However, in the case of the PA, the situation is essentially reversed. As discussed above, the liturgical argument—or argument from tradition—is very weak. Nonetheless, in view of the PA's

---

19. An additional indication of the PA's marginal status is the fact that in Greek usage, for example, the PA frequently does not even appear as a reading for holy women, but only as a reading for the rite of confession of women, ΘΕΙΟΝ ΚΑΙ ΙΕΡΟΝ ΕΥΑΓΓΕΛΙΟΝ, 600. This is significant considering that the sacrament of confession has largely fallen into desuetude among the Greeks, and that even when it is practiced, a gospel is almost never read.

20. ΘΕΙΟΝ ΚΑΙ ΙΕΡΟΝ ΕΥΑΓΓΕΛΙΟΝ, 3. See St. Athanasius Academy of Orthodox Theology, *Orthodox Study Bible*, 1357.

21. *The Lenten Triodion*, 412.

profound theology (more on that below), one would certainly want to make up for this virtual absence. And to do so, Eastern Christians would need to become more like their Evangelical brothers and sisters, by relying more on bible study, rather than just the bible's liturgical proclamation.

Incidentally, if it is not yet clear, everything that I have written thus far is not intended to diminish the importance of the PA as God's Word, but only to argue that certain scholars have gone about arguing for its inclusion in the Bible in untenable ways. Of course the PA should be in the Gospel of John! But it should be there because the Church eventually made the decision that it belongs there.

THE SIGNIFICANCE OF CONFESSIONAL, OR DENOMINATIONAL, TRADITIONS

To introduce my third question, let me quote from Dr. Raith's invitation to speak at this conference. "Please keep in mind that the conference is both a theological and ecumenical venture, so if there's any way explicitly to bring your own tradition into your response, and highlight differences, similarities or points of convergence, that would be excellent." Thus my third question: What, in fact, is my tradition? Of course, it may seem odd to have saved this question for the end of my paper, but in view of what I will be asserting below, the deferral is fitting.

In answer to the question about my tradition, by now it may be obvious that I am Catholic (especially as that is how I am listed in the program). But as a member of an Eastern Catholic Church of the Byzantine Tradition I would normally contribute insights derived from what is generally associated—whether exclusively or not—with Eastern Orthodoxy. This is in keeping with Vatican II's exhortation to Eastern Catholics to maintain and foster their particular spiritual patrimony,[22] which generally coincides with that of the Orthodox. At this conference, however, that won't do—or at least it won't do in that I need to avoid redundancy. Dr. Parsenios is with us; and while I might be able to provide the perspective of an Orthodox in communion with Rome, George is able to provide the perspective of an Orthodox in communion with the Orthodox.

One might ask, however, what is the purpose of inviting an apparently "marginal" Catholic to represent the Catholic tradition at a conference like this. I have no idea what the organizers intended, but I would note that while Eastern Catholics account for only one percent of Catholics worldwide— and so might be viewed as eccentric representatives of Catholicism—they

---

22. *Orientalium ecclesiarum*, par. 6.

remind us of the obvious fact that thinking and acting *kat holon* is not only a notional dimension of Catholicism, but constitutive of it as an institution. And this was so—though in very wounded ways—long before Vatican II. Thus, one should never be allowed to speak of Catholicism without somehow acknowledging this. The low quantity of persons proclaiming certain truths should not be allowed to muffle the quality of those truths. Besides, history teaches us how exceptions sometimes become the rule.

But drawing attention to my own "hyphenated" Catholicism serves another purpose. I am convinced that increased "hyphenation" is the only way to proceed as we Christians attempt to seek the Truth not only together—but effectively. One notes, for example, the title of George Weigel's seminal book: "Evangelical Catholicism."[23] Can we hope for books espousing "Catholic Orthodoxy," and/or "Catholic Evangelicalism"?[24]

This leads to the issue of what our "confessional" or ecclesial categories ultimately mean—especially in an ecumenical and even anti-authoritarian age. For those gathered here, it will hardly be news that in the search for truth—and *the* Truth—our ecclesial traditions are sometimes heavy—if albeit necessary—burdens. This is simply a nuanced version of the maxim that "'confessional scholarship' is an oxymoron."

Having said this, however, let me note that the idea of identifying a scholar according to his/her ecclesial affiliation is not as detrimental to the

---

23. Weigel, *Evangelical Catholicism*.

24. Speaking of the need to overcome binaries with "hyphens," note how differently the PA figures in Catholic scripture commentaries that are "critical" as opposed to "spiritual." The PA always figures in the latter, and almost never in the former. It would be helpful for the two types of commentary to enter into greater dialogue—or "hyphenation"—as it were. For some of the critical commentaries that illustrate the absence of reflection on the PA, see Kelly and Moloney, *Experiencing God in the Gospel of John*; and Ellis, *Genius of John*. Even a Byzantine Catholic commentary does not reflect on the PA, relegating it to a footnote: Custer, *Holy Gospel*, 309. Conversely, examples of "spiritual" commentaries by Catholics that do include—frequently profound—reflection on the PA are: Daloz, *Nous avons vu sa gloire*; Zevini, *Commentaire spirituel de l'Évangile de Jean*; Gargano, *Lectio divina su il Vangelo di Giovanni*; and Desjeux, *Voir l'invisible*. Incidentally, such spiritual commentaries usually do not even allude to the PA's disputed status.

It may be worth mentioning that the Eastern theological tradition is noted for its synthesis of theology and spirituality. Thus it is not insignificant that when we turn to Orthodox commentaries, we see that even Paul Nadim Tarazi, a scholar who tends to strongly promote critical methods, especially redaction criticism, dwells on the PA. *The New Testament: An Introduction*, 181–83. In addition, one of the few modern full-length commentaries on John by an Orthodox scholar also displays this synthesis of "criticism" and "spiritual edification" as regards the PA. Papadopoulos, *The Gospel of St. John*, 131–33.

search for truth as it might seem.[25] To begin with it can apprise the audience of the speaker's "preconceptions," "biases," and "prejudices"—a very postmodern concern, incidentally. But put more positively, it can alert us to the kind of tacit knowledge that may be guiding the speaker's formulations. And when this tacit knowledge has been formed in a particular worship tradition, it is a vital knowledge indeed.

Moreover, I did add the word "necessary" in my reference to tradition as a possible "burden." This is not only because of the truism that one can never wholly escape one's present and past history—and should never be allowed to pretend that he/she has done so—but more importantly because the requirement to admit one's tradition can facilitate a retrieval, or sharing, of theological wealth that otherwise might be lost. Frequently it is only because we have been asked to contribute insights from our respective traditions that we go searching for pearls that might otherwise go unnoticed.

This brings me back to the PA and a dimension of my own tradition. Churches of Byzantine usage (ideally) employ the Septuagint as their version of the Old Testament. When we read the PA with an appreciation for its intertextuality with the Septuagint—the natural locus to seek such correlations with the OT[26]—we find a thoroughly inspiring, not to mention enlightening—connection with Exod 32:15 and 31:18. This, of course, is the account of God's bestowal of the Decalogue. Chris Keith analyses the use of καταγράφω in John 8:6 and γράφω in John 8:8 and notes how the use of the compound verb in the former and the simple verb in the latter creates a parallel between "Jesus' writing in the ground in PA with God's writing of the Decalogue in Exod 32:15." There, "the verbs appear in a similar syntactical arrangement, and also like John 8:6, 8, as synonyms."[27] He adds: "Increasing the likelihood of this interpretation is that both God and Jesus use their fingers in the process (John 8:6, Exodus 31, 18). According to PA's interpolator, not only is Jesus literate, he is divinely so."[28] (Professor Jeffrey has appropriately drawn attention to the image of Christ writing.)

Keith highlights other parallels between the PA and these sections of Exodus, all of which evoke Jesus's divine authority. Consequently, whether one accepts an interpolationist approach or not, and whether or not one

---

25. For those unacquainted with the publicity surrounding the conference at which this paper was presented, each presenter's denominational background was listed in parentheses.

26. See, for example, Müller, *The First Bible of the Church*. More generally, for a recent discussion of the Septuagint's vital importance, see Law, *When God Spoke Greek*. Some Evangelicals might find Law's book disturbing, but its probity is very compelling.

27. Keith, *Pericope Adulterae*, 257.

28. Ibid.

agrees with Keith's hypothesis that the (alleged) interpolation was intended to demonstrate our Lord's grapho-literacy, the believer is drawn into a profound affirmation of Jesus's divinity. And this affirmation—so necessary in our day—is certainly aided by recourse to the Septuagint.

I mentioned above that Professor Jeffrey's thinking certainly conforms to the formal dimension of the Paradosis. As noted, that "formal dimension" is the "the very ὑπόθεσις of the sacred books—their fundamental coherence due to the living breath passing through them, transforming their letter into a 'unique body of truth.'" Consequently, whatever other "hypotheses" one is willing to accept about the PA, as Professor Jeffrey has written: "The import of this particular narrative is confirmed in the full canon of Scripture, after all, which everywhere affirms that the Law is just, but that righteous judgment from the Law cannot be given except by that one who has fulfilled the Law. He who both authored and fulfilled the Law is the singular source of the grace and mercy we have been offered. This is the primary evangelical meaning, I suggest, of the *pericope adulterae*." It is also, I would submit, the Catholic and Orthodox meaning, and "how good and pleasant it is when brothers dwell in unity" (Psalm 133 [134]).

Researching the question of the PA's authenticity, I noticed an academic title that I thought would be of use. The volume is called *Is John's Gospel True?* However, for us, it is useful primarily in adding urgency to the exhortation with which I will end my paper below. This is how the author ends his book:

> Our major conclusion follows ineluctably. The fourth gospel is profoundly untrue. It consists to a large extent of inaccurate stories and words wrongly attributed to people. It is anti-Jewish, and as holy scripture it has been used to legitimate outbreaks of Christian anti-Semitism. . . . What the churches do about this is a matter for them. On past form, most of them will do precious little, and false belief will continue to flourish among them.[29]

This is the intellectual climate that most of us work within. Of course, this author and thinkers like him will probably never be convinced of the truth of John's Gospel by anything that we theologians write or say. But what we churches can do is work together to replace the tacit knowledge that leads people to reject the Gospel's truth by bringing them to a new "bias"— a positive "bias"—derived from their witnessing the love with which the Father loves the Son dwelling in us (cf. John 17:26)—Catholics, Orthodox and Evangelicals.

---

29. Casey, *Is John's Gospel True?* 229.

Response to Professor David Jeffrey

GEORGE PARSENIOS (ORTHODOX)

DAVID JEFFREY HAS WRITTEN an interesting and insightful paper on the *pericope adulterae* (hereafter *PA*). He has not only covered all of the relevant issues of interpretation in an efficient and creative fashion, but has at every turn looked with fresh eyes at scholarly consensus and received opinion. I am glad to have been given the chance to read his essay and to respond to it in this forum.

Like Caesar when he described Gaul, Professor Jeffrey divides his paper into three parts, and each of these three parts has subdivisions within it. I will devote most of my response to the first of his three parts, the one in which his chief concern is to determine whether or not the *PA* has its real and natural home in chapters 7–8 of the Gospel of John. Professor Jeffrey believes that the *PA* is Johannine. To support his view that we should take more seriously the Johannine character of the *PA*, Professor Jeffrey underscores the legal quality of the passage. He follows Allison Trites in arguing that these legal resonances connect the passage closely to the Gospel of John, since John gives the life of Jesus a uniquely legal shape. I appreciate this line of reasoning, and I will reflect on this approach in various ways in the comments that follow. After addressing questions of Johannine authenticity, I will then turn, very briefly, to questions of the place and function of the passage in the Orthodox Church.

I will begin with legal questions, and how they relate to the question of authenticity. My attention will first turn to the work of Trites, since his argument is the basis of the argument made by Professor Jeffrey.[1] Trites focuses on what he calls the "controversy pattern" of the Gospel of John, a feature of the book which more recent scholars have labeled the Johannine "lawsuit

---

1. Trites, "Woman Taken in Adultery," 137–46.

motif."[2] By using the phrase "lawsuit motif," scholars draw attention to the fact that the life of Jesus in John has a uniquely legal shape. The *PA* also contains legal themes and contains legal language. This basic legal connection between the *PA* and the Fourth Gospel is suggestive, but it remains to be seen whether this surface similarity reflects deeper and more extensive ties—ties that bind the *PA* to the Gospel of John with greater certainty. I believe that no such ties exist. Let me explain.

When Trites turns to the part of his argument in which he coordinates the *PA* with the Gospel of John, he writes, "Perhaps enough has been said to make the controversy-pattern of John 1–12 clear. But of what relevance is this fact to the genuineness of the *Pericope Adulterae?* Simply this, one finds precisely the same type of controversy language, imagery and terminology which is to be observed in the rest of John 1–12."[3] To prove this case, Trites finds specific linkages with John in the *PA*, such as the threat of stoning. The woman is condenmned to stoning at 8:5 just as Jesus is almost stoned to death at John 8:59, 10:31, 11:8. Trites also notes that the *PA* contains words like *katêgorein* (to prosecute, 8:6) and *katakrinein* (to condemn, 8:10). These are definitely legal terms and they are definitely used elsewhere in John (*katêgorein*, 5:45; *krinein*, 3:17, etc.). But these facts prove little. The mere presence of legal language or themes does not resolve the question of Johannine provenance. All of the canonical Gospels raise questions related to law, guilt and innocence in the life of Jesus. Merely showing that the *PA* uses legal language does not necessarily make it Johannine any more than it makes it Matthean, Markan, or Lukan.

But the most suggestive part of Trites's argument—and by suggestive, I mean the one that provides the best way for me to explain my reservations about Johannine authenticity—comes where he describes the basic structure of the *PA*. He writes that the passage "presupposes a juridical situation in which the woman is the accused, the scribes and Pharisees are her accusers, and Jesus is placed in the role of judge."[4] The last part—the one in which Jesus is cast in the role of judge—is the least Johannine, at least as Trites understands the role of a judge. The judicial decision that concludes the *PA* is the most famous part of the entire episode, where we read, "Jesus said to her, 'Woman, where are they? Has no one condemned you?' She said, 'No one, sir.' And Jesus said, 'Neither do I condemn you. Go your way, and from now on do not sin again'" (8:10–11). The men who were so quick to

---

2. See especially Lincoln, *Truth on Trial*; Parsenios, *Rhetoric and Drama in the Johannine Lawsuit Motif.*

3. Trites, "Woman," 144.

4. Ibid.

condemn the woman earlier have recognized that they are not without sin, so cannot cast a stone. The sense of non-judgment here is reminiscent of that expressed in Matt 7:1: "Do not judge, lest you be judged." The sentiment also seems, at first glance, to fit within its Johannine context. At John 8:15, for instance, Jesus disavows any desire to act as a judge when he says, "You judge according to the flesh, I judge no one." But things are not quite as they seem. After just a little more scrutiny, the Johannine concept of judging, not only in chapters 7–8, but in the Gospel of John more broadly, is of a wholly different order from the concept of judging in the PA, and the concept of judging in the PA is far more at home in the synoptic portrayals of Jesus.

There are two ways in which this is so. First, Jesus is not consistent in his claims not to judge in John 7–8. If 8:15, says, "I judge no one," we have to coordinate that sentiment with John 8:26, where he says, "I have much to say about you and much to judge," or John 9:39, where Jesus says, "For judgment I came into this world, that those who do not see may see, and that those who see may become blind." If Jesus denies that he is a judge, he also affirms that he is a judge in the same breath. Why is this so? To understand this feature of Jesus's teaching in John, we have to look to Johannine theology more broadly. The concept of judging is not the only feature that bears this stamp of inconsistency. Indeed, every major theme in Johannine theology seems to operate in this way. For instance, Jesus can claim "I and the Father are one" (10:30) which implies equality with God, and yet he can also say, "The Father is greater than I" (14:28). In the same way, the Gospel of John closes by insisting that the signs of Jesus were written in order to lead people to believe in him (20:31), but sometimes people who believe the signs are actually rejected (2:23–25). At other times, those who seek signs seem to be rebuked (4:48). Such opposing statements are not reconciled. Likewise, Jesus insists that seeing him and believing in him are closely connected (6:30, 40), but then he says in his conversation with Thomas, "Blessed are those who do not see and yet believe" (20:29).

I follow scholars like C. K. Barrett who classify these "inconsistencies" in Johannine thought under the category of the Johannine dialectic.[5] The term dialectic means that opposing and irreconcilable realities are put in conversation with one another and the resulting tension is not resolved. The goal of this dialectical approach is to come to grips with Jesus as the one in whom the Word became flesh. Jesus is both the immortal God and mortal flesh, and he resides in eternity as well as within history. The dialectical style allows John to hold in tension these two irreconcilable aspects of Jesus's

---

5. Barrett, "Dialectical Theology"; Hengel, *Johannine Question*.

person. St. Ephrem the Syrian relies on the poetic form to accomplish the same task when he says,

> Who will not give thanks to the Hidden One, most hidden of all,
> Who came to open revelation, most open of all,
> For he put on a body, and other bodies felt Him,
> Though minds never grasped Him *(Faith, 19.7)*?

Jesus is both revealed and concealed, the immortal Word and mortal flesh. This is as true for John as it is for Ephrem. It is in this sense that he is equal to the Father, and, at the same time, the Father is greater than him. And it is in this sense that he is a judge, and yet not a judge. This dialectic is what drives the disavowal of judging in John 7–8. By contrast, the concept of judging in the *PA* seems to be of a very different order. The disavowal of judgment in that passage seems to fit more in the synoptic realm, as noted above, where the meaning is, "judge not, lest you be judged." This is a very different motive for not judging.

The second issue related to judging in John 7–8 has its origins in the Johannine dialectic as well. If Jesus is the Word made flesh, his opponents look at him and see only flesh. The crowds in John 6:42 illustrate the confusion. They say, "Is not this Jesus, the son of Joseph, whose father and mother we know? How does he now say, 'I have come down from heaven'?" The same question drives the discussion in John 7–8, where people wonder whether or not Jesus is a mere man, or someone greater. We read,

> When they heard these words, some of the people said, "This is really the prophet." Others said, "This is the Christ." But some said, "Is the Christ to come from Galilee?" (7:40-41)

In response to this confusion in determining his identity, Jesus says at John 7:24, "Do not judge according to appearance." This admonition alerts us to the fact that there are really two stories running through the Gospel, one on the level of appearance, the other on the level of reality and truth. Those who judge Jesus on the level of appearance believe that he is a blasphemer and they condemn him to death, while those who judge him on the level of reality believe that he is the Son of God and the Messiah, and his apparent condemnation is actually the condemnation of his opponents. The one being sought is actually the seeker; the defendant is actually the judge. This legal reversal culminates in the trial of Jesus before Pilate, a trial which some scholars have called the trial of Pilate before Jesus, to underscore the legal reversal inherent in the scene.[6]

---

6. For discussion, see Parsenios, *Rhetoric and Drama*, 36-38.

The motif of reversal appears long before the final trial, though. John 9 offers a good example. The passage begins with the blind man being called a sinner, and then continues with both the blind man and Jesus being regularly called sinners and being regularly interrogated by their accusers. By the end of the scene, however, Jesus is no longer the defendant, but the judge, while those who think they see and who think they are without sin are shown to be blind sinners.

The same reversal operates in John 7–8. Jesus begins the episode as a defendant who defends his testimony against his judges and accusers. By the middle of chapter 8, however, he ends the episode not in the role of defendant, but in the role of judge: "I have much to judge…" he says (8:26). Thus, Jesus's role as judge in John 7–8 must be seen through the prism of legal reversal. Later in his paper, Professor Jeffrey cites the important passage noted above from John 7:24: "Judge not according to the appearances, but judge with a righteous judgment," and he does so in connection to the debates between Jesus and his opponents over the Law. Again, though, the issue in the *PA* is whether or not the judges are hypocrites, who profess but do not follow the Law. When the Gospel of John refers to the teachers of the Law who do not follow the Law, there is more at stake than hypocrisy. The issue at hand is the identity and innocence of Jesus. The opponents of Jesus do not judge him justly because, even as they use the Law to condemn him, they do not recognize that the Law is actually written about him:

> If you believed Moses, you would believe me, for he wrote of me. But if you do not believe his writings, how will you believe my words? (John 5:46–47).
>
> You search the scriptures, because you think that in them you have eternal life; and it is they that bear witness to me; yet you refuse to come to me that you may have life. (5:39–40).

It follows that Jesus's opponents would not be judging him at all if they judged justly, because they would recognize that he is himself the judge. His role as judge, as noted above, is filtered through the theme of legal reversal. By contrast, the question of whether or how Jesus is judge in the *PA* is of a different order. When he turns the tables on his opponents and shows that they have no right to judge, his reason is their hypocrisy. Once again, this seems much more at home in the synoptic controversies.

Thus, whether we have in mind the issue of dialectical theology or that of legal reversal, the complicated quality of Jesus's judging in John 7–8 has its origin in the soaring Christology of John, where Jesus's role as judge proceeds from his identity as the Word become flesh. The *PA* betrays no awareness of any such thing. Other issues could be multiplied, and they have been listed at length by others, so I will not belabor the point any further. I simply do not believe that this passage is an original part of the Gospel of John.

Two caveats are in order at this point. First, I do not come to my conclusion about the character of the *PA* on the basis of the text critical arguments alone. As Professor Jeffrey notes, these arguments are not so conclusive as is often assumed. The *PA* is often treated on the text-critical level like the famous "Comma Johanneum" in 1 John, where the Trinitarian statement "Father, Word and Holy Spirit; and these three are one" was added to John 5:7. The evidence against accepting the Comma as original to 1 John is irrefutable. No Greek text before 1400 contains the passage, and of the eight that contain it after that date, four do so in the form of marginal notes. The comma appears in the Old Latin text only after 600 and in the Vulgate only after 750. Before 1500, it does not exist in Coptic, Ethiopic and Arabic versions. It seems to have entered the textual tradition due to Trinitarian controversies in Spain and North Africa.[7] The text is obviously late and obviously an interpolation. While the textual evidence against the *PA* is very strong, this evidence is not like that of the Comma. As Professor Jeffrey notes, the passage seems to have been known to Papias, and it does not enter the Greek manuscripts as late as the Comma. It also inspires a great deal of early commentary from major figures like St. Ambrose and Augustine. Clearly it is more accepted in the West than in the Greek manuscripts, but the matter is at least debatable. On text-critical arguments alone, I would give the passage a chance—a slim chance, but a chance nevertheless, at being authentic.

Second, by arguing that the passage is not Johannine, I do not mean to imply that it is not an authentic piece of tradition about Jesus. I see little reason to separate it from the traditional teaching about Jesus. The passage sounds very much like the Jesus of the Synoptic Gospels, who eats with tax collectors and sinners.

And this leads to the final concerns of my paper, the function and purpose of this passage in the Orthodox Church. The fact that this passage is not at home in the Gospel of John does not mean that it is not at home within the life and faith of the Orthodox Church. The first undisputed discussion of the passage by a Greek interpreter is that of Euthymios Zigabenus in 1200. He writes that the passage is not in the most accurate manuscripts, and is marked by an obelisk in those that include it. Nevertheless, he adds, the passage is "not without usefulness" (*amoiron ofêleias*; *PG* 129.1280 C-D). In this sense, it seems to me that the passage falls into the same category as texts like the *Protevangelium of James*. This is something that I would like to

---

7. Painter, *1, 2 and 3 John*, 301–9; Brown, *Epistles of John*, appendix IV.

suggest anyway. No one proposes that the *Protevangelium of James* should be canonical, but its contents are the basis of many traditions regarding the Theotokos, and numerous Orthodox Churches are decorated with depictions of the Nativity of the Theotokos based on the traditions contained in the *Protevangelium*. The *PA* has also had a place in Orthodox life. St. Nikolai Velimirovic wrote a homily on the passage, which he concludes by saying,

> When people do not judge you for your sin, it means that they do not assign a punishment for the sin, but leave that sin with and in you. When God does not judge, however, this means that He forgives your sin, draws it out of you like pus and makes your soul clean. For this reason, the words, "Neither do I condemn thee," mean the same as "Thy sins are forgiven thee; go, daughter, and sin no more."[8]

The woman is like a confessing sinner whose sins are removed by the sacrament. She is not only forgiven in a juridical sense, but made clean, made free from her sin. Lev Gillet says something similar in his brief homily on the passage. First, he recognizes the text critical questions that plague the passage and he writes, "We are not concerned here with textual criticism, though we are quite aware that this incident may not have belonged to the Gospel of John."[9] After this recognition, however, he asks in the spirit of Efthymios Zigabenus, "At present, we can only want to consider the one question, what does the passage say to us?"[10] Like the comments of St. Nikolai Velimorovic, he sees the point of the passage expressed in the freedom the woman now possesses to move forward in a life free from sin, and concludes his homily by announcing, "Jesus is saying, 'I do not refer to the sins which are past, but to the beyond of eternal freedom. I launch you into the beyond. Go into the beyond, be changed, be illuminated, enter into my light now and it will be impossible for you to remain in darkness. . . . You yourselves can be in the same situation, and for you too there can be light instead of darkness. Therefore step boldly out. Step into space—the space which is freedom in Jesus."[11] Thus, to say that the passage is not clearly Johannine, and to wonder about its provenance, is not the same as saying that it does not have a place in the Christian life. The teaching on forgiveness of guilty sinners who are bowed in shame like the woman caught in adultery is very useful in the life of the Orthodox Church. Sins that are confessed are forgiven and erased and removed, and are no longer a burden or a set

---

8. From *Orthodox Life*, 1985, No. 2.
9. Gillet, "Woman Taken in Adultery," 60.
10. Ibid, 60.
11. Ibid, 62.

of shackles that restrain the spiritual life of the one confessing. In this way, the passage is tightly connected to the tradition of the Church, and to the life in Christ, even if it is not so tightly connected to the canonical Scripture. The passage is not in the Orthodox lectionary, and has a dubious status in Scripture. But this does not mean, in the words of Efthymios Zigabenus, that it is not without usefulness.[12]

---

12. The category of "usefulness" is not a minor or insignificant one. The term, and themes associated with it are common in Paul, especially in the Corinthian correspondence, and Margaret Mitchell has shown recently that the pursuit of a reading of Scripture that was "useful" for the Christian faithful was developed by many Church Fathers in imitation of Paul. See Mitchell, *Paul, the Corinthians and the Birth of Christian Hermeneutics*, especially 2, 12, 22 for the discussion of "utility" in biblical interpretation.

Jeffrey Final Response

I AM GRATEFUL TO Fr. Peter Galadza and Fr. George Parsenios, for their thoughtful and spirited engagement of my paper. I have learned much from reflecting on each, and I share their desire that our dialogue in these pages may serve to deepen mutual understanding among ourselves whilst respecting our different ecclesial traditions. As both men have noted, misunderstanding may easily arise when one is considering a passage of Scripture or a point of theology which may be contextualized very differently in other traditions. This is a very important point, and one with which I have been concerned in this essay.

My interlocutors prompt me to acknowledge more fully that one of the limitations of a use-based representation of evangelical readings of Scripture is most precisely the absence of what is central and defining for both Orthodox and Catholic traditions, namely a liturgical context. I should confess that in my attempt to give an account of evangelical scholarship on this debated text it initially occurred to me to bypass the matter of liturgical use (and lectionary) altogether, precisely because it does not, at least in the English-speaking world, much factor in the typical approaches made to the text by scholars from evangelical churches. Yet I resisted the impulse to stereotype, for "evangelical" is a broad-brush term, and it covers not only the classic free-churches, Baptists, "non-denominationals" and Pentecostals in their myriad iterations world-wide, but in some cases Anglo-Catholics, Anglicans, Lutherans, Methodists, Episcopalians, Presbyterians and others, who may use a common lectionary which in some cases overlaps with that of the Roman Catholic Church. Thus, though I have been myself for nearly four decades an Anglo-Catholic in practice, I am still regularly taken to be an evangelical by my peers in the ecumenical academy, and certainly not uniquely so among biblical scholars in my ecclesial tradition. I do not regard this appellation as in the least offensive, for where the Gospel is concerned I remain deeply sympathetic to my evangelical brothers and sisters of the more "reformed" and baptistic stripes. I have sought to represent their thinking fairly on this passage, though not without noticing in some of them a growing appreciation for grounding biblical interpretation not merely in the texts and textual history, but in the worship usage of the Church historically. Clearly, as an Anglican, I approve of this. There is thus in my paper a discernable Catholic element, and it proves to be indispensable to my own tentative conclusions to some of the canonical questions.

The antimony of which Fr. Peter speaks, namely that between "Church-under-Scripture" and "Scripture-under-Church," is a frisson many of us live with personally, and those who are scholars more so than most. Some of the scholars whose work I have instanced early in the paper did not perhaps feel it so much, having a strong Reformation bias to the first pole. Others I instance, such as J. Duncan M. Derrett, held to a form of the antimony with a tacit rather than explicit proviso that if an either-or choice were to be required the first pole is most to be trusted; for one who belonged to a church founded by Henry VIII this caveat is not to be wondered at. Still others who might be described theologically as evangelical tend to modify the antimony toward the second pole when they begin to sense the need for an authority greater than that of the solitary Bible-reader, especially if they have experienced situations of pulpit abuse in which the authority of a "strong reader" seems to assimilate and replace the authority of Scripture. A little historical recollection will suggest that this tension has been a perennial problem in the Church both East and West, and continues to be a problem in Christianity world-wide. Not surprisingly, many evangelicals who convert to Orthodoxy or to Rome do so because they have concluded that the Holy Spirit is more likely to be heard speaking clearly through the communal witness of the Church down through the ages than through the claims of forceful contemporary personalities whose "original" interpretations of the Bible are often impressionistic and excessively attuned to the market mores of popular culture.

One can recognize a sympathetic shift in recent evangelical biblical scholarship—even be a part of it—without deriding the more synchronic and culturally conditioned search for authentically grounded faith on the part of those who remain squarely in the evangelical fold. For one who we might think of as a "stereotypical evangelical" in American culture, to "stand alone on the Word of God" can seem rationally enough to be on a higher ground with clearer conscience than to imagine being subject to institutions that have historically often failed their highest principles and abused their authority. Awareness of political and ecclesial mischief, experiences of anxiety over theological divisiveness, revulsion occasioned by clerical abuse, or of scandal occasioned by apparent ecclesial complicity with injustice, even tyranny, is more than enough for some people to maintain a distrust of institutions which lay claim to spiritual authority. Accordingly, however incomplete in their understanding of the matter, many evangelicals will have been heartened by the apparent loosening of the claims of papal infallibility and primacy that seem to be emerging in the recent meeting of Patriarch Bartholomew and Pope Francis, because it seems to them a step in the right direction. A little sympathetic imagination goes a long way to opening meaningful dialogue with such people.

I have some specific indebtedness to my responders. To Fr. Galadza I owe an introduction to a Greek lectionary of the eighth century in which the *pericope adulterae* does occur; I would never have found this exceptional text without the help of an accomplished liturgist! And he was right to suggest that the work of Chris Keith deserved more space than originally I gave it; I was glad to make amends in my paper itself, and not just because Keith's conclusions are substantially compatible with my own. From Fr. Parsenios I have learned that on the walls of Russian Orthodox churches the scene from John 7:53—8:11 is depicted in places reserved for hearing confessions. This seems to me to be a striking example of visual exegesis and a compelling reclamation of this passage in the northern reaches of Orthodox parodisis. While Parsenios focusses on Trites's paper more than I do myself (perhaps because Trites's approach is forensic), I am entirely in agreement with him when he concludes his review by noting with regard to the challengers of Jesus, "the opponents of Jesus do not judge him justly because, even as they use the Law to condemn him, they do not recognize that the Law is actually written about him." On the canonical question he and I must for now register divergent opinions, however; whatever my residual dubieties about whether John himself composed the account of the woman taken in adultery and placed it just where we find it in a majority of texts after the fourth century, I would not relegate it to the level of a pseudopigraphical text such as the *Protoevangelion of James*. At this point, on literary grounds as well as historical and text-critical evidence I regard the *pericope adulterae* as an authentic Jesus story, and am content that St. Jerome, the Codex Bezae and the Council of Trent all made the right judgment.

In conclusion, I would like to reiterate that this assignment was conceived by me as a request to represent evangelical scholarship and approaches to the text more than to be an evangelical expositor making a case for a specific and singular evangelical reading. That necessitated in my view a fair but sympathetic examination of evangelical attempts to make a case for canonicity based on the scholarly strategies and methods that called that status into question. Much in recent evangelical attempts to defend the authority of Scripture through taking on academic critics on their own grounds has, however understandable, proved ineffective. The particular examples I chose—Zane Hodges, A. F. Johnson, Edward F. Hills, and finally Alison Trites—all still betraying the anxieties of evangelical forays into text-criticism in their period to some degree—are nevertheless part of a trend toward considering far more carefully both literary analysis and church-historical context. I presented Derrett as an exemplar of future developments, one whose evangelical convictions are always evident, but whose philology and churchmanship alike move him into much more secure and ecumenically comprehensible territory.

In my delivery I ended on a note of caution where evangelical are concerned, though I may have been misunderstood. Let me be clear: I intended my excursus not merely to be descriptive, but also to be moderately self-critical of the tradition I have been asked to represent. If I may reiterate: too narrow a fixation on text-critical matters has frequently, however otherwise intended, not so much buttressed evangelical efforts to defend a high view of Scripture as inadvertently to misdirect focus away from the role of Scripture as the whole counsel of God. The greater value of some of these evangelical text-critical labors, I have suggested, is gradually to have combined cultural understanding, philological insight and literary analysis in such a way as to read the text more canonically. This development has tended to move evangelicals closer to traditional Catholic views of the *pericope* than to Calvinist or liberal Protestant readings. That does not mean that there is not a need for further course correction in evangelical readings, of course, either in this instance or more generally; on the matter of authority I submit that among other *desiderata* we evangelicals need to take the Law itself more seriously, and to take the person of Jesus as the singular fulfilment of the Law most seriously of all. Antinomianism among us sub-culturally has been no help to just interpretation, and not only in regard to this passage. The import of this particular Jesus story is confirmed in the full canon of Scripture, after all, which everywhere affirms that righteous judgment from the Law cannot be given except by one who has fulfilled the Law. He who both authored and fulfilled the Law is the singular source of the grace and mercy we have been offered. This I take to be the primary evangelical meaning of the *pericope adulterae,* though I think it to be compatible with the understanding of all traditions in which this text is read.

CHAPTER 3

John 11:1–44
God Who Raises the Dead

TIMOTHY GEORGE (EVANGELICAL)

It may well be the case that the Gospel of John is not only the favorite among the four canonical gospels but also the most beloved book in the entire New Testament among Christian peoples of every age and every tradition. That it holds such a place of high esteem among evangelicals is beyond question. I myself recall how, as a young boy first learning to read, it was the Gospel of John that riveted my attention: the power and poetry of it, the dazzling symbols of light and darkness, life and death, of the Word who was made flesh and dwelt among us—the Word who came from so far away, from the bosom of the Father, to embrace so deeply the realm of human troubles, finally to undergo death on a cross.

The first verse I learned to memorize was John 3:16, everyone's favorite text in the New Testament until, as someone said, it was recently displaced by Matt 7:1, "Judge not—anyone for any reason whatsoever!" On Easter Sunday, John 11—which is the theme of my talk—vied with John 20 and 1 Corinthians 15 as the sermon text of choice for preaching on the resurrection of Jesus. In the *Book of Common Prayer*, the "Order for the Burial of the Dead" begins with a recitation of John 11:25–26: "I am the resurrection and the life, saith the Lord: he that believeth in me, though he were dead, yet shall he live: and whosoever liveth and believeth in me shall never die." It concludes with a collect in which this verse resonates again: "Oh merciful

God, the Father of our Lord Jesus Christ, who is the resurrection and the life; in whom whosoever believeth shall live, though he die; and whosoever liveth, and believeth in him, shall not die eternally. . ."

One reason why evangelicals have been so devoted to the Gospel of John is its explicitly evangelistic thrust. As a young Christian, I was taught to memorize what has been called the purpose statement of the entire gospel, John 20:31: "But these are written that you may believe that Jesus is the Messiah, the Son of God, and that by believing you may have life in his name." The great Baptist missionary pioneer William Carey went to India in the 1790s with the intention of translating the Bible into Bengali in order to share the message of Christ with the indigenous people there. But he first issued a translation of the Gospel of John, which his helpers took into the rice fields and market towns of northern India. There are reports of some villagers coming to faith in Christ simply through reading Carey's translation of the Gospel of John. They discovered in its pages, it was said, the one for whom they had been waiting all along.

Persons might have come to faith by simply reading John, but John itself cannot be read simply. From the second century on, when Tatian constructed his *Diatessaron*, the place of John within what Irenaeus called "the fourfold gospel" has been a difficult issue to unravel.[1] How the gospel "according (*kata*) to John" relates to the gospel "according to Mark," "according to Luke," and "according to Matthew" is a question well known and much-debated. It did not take the rise of the historical-critical study of the Bible in the nineteenth century to point out this puzzle. Eusebius, Epiphanius, and Augustine, among others in the early church, tried to explain the seeming discrepancies between John and the synoptics. Eusebius of Caesarea believed that John was aware of what Mark, Matthew, and Luke had written earlier, that John accepted their reports as true, and that John had a rather different and distinctive perspective to present. John set out to write what Clement of Alexandria called "a spiritual gospel," not spiritual as opposed to historical but spiritual in the sense of containing a deeper, richer, more textured meaning than what might be found on the surface of the text.[2]

Among the ancient Christian writers, the two most prolific preachers, judging by the number of extant sermons we have from their hand, were St. Augustine—we have more than one thousand of his sermons—and St. John Chrysostom—we have more than eight hundred of his. Both left us extensive homilies on the Gospel of John. Augustine begins his series on John by comparing the gospel to a high mountain, a reference back to Psalm

---

1. Irenaeus, *Against Heresies*, 3.11.8.
2. Clement of Alexandria, *Hist. Eccl.*, 6:14.7.

121:1: "I lift up my eyes to the mountains—where does my help come from? My help comes from the Lord, the maker of heaven and earth." John is a high mountain on which we stand to see the wonders of God's redemptive work. Even so, this is a mountain shrouded in mystery, for John the Gospel writer was a fallible, limited human. As Augustine put it: "I venture to say, my brethren, perhaps not John himself spoke of the matter as it is, but even he only as he was able; for it was man that spoke of God, inspired indeed by God, but still man . . . therefore, my brethren, if you would understand, lift up your eyes to this mountain, that is, raise yourselves up to the evangelist, rise to his meaning."[3]

Chrysostom uses another image. Reading John, he said, was like listening to beautiful music. To appreciate the symphony of John's gospel requires more than a brilliant mind well-trained in the theories of Plato and Pythagoras. No, appropriating John requires spiritual formation. Indeed, the gospel writer himself "made ready his soul as some well-fashioned and jeweled lyre with strings of gold and yielded it for the utterance of something great and sublime to the spirit."[4] And so "if a man cannot learn well a melody on pipe or harp, unless he in every way strain his attention: how shall one, who sits as a listener to sounds mystical, be able to hear with a careless soul? . . . for it is not otherwise possible for a man to gain from hence anything great, except he have first so cleansed anew his soul."[5]

JOHN 11 IN JOHN'S PLOT

With that in mind, let us turn to the remarkable account of Jesus's raising of Lazarus from the dead recorded in John 11:1–54. Within the narrative structure of John's gospel, this passage plays a pivotal role: It is at once the culmination of the Book of Signs (John 2–12) and, along with chapter 12, the transition to Book of the Passion (John 13–20). The closing verses of chapter 11 present Jesus's raising of Lazarus as the crux of the conspiracy that will end in his crucifixion at Calvary. The sensation of having brought back to life a man who was certifiably dead could possibly explain why Jerusalem was thronged with onlookers crying "Hosanna!" when Jesus entered the city on Palm Sunday (cf. John 12:12–19).

Because of the decisive role the Lazarus story plays in the gospel's plot line, it is redolent of both *analepsis*, a glancing back at what has already come before, and *prolepsis*, a foreshadowing of what is yet to happen. One

---

3. Augustine, *Homilies on the Gospel of John*, 7:7–8.
4. Chrysostom, "Prooem" in *Hom. in Iohan.*
5. Chrysostom, *Homilies on the Gospel of John*, 14:1–3.

indication of this is the small detail given in 11:2 identifying Mary, the sister of Lazarus, as "the same one who poured perfume on the Lord and wiped his feet with her hair." This is presented as though the reader were already aware of it, although the event itself will take place only in chapter 12. The glancing back is seen in the statement of the Judeans at the tomb of Lazarus in 11:37, in which "some of them said, 'Could not he who opened the eyes of the blind man have kept this man from dying?'"

In all of this, John is teaching his readers how to become a wise *semeistokos*, that is, one who is able to stand on the mountain of John 11 and see, with an eagle's eye, a more distant vista. In this way, John is telling us precisely that Jesus has come to open up for us the way to the heart of the heavenly father. "I and the Father are one," he says in John 10:30 and again later in John 12:49: "For I have not spoken on my own, but the Father who sent me commanded me to say all the things that I have spoken. I know that his command leads to eternal life. So whatever I say is just what the Father has told me to say"—and, we may presume in John, to do just what the Father has told him to do.

Throughout the Gospel of John, the recurrent question is, over and over again, who is Jesus Christ? Many answers are given: the Lamb of God who takes away the sin of the world, Messiah, Son of God, the King of Israel, the Son of man, a teacher who has come from God, the bridegroom, the Savior of the world, a sinner, a Samaritan, a demon-possessed man, a blasphemer, Joseph the carpenter's son—"Didn't this guy play basketball for Nazareth High last year?" Jesus, of course, answers the question of his identity with his powerful "*ego eimi*" statements, including the climactic "I am the resurrection and the life" in John 11:25.

But behind the persistent Christological focus of the Gospel of John, there is a bigger or, if you will, a deeper question: Who is the God that Jesus of Nazareth has come to reveal? As C. K. Barrett put it, "There could hardly be a more Christocentric writer than John, yet his very Christocentricity is theocentric."[6] This recognition of what we might call "the theology behind the theology" in the Gospel of John has been explored by several scholars, including Marianne Meye Thompson. In her insightful book, *The God of the Gospel of John*, the question is: What kind of God is the God whom we know in Jesus Christ? Or, as Thompson quotes her teacher D. Moody Smith:

> The fundamental question of the Fourth Gospel is the question of God, not whether a God exists but who is God and how God reveals himself. Thus the fundamental question or issue of the

---

6. Thompson, *God of the Gospel of John*, 7 n. 17.

gospel can be stated as the nature of revelation. What God is revealed and how is God revealed.[7]

In John 11, the character of God, "the God who raises the dead," to use a distinctive Pauline expression (see 2 Cor 1:9), is revealed in three surprising, unexpected actions that Jesus took. Each of these acts poses a question about the character of Christ and the nature of the God he came to reveal. Jesus *waited* (11:6): Why the delay? Jesus *wailed* or raged (11:33): Why the anger? And Jesus *wept* (11:35): Why the grief? These acts give insight both into Jesus's intentionality and his emotionality, and they do so with an intensity found nowhere else in the gospels. It is no wonder that commentators across the centuries have been confounded by the Jesus of John 11. In the reception of John's gospel in the history of the church, each of Jesus's surprising acts in this chapter addresses a major distortion of the Christian faith: deism, stoicism, and docetism.

JESUS WAITED: WHY THE DELAY?

The raising of Lazarus took place in wintertime, around the Feast of the Dedication in Jerusalem. The immediate context shows Jesus in peril as his adversaries among the Judeans threaten to stone him to death because, as John tells us, he, being a man, had "made himself God" (10:33). Earlier they had demanded of Jesus, "If you are the Christ, tell us plainly" (10:24).

This is the favorite text of evidentialists of all kinds, including King Herod in *Jesus Christ Superstar*: "Just to prove that you're no fool, walk across my swimming pool!" (cf. Luke 23:8–9). Tell us plainly. Don't be so elusive. Show us your stuff! In the synoptics, when the Pharisees ask Jesus for a sign, they are told that no sign shall be given this generation, and Matthew adds, "except the sign of Jonah" (Mark 8:12; Matt 12:38–42; Luke 11:29). But in John seven great signs are given. This "tell us plainly" in John 10 is answered by Jesus's public raising of Lazarus in John 11. But the clarity of the miracle is shrouded in ambiguity because Jesus does not come to Bethany immediately. When Jesus hears that Lazarus is ill, he deliberately delays. He stays where he is two days longer. In the meantime, Lazarus dies. Why this strange delay?

One answer is to say that Jesus wanted Lazarus to be really dead, good and dead, before he brought him back to life. This theory refers to the rabbinic belief that the soul hovered around the body for three days after the time of death, departing only when decomposition had set in (Carson, 411).

---

7. Smith, *Theology of John*, 75.

The fact that the body of Lazarus gives off a malodorous stench after four days in the grave makes the miracle more verifiable, more undeniable, more spectacular. This motif fits the pattern of the other sign-miracles in John, all of which are, we might say, miracles-plus. In John 2, Jesus turned water not just into wine but into Cabernet Sauvignon of exquisite quality; the man healed in John 5 had been paralyzed for thirty-eight years; in John 9 the man given sight had been blind from birth; there were twelve baskets of leftovers after the feeding of the 5,000, and so on.

But there is more to it than this, for this is not the first deliberate delay in Jesus's ministry. At Cana, Jesus's irritation with Mary is not so much with what she asked him to do but with the insistence that he do it right then and there, on the spot. "My hour has not yet come," Jesus told Mary. Jesus will not be coerced into action, even by those closest to him, as Leon Morris says (Morris, 480). In John 4, there is a foreshadowing of John 11 when Jesus stays with the Samaritans for *two extra days* before departing for Galilee. Again, Jesus's delay there, as in John 11, resulted in many coming to faith (4:39–42; cf.11:45). More troubling is the delay of Jesus when the disciples are on the sea in the storm. We are told that "it was now dark, and Jesus had not yet come to them" (6:17). Now, as Lazarus lingered at the portal of death, as Martha and Mary were wracked with anxiety, straining every nerve to hear any word from the Master, it was again dark, the storm was raging, and Jesus was nowhere to be found. He had not yet come to them.

While he waited, Lazarus died. Almost as though to fend off the thought that Jesus might be indifferent or callous to the plight of his friends in Bethany, the author of the Fourth Gospel inserts this comment: "Now Jesus loved Martha and her sister and Lazarus" (11:5). We need to be reminded of this because of the unbearable tension between Jesus's love and his inaction, his delay. It is this tension that carries the story forward, seen and felt in the same question repeated three times in John 11—first, from Martha's lips in verse 21: "Lord, if you had been here, my brother would not have died"; and Mary in verse 32: "Lord, if you had been here . . ."; and finally from the Judeans in verse 37: "Could not he . . . have kept this man from dying?" If only he had been here.

John gives us a God who does not fit neatly into the comfortable theodicies of our postmodern sensibility: the god of process or openness theology, a god who means well, perhaps, but who, at the end of the day, is impotent in the face of radical evil. John's God is closer to the God of the Negro spiritual, born of slavery and suffering: "The Lord, he may not come when you want him to, but he's always right on time." This is also the God of John Calvin, who in his *Commentary on John* declares: "But as Christ is the unique mirror of diving grace, his delay teaches us that we should not judge

God's love through present circumstances.... Although Christ may delay, he never sleeps or forgets his own people."[8]

John's way of accounting for Jesus's delay is to connect it with the manifestation of God's glory. The illness of Lazarus, Jesus says, is not unto death (*pros thanaton*), though he will die, but it is rather for "the glory of God, so that the Son of God may be glorified by means of it" (11:4). The theme of glory frames the miracle story, as Jesus will later say to Martha: "Did not I tell you that if you would believe you would see the glory of God?" (11:40).

Glory, of course, is the great theme of the entire Gospel of John, announced at the beginning in the key verse 1:14 ("We have beheld his glory"). Glory connected directly to the signs (2:11; 7:39; 9:3; 11:4, 40). But glory in John, though it breaks through in the miraculous signs, is not primarily about the glitter and the glow of the supernatural. In John, Jesus is glorified when he is "lifted up," when he is lifted up on the cross (see 3:13–15; 12:16, 31–43).

The glory of God is seen in the Lazarus event not merely in Jesus's bringing back to life a man four days dead—one who must, after all, die yet again—but in the significance of this event in propelling Jesus toward the cross, toward his being glorified by being lifted up. The irony of the miracle in John 11 is that Jesus calls forth Lazarus from one grave in order that he himself might enter another one.

JESUS WAILED WITH RAGE: WHY THE ANGER?

Once Jesus's too-late arrival in Bethany has taken place and his encounter with the two grieving sisters with their identical question ("Lord, if you had been here...") has happened, we are given an insight into Jesus's own emotional reaction to the scene around him. In 11:33, we are told that Jesus "was greatly disturbed in spirit and deeply moved" (NRSV) and then in 11:35 that "Jesus began to weep." Given the deep sadness of the occasion and the close proximity of these verses in the text, it is tempting to elide these two reactions of Jesus into a single response or mood. Many commentators have done just this, but I think that it is a mistake to do so, for we are being told two rather distinct things about Jesus here and, consequently, about the God he came to reveal. So, we shall consider the outburst of Jesus in verse 33 as distinct from his weeping in verse 35.

In verse 33, the author of the Fourth Gospel links two verbs to describe Jesus's response to the situation: *embrimâsthai* and *tarásso*. *Tarásso* means "to shake," "to stir up," "to be troubled." It is one of John's favorite verbs. For

---

8. Calvin, *John*, 272.

example, it is used of the troubling of the waters at Bethesda in 5:7, and it recurs five times in four consecutive chapters (11:33; 12:27; 13:21; 14:1, 27.) It is a word that conveys a sense of being upset, overwhelmed, floored or, "punched in the gut," as we say in English.

One of the marks of the Johannine Christ is that he experienced such buffeting, as we see in 12:27–28—"Now my soul is troubled. And what should I say—'Father, save me from this hour'? No, it is for this reason that I have come to this hour. Father, glorify your name.'" But the verb with which *tarásso* is linked in 11:33, *embrimâsthai*, which is here intensified to *enebrimēsato tō pneumatic*, is unique to John in this text, though it is found elsewhere in the Septuagint and the synoptics (Mark 1:43; Matt 9:30; Mark 14:5; Matt 12:18).

In his John commentary, the great Baptist New Testament scholar, George Beasley-Murray, points out a major disagreement between the English and German traditions of biblical scholarship in the translation of this word. The NIV's "deeply moved in spirit," the Good News Bible's "his heart was touched," or the New English Bible's "sighed heavily" are all softened versions of the KJV's "he groaned in the spirit and was troubled." However, in the Reformation both Luther and the Zurich Bible used a German word, *ergrimmte*, to render this unusual Greek word. *Ergrimmte* comes into English as "he became angry, disgusted, enraged." Schnackenburg speaks for the German tradition when he declares: "The word *embrimâstahi* . . . indicates an outburst of anger, and any attempt to reinterpret in terms of an internal emotional upset caused by grief, pain, or sympathy is illegitimate."[9]

In an important study on "The Mental Attitude of Jesus at Bethany," Cullen I. K. Story sights evidence from classical and patristic sources that support the German rendering of *embrimâsthai* as involving anger on the part of Jesus and not mere sorrow or sympathy. The first of these is from Aeschylus in his play *The Seven against Thebes*, in which this verb refers to the snorting of a warhorse about to charge into battle (cf. the movie *War Horse*). The image is that of an enraged animal, grunting and growling, nostrils flaring, bellowing with anger and rage. However we translate this unusual word in the context of John 11, it at least means that Jesus experienced indignation, revulsion, outrage.

But, however much we appeal to anthropomorphic language or to Calvin's favorite trope of accommodation, the question remains: Can God get mad? Can Jesus become as angry as this verb seems to imply that he did? Among those who have shrunk from entertaining such a possibility is none other than the great Augustine—to which Calvin, who quotes Augustine

---

9. Schnackenburg, *Gospel According to St. John*, 2:335.

more than 1,000 times in his *Institutes* (usually quite favorably), respectfully disagrees at this point.[10] But for those who are willing to allow the text to mean what it seems to say, that Jesus experienced indignation and outrage as he prepared to raise Lazarus from the dead, the question remains: At what or whom was Jesus angry?

Many have attempted to answer this question. Phillip F. Esler and Ronald Piper, in their book *Lazarus, Mary, and Martha*, summarize five major views among various scholars as to why exactly Jesus might have become angry at this point. I shall list these five views not in the order that Esler and Piper present them but on a scale of what I consider least to most likely. First, there is Cullen Story's idea that Jesus might have been angry with himself because, after all, the delay in his arrival had precipitated the crisis. Second, some have suggested that Jesus was angry at the thought of his own impending death (Sprosten North). Third, he might have been angry at those among the Judeans, especially the Pharisees, who were already conspiring to have him killed. Fourth, many commentators have suggested that the focus of Jesus's anger was the lack of faith on the part of Mary and those among the mourners who refused to believe (Bultmann). However, it is best, I think, to regard Jesus's anger as directed against Satan, the Evil One himself, who presides over the realm of death, wreaking havoc throughout God's good creation.

It is well known that John has no temptation narrative with Jesus and Satan in direct confrontation. Nor does he record the exorcisms so prominent in the synoptics. In John, Satan is a shadowy figure, though he is not absent. For example, in 8:48 Jesus is accused of being in league with the devil; in 12:31 Satan is referred to as "the prince of this world" whose defeat will be accomplished by the "lifting up" of Jesus on the cross; and in 13:2 the devil is said to have inspired Judas to betray Jesus. What we have in John 11 is Jesus's direct confrontation with Satan, his pursuit of him, and his attack against him at his most formidable point, the realm of death.

Shortly before his death in 1991, the British New Testament scholar Barnabas Lindars published an essay, "Rebuking the Spirit: A New Analysis of the Lazarus Story of John 11," in which he argued that behind the Lazarus story as we have it in John 11 are the "traces of an earlier raising story in which exorcism plays a key role."[11] Whatever one makes of Lindars's source-critical theory (and it seems far-fetched to me), he is not wrong to associate the anger expressed by Jesus at the tomb of Lazarus as directed against Satan and his pomp.

10. Calvin, *Commentary on John* 11:33.
11. Lindars, "Rebuking the Spirit," 89–104.

It is clear that Jesus is the aggressor, not the victim, in this scene. What we have here is not so much a sudden upset as an "undying hostility to the forces of evil, coming to the surface at the very sight of them."[12] There are many echoes of this motif in the early Christian tradition. For example, in the apocryphal Gospel of Bartholomew from the third century, Jesus is depicted on the Last Day as leading the apostles and Mary from the Mount of Olives toward the eastern gate of Jerusalem to recapture the city from the Evil One. In this assault, Jesus is said to have threatened or rebuked (*embrimēsamenos*) the demons of the underworld, even as he beckons Michael the archangel to sound his mighty trumpet.[13] Likewise, in the life of Antony, as told by Athanasius, the great father of monasticism gradually withdraws from the softer life of the city into the far reaches of the desert, eventually making his abode in the graveyard and tombs of the dead. He does so not (as some of my students allege when I have them read this story) because he is psychologically imbalanced and just needs to see a good shrink but rather because he is a prize-fighter for Christ doing hand-to-hand combat with the devil. Something similar, I suggest, is going on here in John 11. And so it is not the weeping sisters and their friends, the unbelieving crowd around them, or the plotters seeking his death who evoke this intense expression of anger and revulsion on the part of Christ. Rather, this strong emotion, as Herman Ridderbos has put it, "is the revulsion of everything that is in him against the power of death."[14] Or, as Calvin comments: "Christ does not come to the sepulcher as an idle spectator, but like a wrestler preparing for the contest. Therefore no wonder that he groans again, for the violent tyranny of death that he had to overcome stands before his eyes."[15]

This perspective challenges both our contemporary understanding of death and the modern view of God. When I was a student at Harvard, I recall hearing Elizabeth Kübler-Ross speak on her best-selling book, *On Death and Dying*. Her work helped to normalize and domesticate death in our culture. She carefully and clinically explained the various stages of grief related to death.[16] She taught us to consider all of this in a calm and therapeutic manner, and no doubt many people found solace in such construals. So death becomes a normal, controllable, and manageable part of human

---

12. Ibid, 93.
13. Hennecke, *New Testament Apocrypha*, 1:496, "And he led them down from the Mount of Olives, and threatened the angels of the underworld, and beckoned to Michael to sound his mighty trumpet in the height of heaven. Then the earth was shaken and beliar came up, held by 660 angels and bound with fiery chains."
14. Ridderbos, *Gospel According to John*, 402.
15. Calvin, *Commentary on John 11: 38*.
16. Kübler-Ross, *On Death and Dying*.

life. This perspective fits comfortably into the positivist, materialist, and secularist presuppositions of our time.

The New Testament, on the other hand, presents death as a violent intrusion, an illicit disruption, a trespasser, a foe or enemy to be overcome. Indeed, Paul refers to death as "the last enemy" to be destroyed by Christ, who will stomp it under his feet on the day of resurrection (1 Cor 15:25–26). In the meantime, God does not sit idly by observing with cool detachment the sufferings of his people and the ragings of Satan. This is the God of deism, the God Thomas Hardy once referred to as "a dreaming, dark, dumb Thing that turns the handle of this idle show."[17] This is the God who is at the root of so much contemporary atheism. But the God of the Gospel of John is the God who challenges evil at its strongest point, a God who becomes indignant and angry in the face of death and evil. What we have in John 11 is not so much sinners in the hands of an angry God (though there is much about judgment in John) but rather sin itself, in its most intrusive, death-dealing effect, confronted by an angry Christ.

JESUS WEPT: WHY THE GRIEF?

The first surviving commentary we have on the Gospel of John, indeed on any of the New Testament writings, is by Heracleon, a disciple of the gnostic Valentinus. The work of Elaine Pagels and others have highlighted the popularity of John within the gnostic communities. For this reason, the canonicity of John, along with the Book of Revelation, which is believed to be written by the same author, was questioned by some in the early church. The battle for the Johannine part of the Bible has continued down to our own day with Ernst Käsemann famously criticizing John's "naïve docetism" and declaring that "the Church committed an error when it declared the Gospel to be orthodox" since "neither apostolic authorship nor apostolic content can be affirmed for it."[18] Does John give us a genuinely human Christ at all? Käsemann, among others, thinks not and explains those features in John where Jesus's humanity is on display—the mention of his parents and brothers (2:1–11; 6:42; 7:3, 10), his asking for a drink of water at the well in Samaria (4:6), and his weeping at the grave of Lazarus (11:35)—as either interpolations by a later editor trying to make John more "orthodox" than

---

17. Thomas Hardy, "The Dynasts," 2:254.

18. Käsemann, *Testament of Jesus*, 73–76. See Thompson's discussion of the debate on John between Käsemann and Bultmann in Thompson, *Humanity of Jesus in the Fourth Gospel*, 1–11.

he really was or, in the case of Käsemann, a newly constructed portrayal of Jesus made from whole cloth.

The declaration of Jesus's weeping in the text as it stands challenges all docetic and gnostic readings of the Gospel. The Greek word *dakruō*, given here in the aorist tense, is found nowhere else in the New Testament, although the cognate noun *dákruon* occurs ten times in other places. As used of Jesus in this setting, *dákrusen* means more than to shed a few tears. It means something like "he burst out crying" or, as one scholar has put it, "Jesus bawled" (Bruner, 676). The anger Jesus displayed in verse 33 is still simmering inside Christ, as the repetition of the word *embrimâstahi* indicates. However, as Schnackenburg argues, something other than anger is on display in Jesus's tears (Schnackenburg; Schenck, *And Jesus Wept*, 224). The tears of Jesus in verse 35 show his deep identification with those who are grief-stricken. It reveals the breaking of his heart for others whose own hearts are broken. Here Jesus weeps with those who weep, even as he learned obedience through what he suffered. As the writer to the Hebrews puts it: "In the days of his flesh, Jesus offered up prayers and supplications, with loud cries and tears, to the One who was able to save him from death, and he was heard because of his reverent submission" (Heb 5:7). Calvin warned against our treating Christ as a stern Stoic, a savior impervious to the sighs and groans of his brothers and sisters (Calvin on John 11). Ridderbos also warns against idealizing interpretations of Jesus's tears in this text. Jesus "strides to the tomb, not in the sovereign apathy of the great Outsider, but as the One sent into the world by the Father, as the Advocate who has entered human flesh and blood" (Ridderbos, 404). On display is not only the divine authority of Jesus but also his deep human involvement in the death of his friend and its effects on those who mourn his loss.

In their fascinating study of John 11, Philip Esler and Ronald Piper devote a chapter to "The Raising of Lazarus in Early Christian Art." They point out that in Aldo Nestori's definitive repertoire of the paintings of the Roman catacombs, the raising of Lazarus is the second-most represented. (Depictions of the Good Shepherd is number one with eighty-five instances, with Lazarus coming in second with sixty-six, and Jonah, another resurrection motif, with sixty-five.)[19] Jesus is often depicted with a magician-like wand and sometimes simply with his hand extended, calling forth the dead men from the grave. The stark reality of death is not minimized in these frescos, nor is the outpouring of grief from Martha, Mary, and their friends, Jesus included. But in an age when Christians were subjected to violence, persecution, and martyrdom, John's account of Jesus's raising of Lazarus as-

---

19. Esler and Piper, *Lazarus, Mary and Martha*, 132.

sured the catacomb Christians that death, however and whenever it came, was not the final word.

Though much has been made of the so-called "realized eschatology" in the Gospel of John, Jesus's "I am the Resurrection" statement in John 11:25 does not cancel out the earlier statement of Jesus in John 5:28–29, "The hour is coming when all who are in their graves will hear his voice and will come out." Jesus stands at the grave of Lazarus and shouts out his name: "Lazarus, come forth!" "My sheep hear my voice and know my name," he has already said in chapter 10, and now he calls one of his sheep by name and does so with a loud voice (*ekraugasen*, 11:45). As my friend Dale Bruner says, it was "the roar heard round the world."[20] Spurgeon says that if Jesus had not specified Lazarus by name, then the general resurrection foretold in John 5 would have happened right there on the spot! So John 11 is about both the sharing of new life in Christ here and now—"he that believes in the Son has life already"—and also about the radical disturbance of the present order of things by the awesome in-breaking of apocalyptic.

In *The Brothers Karamazov*, Dostoevsky wrote:

> I believe like a child that suffering will be healed and made up for, that all the humiliating absurdity of human contradictions will vanish like a pitiful mirage, like the despicable fabrication of the impotent and infinitely small Euclidean mind of man, that in the world's finally, at the moment of eternal harmony, something so precious will come to pass that it will suffice for all hearts, for the comforting of all resentments, of the atonement of all the crimes of humanity, of all the blood that they have shed; and that it will make it not only possible to forgive but to justify what has happened.

Such a view of time and eternity, of the setting right of accounts gone horribly wrong, can only make sense in light of the God revealed by what we have seen in John 11 through the delay of Jesus, his anger in the face of radical evil, and his weeping with those who weep.

---

20. Bruner, *Gospel of John*, 681.

What is Dearest to Us?
A Response to Timothy George

MICHAEL WALDSTEIN (CATHOLIC)

IN SEARCH FOR AN OPENING STATEMENT

WHEN I BEGAN WRITING my talk, I planned an opening statement that would make an impact on an Evangelical audience. This was my first draft.

> *I am a Catholic. I admit it.*
> I am—not a Christian, but a Catholic.
> I worship—not God, but the Virgin Mary.
> I read—not the Bible, but papal encyclicals.
> I think—not my own thoughts, but those of the Pope.

On second thought, I threw this draft into the trash. To mislead you about what being a Catholic is—that would be to play a bad trick on you. Your laughter about it leads me to suspect that the trick would not have convinced you anyway.

Then I wrote a second draft.

> *I am a Catholic. I admit it.*
> On my iPad I have an app called iProtesThump. The latest version, iProtesThump Professional 7.0, just came out.
> You may wonder, What does iProtesThump do?
> iProtesThump thumps Protestants. It measures their degree of protestanticity, displays that degree on the Richter scale, downloads the Catholic answer most suited to the value measured in the disgruntled theological earthquake, and delivers

> the solid Catholic answer in a deep basso voice, like the voice of God in an expensive Hollywood movie.
>
> I am ready to respond to Prof. George. I will not even have to open my mouth. I'll just connect the iPad to the sound system. Designed in California, assembled in China. Nevertheless, it works quite well.

I threw out this second draft. A text of Luther came to mind after meditating on Luther's reaction to the news that a Council would be held at Trent and that Protestants were not invited.

> We should take him—the Pope, the Cardinals, and whatever riffraff belongs to his Idolatrous and Papal Holiness—and, as blasphemers, tear out their tongues from the back, and nail them on the gallows in the order in which they hang their seals on official documents, even though all this is mild compared to their blasphemy and idolatry.
>
> Then one could allow them to hold a council, or as many as they wanted, on the gallows, or in hell among all the devils.[1]

Luther's protest is too wounded and too wounding, too bent out of shape by evils in the early Renaissance Church, too corroded by bitter hatred and white-hot anger, to make jokes about. That is why I threw out the second draft.

I have read many books and papers filled with disgruntled Protestant protests and I often worry about the temptation of becoming a disgruntled protester in response. If one gives in to this temptation, one turns Catholic theology, not perhaps into Protestant, but protest squared.

These worries dissolved into thin air when I began reading Prof. George's paper. Far from making me disgruntled, the paper made me deeply and gratefully gruntled, if that is the word I am looking for. I felt that I was meeting a brother in Christ. What captured me from the beginning was Prof. George's opening statement, which he chose with much wisdom and to great effect. He recalls the first Scripture passage he memorized. "God so loved the world that he gave his only Son . . ." (John 3:16). It was the first, he explains, because it was "everyone's favorite text in the New Testament." It is my favorite text too. This goes to prove, by the way, if proof were needed, that I belong to the category of people called "everyone."

Prof. George's opening statement led me to write a third version of my opening statement. I wrote it as an echo of his, inspired by his. Here it is. It

---

1. Luther, "Against the Roman Papacy," (LW), 41:308.

is the real one. I did not throw it into the trash. I hope I never will, though doubtless it could be expressed much better.

I am a Catholic. I admit it. For me personally, being a Catholic means what it means for countless other Catholics, including the Pope. It means embracing the Good News. Three attributes of the Good News stand out. One can arrange them following the triad of truth, goodness, and beauty (or, at the maximum degree of beauty: glory).

1. *True:* The Good News is news, which is to say it corresponds to what is real. If the Gospel were not true as news, it would tell us nothing, nor could it ever be *good news*. A mirage of water in the desert is not good news for a lost wanderer dying of thirst, because it is not news in the first place.

2. *Good:* Exactly because the Gospel is *true*, it can be really *good*. Truth is the first condition of its goodness. The main reason for the Gospel's goodness, of course is its content. The lamb's gift of self in "carrying away the sin of the world" (John 1:29) is so good, that it dearest to those who embrace it, dearer than anything else. Its outstanding goodness moves us to make a radical gift of self in return, in which we find our own good. St. Bernard puts it in a nutshell.

    In the first work [i.e., creation] he gave me myself, in the second [i.e., redemption] himself, and where he gave himself, he gave me back to myself. As one given and given back, I owe myself for myself, and owe myself twice. What shall I render to God for himself? Even if I could give myself back to him a thousand times, what am I to God?[2]

3. *Beautiful/Glorious:* That he gives himself as Bridegroom, that he "has the bride" (John 3:29), that she is the great city who becomes his "wife" (Rev 21:2.9), this is good beyond all reckoning. The beauty of this event goes beyond all bounds. It is not only good, not beautiful in the limited way other things are, but glorious.

In conclusion, to embrace the Gospel as true, good, and glorious, to love this truth, goodness, and glory, to hold it dearest, dearer than anything else, this is what it means for me to be a Catholic. I realize that in many ways I fall short of being radically Catholic.

There is another way of saying what I have just said. It comes to the same thing. I am not as familiar with it, but you might be. For me to be a Catholic means accepting Jesus Christ as my personal Lord and Savior.

What I mean by "*my personal Lord and Savior*" is that:

---

2. Bernard of Clairvaux, *De diligendo deo*, ch. 5, par 15; emphasis added.

- He is Lord and Savior *primarily of the whole world*, of which I am *a personal part*;
- He is Bridegroom *primarily of the whole Church*, of which I am *a personal part*;
- He is, in short, the *common good* of the whole, of which I am *a personal part*.

It is precisely on the most intimate and personal level of myself, as "I," that I am a part, related to a whole that is greater than I. The Church is my mother, not only in the sense that by the power of her Bridegroom she gave me new birth from above by water and the Spirit, but also that she continues to nourish me by the Eucharist, by the Bridegroom's body and blood, by the sacrament in which his gift of self and my returning gift of self are uniquely concentrated. Growing up to maturity does not mean leaving my mother's womb, as it did when I was born from my physical mother and once again when I left my parents' home to build my own life. It means growing more thoroughly into the Church, becoming more part of her as a responsible person. The greater whole does not take away my personal responsibility, but defines that responsibility in its nature.

Since I am emphasizing this point so strongly, you might get the impression that I am trying to smuggle elements of Catholic sensibility about the priority of the Church over the individual person into Evangelical language to undermine the Evangelical emphasis on the individual person. That impression would be a mistake. There is no opposition, but a necessary mutual implication between the personal and the communal. What I said is simply biblical. Immediately after he states the most general principle of moral life, Paul's Letter to the Romans emphasizes the membership of each person in the body of Christ, the unity of the Church as the very first concrete moral principle: we are members of each other and should think of our own "I" accordingly, refusing notions of ourselves that set us apart by ourselves (see Rom 12:1–4).

The same emphasis on membership is also part of your Protestant heritage. Despite the intensely burning anger that acted on his relation to the Church like sulfuric acid, Luther's sensibility was in many respects Catholic. An important testimony is found in his commentary on Psalm 45, the Messianic Wedding Psalm, when he comments on the words, "At your right hand stands the queen, clothed all in gold" (Ps 45:9).

> And this I know too, that he has become the Bridegroom and has communicated to his bride, the Church, all that he has. I am a part of his Church (*eius Ecclesiae ego sum pars*). For I have

sure signs and pledges, namely, Baptism, the Gospel, the Eucharist, that witness to the fact that I am a member (*membrum*) of Christ."[3]

This queen, which is the Church, is not an impersonal organization. It is not "organized religion." If anything, it should be called "organic religion." It has a personal center in the mother of Jesus. She is not only the first member of the Church, but in some way the connecting middle. Membership in Christ's body means also a particularly close and personal relationship to her.

Here, then, are the three themes on which I will focus below in looking at some passages of John that complement the text Prof. George focuses on, the raising of Lazarus (John 11): the unity of the Church, the Eucharist, and Mary.

DISPLACING GOSPEL BY LAW

First, however, let us continue with Prof. George's opening statement. Immediately after noting that John 3:16 was "everyone's favorite text in the New Testament," he adds "*until, as someone said, it was recently displaced* by Matt 7:1. Judge not—*anyone* for *any* reason whatsoever" (emphasis added). There is a clear ironic tone in these words. They express a judgment about a terrible sickness that is increasingly infecting Christians.

Let us look closely at the new favorite. Jesus says, "Judge not, that you may not be judged" (Matt 7:1). The words "anyone for any reason whatsoever" are added by Prof. George's source. After prohibiting judgment, Jesus goes on to explain under what circumstances we *can* judge. "First take the log out of your own eye, and then you will see clearly to take the speck out of your brother's eye" (Matt 7:5).

Immediately after these words, Jesus makes a statement that is likely to strike our non-judgmental nostrils as the very stench of judgmental bigotry. "Do not give what is holy to the dogs, and do not throw your pearls before the swine" (Matt 7:6). It looks like we cannot escape from judging in some circumstances whether we are faced with "the dogs and the swine" or not. Our revulsion from the stench of judgmental words, by the way, shows how judgmentally non-judgmental our spiritual nostrils have become.

Yet, the problem of the re-entry of judgment is a small problem compared with what the word "displaced" shows. John 3:16 was recently *displaced* by the new favorite.

---

3. Luther, "Lectures on Psalm 45" (LW), 12:262; (WA), 4.2:555–559.

The most important difference between the old favorite and the new is that "God so loved the world" is Gospel, that is, good news about a fact that really happened. "Don't judge!" by contrast, is Law, that is, a commandment about an act to be avoided or performed. It commands the sort of thing Paul calls a work of the Law.

If there is anything to be learned from Paul's Letter to the Galatians, it is that displacing the Gospel by confidence in works of the Law is not a good idea. It means betraying Christ. Anyone who promotes reliance on works of the Law rather than faith in the Gospel is accursed, Paul says; those who listen and agree with such a displacement of the Gospel are foolish and bewitched. They have fallen from life according to the Spirit into flesh (see Gal 1:6–9; 3:1–3).

Suppose that, contrary to my evident age of sixty, I were a young man who very much wants to get married. It would be a mistake for me to forget that the main thing about marriage is having a spouse. It does me little good to be committed to norms that govern sexual behavior, or to family values. These will not make me the least bit married. They don't answer my desire to get married. I could still be sitting in an empty house, staring at a television screen all by myself, alone.

Marriage without a wife is marriage without good news. The good news is that my wife made the astonishing decision to give herself to me, astonishing, because I know I don't deserve it. She, by the way, knows this too. My wife (and then our children)—this is what is dearest to me in marriage.

Of course, there is an important place for the Law and for the works of the Law characteristic of marriage. They enter the scene immediately, together with the gift of self between husband and wife. If one or both of the spouses act contrary to the law of love, they wound or even destroy their shared life. When they act in accord with the law of love, they build and preserve their union. Yet such works of the Law have their important place *only in second place, after* the first great good, not "after" in time, but "after" in being constitutive of marriage.

It is worth listening to Luther again, this time on the primacy of the spouse and his gift of himself. "God so loved the world that he gave his only Son . . ." Married love, that is, spousal love, burns like fire and seeks nothing but the spouse. It says, "I do not want what is yours; I want neither your silver nor your gold, neither this nor that; I want to have you yourself; I want to have you totally or nothing." All other loves seek something other than the beloved: this one alone wants to have the beloved's own self totally . . .

> This is truly, Paul says, a great sacrament, that is, the married state signifies something truly great. Is it not something great

that God is made man, that he gives himself to be man's own and wants to be his, just as the man gives himself to the woman and is hers? But if God is ours, then everything is ours.[4]

"I will take you as my wife" (Hos 2:19). These are wonderful words. He does not say, "I will make a covenant," as He said to the fathers, but, "I will take you as my wife." There is on earth no love more burning (*ardentior*) than that between bridegroom and bride. The bridegroom hands over to the bride, not a gift, but himself (*non munus sed seipsum tradit sponsae*), the innermost affection of his heart and all that is his.[5]

THE JEFFERSON BIBLE AS AN EXAMPLE OF DISPLACING GOSPEL BY LAW

There are some people who might doubt that the displacement of Gospel by Law is a problem for us Americans Was not the founding of America a founding with truly Christian roots? Do our roots not protect us from what happened to the Galatians?

Even if the answer to the first question were "yes," the answer to the second could still be "No." Unfortunately, the answer to both questions is most definitely "no." The roots of the Galatian problem, which gained prominence later in the Pelagian heresy, lie deep within the American tradition. The author of the *Declaration of Independence* is also the author of a book to which he gave the title, *The Life and Morals of Jesus Christ* or, on the book's spine as he had instructed the book binder, *Morals of Jesus*. He explains his project in a letter to John Adams.

> In extracting the pure principles which he [Jesus] taught, we should have to strip off the artificial vestments in which they have been muffled by priests, who have travestied them into various forms, as instruments of riches and power to them. We must dismiss the Platonists and Plotinists, the Stagyrites [i.e., Aristotelians]... and Scholastics...
>
> We must reduce our volume to the simple evangelists, select, even from them, the very words only of Jesus, paring off the Amphibologisms [lit. words that throw their meanings in several directions or around, i.e., words of Jesus unconnected with his real intentions] into which they have been led by forgetting often, or not understanding, what had fallen from him, by giving

---

4. Luther, "Sermon on the Estate of Marriage" (LW), 44:9–10; (WA), 2:167–8.
5. Luther, "Lectures on the Minor Prophets, Hosea 2:19" (LW), 18:13; (WA) 13:11.

their own misconceptions as his dicta, and expressing unintelligibly for others what they had not understood themselves.

There will be found remaining the most sublime and benevolent code of morals which has ever been offered to man.

I have performed this operation for my own use, by cutting verse by verse out of the printed book, and arranging, the matter which is evidently his, and which is as easily distinguishable as diamonds in a dunghill.[6]

The first and most important thing to note is that the fruit of Jefferson's labors is, as he puts it, "the most sublime and benevolent *code of morals* which has ever been offered to man" (emphasis added). Jefferson's reworked New Testament is a book of Law, not of Gospel.

To produce this book, Jefferson laid out four printed editions of the New Testament on a table: Greek, Latin, French, and the King James Version. He first distinguished the diamonds from the dung, that is, Jesus's very own words from the confused Platonizing non-sense placed on his lips by ignorant priests hungry for money and power. He then used a sharp knife to cut away the dung from the diamonds and kept the diamonds as the only thing worth preserving. Arranging the diamonds in the order he saw fit, he glued them on quires of blank paper and finally had them bound as a book.

If Long John Silver had observed Jefferson at work, he would probably have cautioned him against this method. Silver's fellow-pirates in *Treasure Island* become dissatisfied with his leadership and hand him "the black spot," the official notice that they had condemned him to death.

> "The black spot!" I thought so, Silver observed.
> "Where might you have got the paper? Why, hillo! look here, now: this ain't lucky!
> You've gone and cut this out of a Bible. What fool's cut a Bible? . . .
> Well, you've about fixed it now, among you. . . You'll all swing now, I reckon . . .
> Dick, was it? Then Dick can get to prayers. . . . He's seen his slice of luck, has Dick, and you may lay to that."

Dick left most of the Bible intact and took only a small piece to be used for another purpose. Jefferson cut more than 90 percent of the New Testament away as dung. The King James Version New Testament contains 180,552 words. The English column of *Morals of Jesus* only 22,959. If one counts only diamond grade materials, that is, the morals taught by Jesus, leaving out the

---

6. Cappon, ed., *Adams-Jefferson Letters*, 384.

narrative passages that frame this teaching, the total is less than 10 percent. More than 90 percent of the text, Jefferson judged, is dung.

Among the narrative passages, he allows not a single miracle. Jefferson preserves the story of Jesus's birth, though not from a virgin, and of his death, though without a resurrection. The last sentence of *Morals of Jesus* is, "There laid they Jesus, and rolled a great stone to the door of the sepulchre, and departed."

Jefferson's way of telling the difference between diamonds and dung is not complicated. Works of the Law in conformity with Enlightenment moral principles are diamond. The Gospel itself, encapsulated by "God so loved the world that he gave his only Son . . .," is dung.

What is surprising, given Jefferson's overall intellectual and artistic brilliance, is that he overlooks the inner tensions of his historical reconstruction. The wicked and stupid Platonizing priests of the Early Catholic Church, beginning in the New Testament itself with Paul and John, wove the seamless garment of the Gospel out of thin air, having nothing from Jesus himself to go by and only some loose metaphysical threads from Plato. Then they draped this garment over a simple proto-Free-Mason from Galilee, a reasonable and eloquent man, interested mainly in flat-footed moralizing of the sort practiced in the European Enlightenment. Jefferson's Jesus was certainly ahead of his time—by close to 1,800 years.

Even if one leaves aside the question of truth and evaluates the New Testament and later theological developments as mere works of art, how did the stupid priests manage to create a figure of dazzling beauty and glory, the Jesus of orthodox Christianity? It is a figure that has been examined and plumbed again and again by the greatest minds of the human race for almost two millennia. It has been found inexhaustible in its inner wealth and fascination. In comparison with such priest-craft, Michelangelo's artistic genius was of little worth.

In Jefferson's eyes, by contrast, the Christian intellectual tradition is worse than worthless. As a matter of principle, it is an intellectual tradition devoted to darkness and confusion, to the refusal of light and truth. Darkness is dear to it, because it keeps ordinary people in a state of dependence on the experts in dark reasoning. This dependence enables the specialists, the clergy, to gain power and money. That is the essence of priest-craft.

Jefferson offers a list of the three men he considers the greatest ever, "my trinity of the three greatest men the world had ever produced." Jesus is not among them, nor are any of the intellectual giants of the Christian tradition.

> Bacon, Locke, and Newton.... I consider them as the three greatest men that have ever lived, without any exception, and as having laid the foundation of those superstructures which have been raised in the Physical and Moral sciences.[7]

These are the thinkers among whom Jefferson is at home. He understands them and agrees with them. It is a rather narrow slice of the Western intellectual tradition. Narrowness of vision due to lack of acquaintance with the broader intellectual tradition, is not in itself a problem. There are many honorable people, especially among politicians, who are ignorant in this manner. Such ignorance becomes a problem, a very serious one, when it is combined with an obscurantist and bigoted contempt for what one does not take enough trouble to understand. It is symptomatic when Jefferson writes,

> I abuse the priests indeed.... The genuine system of Jesus, and the artificial structures they have erected to make the instrument of wealth, power, and preeminence to themselves are as distinct things in my view as light and darkness ... I have classed them with soothsayers and necromancers ... fattening idleness on the earnings of the people.... Cannibals are not to be found in the wilds of America only, but are reveling on the blood of every living people.[8]

The art of blood sucking is not a Catholic privilege, according to Jefferson. Athanasius or Calvin: it makes no difference.

> Now which ... is the true and charitable Christian? He who believes and acts on the simple doctrines of Jesus? Or the impious dogmatists of Athanasius and Calvin?
>
> Verily, I say that these are the false shepherds.... They are mere Usurpers of the Christian name, teaching a Counter-religion, made up of the deliria of crazy imaginations, as foreign from Christianity as is that of Mahomet.
>
> Had the doctrines of Jesus been preached always as purely as they came from his lips, the whole civilized world would now have been Christian. I rejoice that in this blessed country of free enquiry and belief, which has surrendered it's creed and conscience to neither kings nor priests, the genuine doctrine of one only God is reviving, and I trust that there is not a young man now living in the US who will not die an Unitarian.[9]

---

7. Jefferson to John Trumbull, February 15, 1789.
8. Jefferson to Charles Clay, January 29, 1815.
9. Jefferson to Benjamin Waterhouse, June 26, 1822.

The guillotine is not needed to weed out the poisonous growth of priest-craft. Freedom *of* religion will produce freedom *from* the religions of priest-craft, both Catholic and Protestant. It will be "euthanasia for Platonic Christianity" and Christianity's "restoration to the primitive simplicity of it's founder,"[10] which every American citizen will accept precisely because the pressure of priest-craft will be gone. The new Christianity will be established by the very disestablishment of religion, because it is simply the religion of human nature and of nature's God. There will not be complete unanimity, because human minds diverge, but there will be a substantial enough agreement to keep America on a path of peace and prosperity.

Jefferson's "Christianity" is a hypothesis constructed by historians. It has never been observed in real life. His attempt to steal the name "Christianity" for his version of Jesus's teaching is a ploy, a politically successful deception. It hides, and does so quite effectively for many Americans, that Jefferson is a most decided enemy of the only Christianity that has ever been observed in real life.

THE GLORY OF THE GOSPEL

The Russian philosopher and theologian Vladimir Solovyov wrote a short story that contains a particularly eloquent response to Jefferson. In that short-story the Anti-Christ, who has become emperor of the whole world (sufficient proof that the republican Jefferson cannot be identified with Solovyov's Anti-Christ), offers Christians gifts, provided they support him whole-heartedly.

To the Pope and Catholic leaders in general he offers world-wide moral authority for the common good of peace and justice; to Protestants he offers a splendidly endowed world-institute of free and unfettered inquiry into the Scriptures; and to the Orthodox a world-museum of Christian archeology and the re-instituting of sacred customs.

Solovyov's irony in this passage is biting, particularly toward his own Russian Orthodox. He is quite correct in seeing the reduction of the Gospel to moralism as a disease that by preference infects Catholics. That others can be infected as well is demonstrated beyond any doubt by Jefferson's revision of the New Testament. Whatever the right way of classifying Jefferson may be, if there is a right way at all, "Catholic" certainly is not it.

Many Christians accept the Emperor's offer, but Pope Peter II, the Protestant Professor Ernst Pauli (which one can render in English as "Earnest of Paul) and the Orthodox Elder John refuse, together with a small number of

10. Jefferson to John Adams, October 12, 1813.

followers. When the majority of Christians leave to join the Emperor on the great dais of the Council Hall, the Pope, the Professor, and the Elder move closer to each other in several senses of the word "close."

Then the Anti-Christ says to them in a tone of sadness, "What more can I do for you? Strange men! What do you want of me? I do not know. Tell me yourselves, you Christians forsaken by most of your brothers and leaders and condemned by popular feeling: What is dearest to you in Christianity?"

The Elder John, rises up "like a white candle," as Solovyov puts it, and answers gently, "Great emperor! Dearest to us in Christianity is Christ himself—He himself. Everything rests on him, for we know that in him all the fullness of Godhead dwells bodily."[11]

This answer given by the ancient Orthodox Faith in the person of the Russian Elder John is the answer against any reduction of the Gospel to Law. How could the Law be dearer to us than the Bridegroom?

This is why I would like to thank you personally, Prof. George, for your paper, which defends the primacy God's love in giving us the gift of his Son. Devotion to this primacy is what all of need right now. As a small token of thanks, here is a present for you, a little bottle of Nard.

At the beginning of the Lazarus narrative John identifies Mary of Bethany by anticipation as the one who anointed Jesus's feet and wiped them with her hair (John 11:2). When she actually anoints him (John 12:3), John adds that she used pure Nard.

For years I wondered what Nard smelled like. I finally decided to check on Amazon and in two days I had a little bottle like this one. I let a single drop fall on a piece of paper. The smell was very strong and it lasted for several weeks.

Mary used a whole pound of it, which is an enormous amount, about one hundred of these little bottles. The lavish excess is a sign of her overflowing love. I don't wonder any more why "the house was filled with the fragrance" (12:3). It would be enough to fill many houses.

Jesus connects Mary's gesture of love with his own death. When Judas objects to the waste of so much money, Jesus answers, "Let her. [She spent this much money on Nard] in order to keep it for the day of my burial" (John 12:7). The day of burial has not actually arrived, but Jesus is so close to it that it is present to him as the Nard wafts through the house. He himself Jesus must have smelled of Nard all through his passion, even in the tomb.

Prof. George's argument against the sickness identified in his opening statement unfolds some of the wealth contained in the answer given by the Elder John. It focuses on three aspects of the Lazarus story.

---

11. See Frank, ed., *A Solovyov Anthology*, 229–48, esp. 239–41.

1. Jesus does not respond immediately to the call to help Lazarus. He lets him die. Then he waits until Lazarus's rotting body stinks.
2. Jesus's anger when faced with his friend's death shows that judgment cannot be surgically removed from God. In God's judgment, death is a terrible evil, not an innocuous natural event.
3. Jesus's tears about the death Lazarus show the depth and strength of his love, expressing on the human level what the key Gospel text affirms on the divine level, "God so loved the world that he gave his only son . . ."

The first of these raises the most difficult and thorny questions. The questions have perplexed many readers of John. Prof. George's way of answering them them is astonishing and profound. It convinces me completely.

> John's way of accounting for Jesus's delay is to connect it with the manifestation of God's glory. The illness of Lazarus, Jesus says, is not unto death (*pros thanaton*), though he will die, but it is rather for "the glory of God, so that the Son of God may be glorified by means of it" (11:4). The theme of glory frames the miracle story, as Jesus will later say to Martha: "Did not I tell you that if you would believe you would see the glory of God?" (11:40).
>
> Glory, of course, is the great theme of the entire Gospel of John, announced at the beginning in the key verse 1:14 ("We have beheld his glory"). Glory connected directly to the signs (2:11; 7:39; 9:3; 11:4, 40). But glory in John, though it breaks through in the miraculous signs, is not primarily about the glitter and the glow of the supernatural.
>
> In John, Jesus is glorified when he is "lifted up," when he is lifted up on the cross (see 3:13–15; 12:16, 31–43). The glory of God is seen in the Lazarus event not merely in Jesus's bringing back to life a man four days dead—one who must, after all, die yet again—but in the significance of this event in propelling Jesus toward the cross, toward his being glorified by being lifted up. *The irony of the miracle in John 11 is that Jesus calls forth Lazarus from one grave in order that he himself might enter another one* (emphasis added).

This reading seems thoroughly convincing to me, mainly because it is a truly Johannine reading. The most important commentary ever written about the Gospel of John is, of course, the Gospel of John. Prof. George seems to know this principle. He is an attentive reader of this commentary as the main means for understanding the text itself.

Prof. George connects three themes that are central in John:

1. the signs, that is, the miracles performed by Jesus, of which the raising of Lazarus is the most spectacular;
2. the glory of Jesus, the splendor of divine love that breaks through in him;
3. the concrete manner of this glory, namely, its concentration in the Cross of Jesus, when God most fully gives his Son.

Taking these three themes as the guiding thread, I will attempt to follow the example of Prof. George's reading to extend it to three other passages: Cana (2:1–11), Golgotha (19:25–37) and a section of Jesus's prayer to the Father (17:20–23).

CANA AND GOLGOTHA: EUCHARIST AND THE MOTHER OF JESUS

The purpose of the Gospel of John is stated explicitly in chapter 20.

> Now Jesus did many other *signs* in the presence of his disciples, which are not written in this book. But these [that is, *these signs*] are written so that you may come to believe that Jesus is the Messiah, the Son of God, and that through believing you may have life in his name" (John 20:30–31).

In this statement of purpose, one can distinguish the final purpose from the most immediate, and one between them. The immediate purpose, the textual purpose, is to write signs. Signs then lead to faith and faith leads to eternal life (John 20:30–31).

The first of these signs, solemnly recorded as the beginning of all signs, is the miracle of wine at Cana: "This Jesus did as the beginning of his signs at Cana of Galilee and revealed his glory; and his disciples believed in him" (John 2:11). The cleansing of the temple, which follows immediately after the wedding at Cana, moves the reader's attention from the first sign to the last sign. When the Judean authorities challenge Jesus, "What sign can you show us for doing this?" (John 2:18), Jesus answers, "Destroy this temple, and in three days I will raise it up" (John 2:19). John immediately clarifies, "He was speaking of the temple of his body" (John 2:21). Golgotha (always together with the resurrection) is thus the fulfillment of all signs. Cana is the beginning. As beginning and end, Cana and Golgotha are closely tied to each other.

It is important to note what the description of the sign of Cana adds to the statement of purpose in 20:30–31, which listed: signs, faith, and life. It adds the theme emphasis "This Jesus did as the beginning of his signs, in Cana of Galilee, *and revealed his glory*; and his disciples believed in him" (2:11). The sign reveals the glory of Jesus. Glory is the true motive of faith in the disciples. The revelation of glory that is begun at Cana is completed at Golgotha. "The hour has come for the Son of Man to be glorified" (12:23; cf. 13:30–32). Glory appears especially in the Hour of Jesus, in his suffering and death, as the victorious power of love in weakness. In this way, the mention of glory in the Cana narrative leads the reader to compare Cana and Golgotha. The comparison shows an astonishing number of contacts between these two scenes, leading to the conclusion that they were composed as a pair. Each needs to be read in light of the other.

John 2:1–11	John 19:25–35
On the third day there was a wedding in Cana of Galilee, and the *mother of Jesus* was there. 2 Jesus and his disciples had also been invited to the wedding.	Standing near the cross of Jesus were *his mother*, and his mother's sister, Mary the wife of Cleopas, and Mary Magdalene.
3 When the wine (*oinos*) gave out, the *mother of Jesus* said to him, "*They have no* wine." 4 And Jesus said to her, "Woman (*gynai*), what is that to you and to me? *My hour* has not yet come." 5 *His mother* said to the servants, "Do whatever he tells you."	26 When Jesus saw *the mother* and the disciple whom he loved standing beside her, he said to *the mother*, "Woman (*gynai*), here is your son." 27 Then he said to the disciple, "Here is *your mother*." And from *that hour* the disciple took her into his own.
6 Now standing there were six stone water-jars (*hydriai*) for the Jewish rites of purification, each holding twenty or thirty gallons. 7 Jesus said to them, "Fill the water-jars with water." And they filled them up to the brim. 8 He said to them, "Now draw some out, and take it to the chief steward." So they took it. 9 When the steward tasted the water that had become wine, and did not know where it came from (though the servants who had drawn the water knew), the steward called the bridegroom 10 and said to him, "Everyone serves the good wine first, and then the inferior wine after the guests have become drunk.	28 After this, when Jesus knew that all was now finished so that Scripture might be fulfilled, he said, "*I thirst*." 29 A jar (*skeuos*) full of sour wine (*oxos*) was standing there. So they put a sponge full of the sour wine on a branch of hyssop and held it to his mouth. 30 When Jesus had received the sour wine, he said, "It is finished." Then he bowed his head and gave over the spirit. . . . 33 But when they came to Jesus and saw that he was already dead, they did not break his legs. 34 Instead, one of the soldiers pierced his side with a spear,

But you have kept the good wine until now."	and at once blood and water came out.
11 This Jesus did as the beginning of his signs, in Cana of Galilee, and revealed his glory; and his disciples believed in him.	35 He who saw this has testified *so that you also may believe*. His testimony is true, and he knows that he tells the truth.

In John, the Mother of Jesus appears only at Cana and Golgotha. Since Cana is the first sign and Golgotha the last, she comprehensively embraces the whole of Jesus's public ministry, the bookends, as it were. She was present before Jesus was born and then gave birth to him. She educated him and then gave birth to him again into his public ministry. At Golgotha she remains behind after his death and receives her enduring role as the Mother of the disciple. "Here is your mother."

At Cana, a wedding provides the context in which Jesus and his Mother are present. Jesus himself is the messianic bridegroom who, veiled in symbolic form, gives the plenty of the messianic banquet to his people. He addresses his Mother as "woman" (*gynai*), a completely unusual mode of address by a son to his mother. He seems to be alluding to the words of Adam. "This now is bone of my bones, and flesh of my flesh; she shall be called woman (Septuagint *gyne*), because she was taken out of her husband" (Gen 2:23). Of course, Jesus's mother is not his bride in a sexual sense, but she is his feminine counter-part nevertheless. The Mother of Jesus also stands in the role of Mother Zion, the mother of all members of the chosen people.[12]

If one reads Golgotha in light of Cana, one is led to see the spousal mystery as the heart of Golgotha as well. And indeed, the same address "woman" (*gynai*) appears there as well. Just as in the great spousal scene in Genesis Eve is drawn from the side of Adam, the community of Jesus draws its life from the side of the new Adam, from the flow of blood (Eucharist) and water (baptism). The Mother of Jesus, in whom this community is present as in its origin, has the role of the new Eve (LXX *Zoe*=Life) as "mother of all the living" (Gen 3:20). The living are represented by the beloved disciple who is told to observe, "Here is your mother" (John 19:27).

On one level, the contrast between the two scenes could hardly be sharper. Cana is a feast of spousal joy, Golgotha a scene of suffering and death. Yet on a deeper level Golgotha already casts its shadow on Cana in the painful words, "Woman what is that to you and to me? My hour has not yet come." It is clear that Jesus understands the words of his Mother as an

---

12. Cf. de la Potterie, *Hour of Jesus*, 113–14.

invitation for "the hour" of suffering and death to begin. By doing what she invites him to do, he begins that hour, which has its focus at Golgotha.

Conversely, Cana shows that the deeper content of Golgotha is the spousal mystery consummated in Baptism and the Eucharist. In the *admirabile commercium* between the bridegroom and the bride, Christ takes on himself what belongs to his bride in her sinful members in order to give her his own life in the flow of baptismal water and Eucharistic blood. As a spousal mystery, Golgotha is at root a mystery of love and therefore of joy.

A sacrament, as Orthodox and Catholics understand it, is a sacred sign, filled with the active presence of the sacred. When you write the word "hot" on a wall in fiery letters that keep their fire at five thousand degrees Fahrenheit, the sign does not only signify heat, but actually communicates it. If you put your hand on this particular sign "hot," it makes your hand sizzle.

The Eucharist is not a mere sign of Christ, as Zwingli would have it, but the anamnesis, the memory of the last supper. It is memorial in the strongest possible sense, not in the sense of mere thought about an event that has long passed away, but as the very presence of that event, as Christ's own saving flesh and blood given to us in his gift to us. In this sense the Divine Liturgy, as our older brothers from the East, from the Greek Church, call the celebration of the Eucharist, is a re-presentation that brings the full power of the original event into our present time.

For Cana, the best word is perhaps not "re-presentation," but "pre-presentation." Even if, despite the presence of water and wine, this pre-presentation does not have a full baptismal and Eucharistic form, since these seem to be released first and decisively in the flow of water and blood on the cross, one and the same event of "the hour" is already in some way present. When the Mother of Jesus points out the need, he answers, "My hour," the Johannine word for the cross, "has not yet come." When immediately after this apparent refusal, he does what she asks, the hour has in some sense come. She then communicates directly with the servants. She does not say, "Do what I tell you, but do what he tells you." That is the Catholic understanding of Mary.

Part of the generosity of God expressed by, "God so loved the world . . ." is that he gives his creatures not only the gift of being, but the gift of acting effectively. "He gave them power to become children of God" (John 1:12). This power is not a detached one that belongs to creatures in competition against God, but only within the stream of gift that comes from God.

John 3:16 is in this way common principle behind both the sacraments and Mary as mother of the Church.

One and the same light, the light of God's glory, shines through both Cana and Golgatha. In and through the spousal mystery of Cana and Golgatha the eyes of faith glimpse "as in a mirror, dimly" (1 Cor 13:12) the final mystery, which is also the end of our pilgrimage: "Father, I want those you have given me to be with me where I am so that they may see my glory which you have given me because you loved me before the foundation of the world" (17:24).

If one arranges the signs written in John as a series, one sees how important this principle turns out to be, already for Baptism, but especially in the Eucharist. The Eucharist appears at the beginning, middle, and end of the signs. The Mother of Jesus accompanies it at beginning and end.

FIRST SIGN: WATER for purification turned to WINE for joy, *MARY PRESENT* (2:1–11)

    2. *Healing* of the official's son (4:46–54)

    3. *Healing* of the lame man by the pool (5:1–18)

FOURTH SIGN: Multiplication of BREAD and the EUCHARIST (6)

    5. *Healing* of the blind man, in Jerusalem (9)

    6. *Raising* of Lazarus (11)

SEVENTH SIGN: Flood of BLOOD and WATER, *MARY PRESENT* (19:25–35)

Six of these seven signs are preliminary. They point ahead to the definitive sign. It is in the definitive sign that the glory of God appears definitively. The term "sign" is not used in the crucifixion scene, but John uses this very term, or alludes to it, three times earlier in the Gospel to prepare the reader.

- "Give us a sign that you can do this" (*semeion*, 2:18), Jesus answers, "Destroy this temple. . ." which John translates, "He was speaking of the temple of his body" (2:20).

- "Just as Moses lifted up the serpent in the desert, so must the Son of Man be lifted up" (3:14). The Septuagint would have been familiar to readers of John's Greek text. "And Moses made a bronze serpent and set it on a sign (*semeion*)" (Num 21:9 LXX).

- "What sign (*semeion*) do you do that we may see and believe you" (6:30). Jesus answers by pointing to himself as the true bread in increasingly clear Eucharistic terms (see 6:32–58).

Even more important than these three texts is the solemn interruption of the narrative immediately after the flow of blood and water out of Jesus's pierced side. "The one who has seen has testified and his testimony is true, and he knows that he speaks the truth, *so that you also may believe*" (19:35). This passage should be read in connection with the purpose of the whole Gospel, which is to write signs, "*so that you may believe*" (20:31), an effect demonstrated by by the very first sign. "This Jesus did as the beginning of his signs, in Cana of Galilee, *and revealed his glory; and his disciples believed in him*" (2:11).

In conclusion, Cana and Golgotha are signs that manifest God's glory. Both scenes, particularly when taken together, show the importance of the Mother of Jesus, as the mother of all the living. Should it be surprising that she from whom the Word took flesh and blood should be closely associated with the life-giving gift of his flesh and blood to us?

Glory is the motive of faith. It is the very pith and substance of evangelical strength and persuasiveness. It is the flashing out of God's love in all its splendor. This, I assume, is the reason why the favorite text mentioned by Prof. George is the evangelical verse par excellence, "God so loved the world . . ." I am completely in agreement when he defends this verse against its displacement by moralism. The evangelical strength of glory is affirmed most fully in a sacramental understanding of the Eucharist and in following Jesus's words, "This is your mother."

THE UNITY OF THE CHURCH AS EVANGELICAL SIGN

To complete this reflection on the evangelistic strength of the Gospel, it is helpful to look at a text in Jesus's prayer to the Father.

> The glory you have given me I have given them
> that they may be one as we are one . . .
> that the world may know that you sent me
> and that you loved them as you loved me (17:22–23).

What an astonishing text. The gift of glory has been given to us. We need to read this text in its context. It is closely related to the immediately preceding verses (17:20–21), where one finds exactly the same grammatical and theological structure, the structure encountered first in the new commandment (13:34–35). In all three texts, an introductory statement is followed by two "that" clauses that sandwich an "as" clause. A third "that" clause follows, which indicates the overall purpose (in 13:35 a separate main clause that indicates the result).

THE FUTURE	THE PRESENT GIFT	THE COMMANDMENT
John 17:20-21	John 17:22-23	John 13:34-35
I do not ask you for them alone, but for those who believe in me through their word,	And the glory you have given me I have given to them,	I give you a new commandment,
that all may be *one*	*that* they may be *one*	*that* you *love* one another
as you, Father, are *in* me and I *in* you,	*as* we are *one*, I *in* them and you *in* me,	as I have *loved* you
that they too may be *in* us,	*that* they may be completed into *one*,	*that* you *too* may *love* one another.
that the world may believe that you sent me.	that the world may know that you sent me and that you *loved* them *as* you *loved* me.	In this all will know that you are my disciples, if you have *love in* one another.

The introductory sentences clearly distinguish the three parallel texts from each other:

- In the first (17:20), Jesus prays to the Father for a future desired result, a result the Father will achieve in due time.
- In the second (17:22) he states a fact: the gift of glory to those who believe in him has taken place. This is the Gospel.
- In the third (13:34) he announces the new commandment, the new Law to love as he loved.

One can see three dimensions of Christian life in these three introductions: the not yet (the future eschaton); the already (the present gift of grace); and good works, at the center of which stands love.

The final element in all three texts is particularly important. The community that flows from the death and resurrection of Jesus receives the gift of glory, which lies at the very heart of its evangelistic persuasiveness. This gift of glory derives from the unity of love between the divine persons, from the mutual "being in" of the divine persons. It flows into the Church in partly visible form as the Church's unity in love, love for each other and love for God.

It is in this manner, Jesus says, that the experience of the encounter with him as the one sent from the Father becomes possible in the present, "that the world may know that you sent me and that you loved them as you loved me." This is how Jesus chose to become contemporaneous with us. He is not only a memory of a distant past gained from books, but present and active, visible in the unity of the Church. It is this visible unity that makes the saving encounter with Jesus possible today, so that the world can recognize him as "my personal Lord and Savior."

CONCLUSION: WISDOM

I would like to conclude with the question how we can read Scripture wisely. What is true theological wisdom?

> There are two kinds of wisdom: one is due to a full use of reason; another to a certain kinship (*connaturalitas*) with what one must judge.
>
> About sexual purity, for example, one can judge rightly after searching with one's reason, if one has studied the science of ethics, but if one has the virtue of purity, one can judge about it by a kind of kinship (*connaturalitas*).
>
> It belongs to the wisdom that is an intellectual virtue to make a right judgment about divine things after reason has made its search, but it belongs to wisdom as a gift of the Holy Spirit to judge rightly about them through kinship (*connaturalitas*) with them. This is why Dionysius says, "Hierotheus [the exemplary theologian] is complete in divine things not only by learning, but also by suffering divine things (*patiens divina*).
>
> This suffering with (*compassio*) and kinship (*connaturalitas*) with divine things is brought about by love, which unites us with God. "The one who clings to God is one spirit [with him]" (1 Cor 6:17).[13]

It seems to me that in this text, originally written in Latin by the pre-eminent Catholic theologian, one can see what most deeply unites us Catholics with our older brothers of the Greek Church, and our younger brothers of the Evangelical churches. The text's argument is base on Scripture, but an important stimulus for understanding 1 Cor 6:17 comes to Thomas from Dionysius Areopagita, one of the pre-eminent theologian of the Eastern tradition. What he says about suffering divine things, about kinship with God through a union produced only by love is, of course, close to what the Elder John says in Solovyov's story. "Dearest to us in Christianity is Christ himself."

---

13. Thomas Aquinas, *Summa*, 2-2.45.2 c.

The Revelation of Christ's Two Natures
A Hopeful Theodicy

John Mark Reynolds (Orthodox)

As a layman[1] responding to an excellent theologian on a text of great importance, I have chosen caution and this caution was encouraged by the request that I engage my religious tradition with the text, so I will write of what I experience when the text is lived out in the life of the church and not attempt to instruct my theological betters on the finer details of the language found in John 11.

I do wonder, however, if some philosophical clarity, particular about God's time and human time might not help our reading of John 11.

The essay by Professor George was blessedly readable and helpful. After reading, I continued thinking about John 11 and its importance in the Gospel. Professor George's emphasis on the *two natures of Christ* and the role of the story of Lazarus in any Christian theodicy were particularly striking to me.

I also appreciated his willingness to take the Bible as a text. Perhaps it is my experience with fruitless discussions of Homeric "sources" or the authenticity of particular Platonic dialogues (Alcibiades I) that has made me dislike such debates in favor of a focus on the *meaning* of the text. The

---

1. I attended a charismatic Bible college, learned a Wesleyan theology, and was shaped by the Book of Common Prayer. I appreciate the Baptist heritage of Houston Baptist University and have been mentored by several Catholic thinkers. My church home is Saint Paul's Antiochian Orthodox Church in Katy, Texas: Western rite, evangelical, and Orthodox.

Scripture is as we have it and when no alternative readings exist[2], then speculation about texts or sources we do not possess strikes me as at best dull and at worst non-falsifiable assertion dressed up as scholarship.

What does John 11 as we have it say? This is the question Professor George *begins* to answer and this approach also is ecumenical. Orthodox, Catholic, and Protestant readers all have the same (or very close to the same) account of the raising of Lazarus. We agree on the data.

One caution to the paper that I cannot address is that the *Jewish* or first century context of the story is (mostly) missing from Professor George's paper, but this is a weakness I cannot address. This causes me concern that we all might be reading the text *too much* through the lens of historical reflection.

Two other features of the essay are commendable: the evangelistic flavor and the piety. George wants people to *become Christians* and knows any of the Gospels had this goal (amongst others) in mind.

George approaches the text piously. He is privileged in reading the text by his sympathy with the author. I am convinced after years of reading great texts and teaching them that sympathy for the goals of the author may not be *absolutely* necessary to grasp the meaning of an account, but for all but the greatest intellects sympathy is most helpful. The greatest intellects can despise an author or his ideas and yet still engage in fruitful dialog with him, Nietzsche accomplished this, but most of us cannot unless we "put on the mind" of the writer and (provisionally) accept his worldview and goals. Sometimes this is very difficult, though scarcely ever has it proved too difficult for me with time. George has the advantage of *being* the sort of Christian who is learned, but also pious and this piety is an advantage. He *wishes* to know the mind of Saint John and to do what the Spirit has led the Evangelist to write.

The danger of pious reading is that it might prevent a *critical* reading, but this is not the case in a good scholar. In fact, our educational system makes it unlikely that any of us will escape a *critical* spirit toward a text, but few of us learn piety.[3] George's essay shows that he has (sympathetically!) read scholars that disagree with his approach to the Gospel of John and the account in John 11. He has a narrowed down his intellectual options without become narrow.

---

2. I am *not* referring to important discussions about places where alternative manuscript traditions exist. The discussion about the place of the John 8 "woman caught in adultery" story is a good example.

3. I learned piety towards texts (starting with Plato, Aristotle, and then John) from my non-Christian Greek professor, Al Geier. He put on the mind of a writer like Charles Williams when he read the author, but did so with a Socratic spirit.

Perhaps, however, George allows his paper to reflect too little on how this text has been lived out in the life of the church. While the paper is scholarly, one way to know how scholars, in any tradition, have understood a passage is how they preached and utilized the text liturgically. If "all Scripture is breathed out by God and profitable for teaching, for reproof, for correction, and for training in righteousness, that the man of God may be complete, equipped for every good work," then how will is this reproof, correction, and training be implemented?

A DIFFICULTY

I am hesitant to attack Professor George's paper, but I do need clarification, perhaps due to my ignorance. George says that the Lord Jesus "waited," "wailed," and "wept." This culminates in the important question: "Can God get mad?"

George is right that anyone with classical training balks at the question for bad reasons. Plato and Aristotle, or at least their followers, declared human passions synonymous with human irrationality. As a result, a traditional classicists wish to say "no" to Divine passions. However, one can accept that in a human person passions have a good place in God's creation and still reject the idea that God is angry as God.

Victorian Christians in the English speaking world often became too prim for passions. For example, *Jane Eyre* juxtaposes the angry God of Mr. Brocklehurst with the loving God of Helen Burns. The God of Victorian fiction is too often nice to the point of weakness.

Instead, of these two bad motives the idea of *divine simplicity* in the Divine Essence combined with the nature of Christ makes me worried about the simplicity of George's question. God does not get angry *in his essence, but God experiences anger in the Incarnation of the Second Person of the Trinity*. Jesus is fully God and fully man, but *without confusion of the natures*. Does God as essentially God get angry? I don't think he can: God knows all and is at rest in his Providence. Does God *experience* anger in the humanity of Jesus Christ? He does, if the witness of Scripture is to be believed.

Jesus is *really angry* and since Jesus is angry in one sense, God is angry. If we pose similar questions of God about the experience of the Savior, we see the importance of a qualified answer to the question George asks. Does God die? Does God get tired? Does God eat dinner with the disciples? The Father and the Spirit are in essence one with the Son, but not in person. God the Father knows the Son and the Son knows pain, anger, death, and the joys of eating in the perfect union (though without confusion) of his divine essence with his human essence. God knows the anger of a man as a man knows anger in the Trinitarian union with the human nature of Jesus, but without changing the Divine Nature essentially.

I wonder if the professor does not underplay this cooperation between the Divine and human natures of Christ, though he frequently mentions it. The Logos humbled himself and chose to limit himself in union with a man's nature. In the perfect cooperation of this union, both natures gave and both natures expressed themselves fully, but without sin. The mistake of the Monophysite is also a danger and George's analysis may come close to it!

What is the psychology of Jesus, the God-man? The "psychology of God" is an area beyond my power and I suspect beyond the power of theologians to describe. Human psychology is also a disputable arena, even if I were to limit myself to classical models of human psychology.

What is the relationship between the will of the Christ and his brain? George provides us no answer or guide to his assumptions and this is dangerous. Reading his paper, George seems to attribute too easily the internal life of the Christ to his Divine nature. If we agree that Jesus Christ was angry, then *God* is angry because of the Union of his nature with human nature, but is he angry because of his Divine nature?

Let me propose that this complex harmonization in Christ's united natures suggests the explanation for his waiting, wailing, and weeping. Jesus waits so God may receive greater glory: His human nature, which one assumes would have left immediately cooperates with his Divine nature. If there is tension between the two, it is a creative tension and not a tension of opposition. Jesus loves Martha and the rest of the community (as John mentions) and this seems a very human reaction. There is no need to note God loves a person, but every reason to point out a man who seems rude or uncaring is doing it from love.

When Jesus "wails" and "weeps," the Divine impassible Love of God *may be* allowing the human nature full expression. As George points out: wailing and weeping is what happens when a man-God faces death and sin. Resurrection of the dead is what happens when the God-man faces death and sin. But what does this say about God?

I am not *sure* what the exact relationship between the Divine psychology and the human psychology is, but I know by Revelation that Jesus had both fully and without confusion of the two natures. I do not know what the relationship between (for example) the Divine Will, the human will, and the human brain of the Christ is, but I doubt George does either.

If a Christian accepts what the historic theological ideas of Divine simplicity and divine impassability, then George's formulations are troubling in their simplicity. God is God's essence is unchanged by the Incarnation, but his relationship to the world is changed. He unites himself in the Second person with a man.

Jesus Christ is victor even in his wailing and weeping, because his Divine nature has the power to heal the wound given to his human nature by sin and death. The psychic scars of the man who stood at his friend's tomb match the scars in the palm of his hands, but these scars are the *birthmarks of a new life!*

TWO NATURES: CHRIST AND HIS BROTHERS

The raising of Lazarus presents difficult philosophical and theological problems that may not be answerable, but the text can still be preached with power and used liturgically. One way to understand the mind of the church on a text is to see how they have used it in "teaching, for reproof, for correction, and for training in righteousness, that the man of God may be complete, equipped for every good work."

For the Orthodox worshipper the commemoration of the raising of Lazarus marks the end of Lent and the start of Holy Week. We turn from our own work of fasting to a recollection of that true Work of which any effort on our part is only a shadow. We take up a cross at his command, but one whose wood and iron has been made sweet by the victory of Christ over death.

If John 11 ends the Book of Signs and begins the Book of the Passion, while for the faithful Lazarus Saturday ends the time of visible signs and begins the season of mystical works. The theology of John 11 is captured in the liturgy and the life of prayer of the faithful. By placing the story at the end of Great Lent, the great spiritual struggle of the church year, the church has commented on the raising of Lazarus.

We are at the end of the struggle of Lent, but at the start of the most intense time of church attendance and worship of the year culminating in the Greatest Feast. Lazarus is raised, but the Christ is not yet risen. We are at the end of the Great Fast, but at the start of the more profound fast of Holy Week. The raising of Lazarus is a hinge for the text and a hinge for the church year. The story gives the reader *hope* and God *glory*: the service focuses on the *hope* of the faithful for the coming resurrection of all the righteous dead and the glory of God.

George is correct that the message of the Gospel is the revelation of God, but this revelation is (as I am sure George would agree) in the person of the God-man. For the first readers of John, the *human* nature even as a wonderworker of Jesus was easy to see and believe. Saint John is emphasizing that this sage, rabbi, exorcist, and miracle worker was the very Son of God.

The God revealed is *not* so much the man-God who weeps, but the God-man who triumphs over death. That Jesus would weep is important, but not unexpected in a rabbi. That Jesus would wait so he could bring forth the three-day dead is even greater. The Gospel of John centers on Jesus as the Son of God and as Professor George notes: "that you (the reader) may believe that Jesus is the Messiah, the Son of God, and that by believing you may have life in his name" (John 20:31).

Each nature works together so synergistically that the duality is hard to see in most of the life of Christ. When the Son of Man eats, his Divine nature is there, but hidden to us. When the Word made flesh speaks, heals, or casts out demons, no man ever has spoken or acted as he speaks and acts. The human seems (almost!) swallowed up in the Divine. The full story of the raising of Lazarus is one of the few moments not part of the Passion itself where each nature in Christ can be heard sequentially and then simultaneously as the text is read to the Faithful.

We see Christ weep, but we also see him worshipped. The weeping Christ commands the tomb opened and (I imagine) with the tears drying on his face commands the dead man not just to *live; but also to come forth.* Lazarus leaves the tomb on his feet: the stinking flesh has been revivified. The focus of the story, and of the liturgical life of the Church, is not on the waiting, wailing, and weeping, but on Life and the source of Life.

LITURGICALLY: IS THIS THE END OF ALL SABBATHS?

Lazarus Saturday is Sunday's service on Saturday: the only time this occurs in the life of the Church and this unique liturgical arrangement grabs the attention of the Faithful. This Saturday is not like other Sabbaths and this is a comment on the nature of the raising of Lazarus.

The Resurrection of Christ a week from Sunday will mark a turning point in liturgical time: we can enter the eternal Sabbath rest of God and commemorate the start of that rest each Sunday. Each Sunday is a little Easter and this will become the primary day of worship for the people of God.

But what of the Sabbath?

As a young man I wrestled with the status of the Sabbath and found Sabbaterianism attractive, but Lazarus Saturday resolves this difficulty for me. Lazarus Saturday is *Sunday*, because the Sabbath, the day of rest, becomes the day of resurrection for Lazarus. He does not sleep on Saturday (as does the Savior), but he comes *forth*.

Christ fulfills the Sabbath rest within his tomb. A week before Lazarus points to the reality that life and coming forth are coming and the Sabbath rest will be fused with divine life. The Church makes Lazarus Saturday a liturgical Sunday and Palm Sunday a liturgical Sunday: back-to-back. Saturday is the first day and the first day has become the seventh day.

The story of Lazarus prepared the church for this truth. A Sabbath follows the triumph of the resurrection of Lazarus where the God-man is in the tomb. Lazarus ascends from hell on Saturday: the Savior descends the next. In the raising of Lazarus time is shown move in both directions: Lazarus *anticipates* the resurrection of Jesus, but he also *experiences* it. He lives again when he comes forth from the tomb, but he comes forth to experience the spiritual life purchased on Calvary.

THE HOPEFUL THEODICY: GOD TAKES ON ALL OUR PAIN

Professor George points to the theodicy of John 11 and it is very powerful. The God-man does not just *know* our pain, but heals our pain. The raising of Lazarus is temporary, of course. Lazarus will die again, but it is a down payment (an image) of the resurrection that will never be reversed.

The God-man *waits* and God gets glory, but healing also comes to many, including Martha and Mary. Martha is allowed to make a confession of Jesus's divinity as powerful, and more complete, than that of Peter. This time her active spirit drives her *out* to Jesus, so she sees him first and dialogs with him. Mary is slower to come, but eventually follows Martha.

In the text, we see that the *waiting* has produced growth in at least Martha: she has passed the test in the school of souls. Her growing pains are not allowed to last a moment longer than necessary as she receives *more* than her reason can demand. She wanted Lazarus *healed of disease, but the Lord Jesus delivered her brother from death.*

Why is this greater if Lazarus must die again? It is greater because we see healings all the time: Divine healing is simply a speeding up of the process that often occurs in a man. We do not see resurrection, because our life is too short. As Plato argues in *Phaedo*, life gives way to death, but death gives way to life. Most of us will not live long enough to see the general resurrection of the dead, so we have our doubts. Lazarus destroyed those doubts once and for all.

Death is no more unconquerable than illness.

If death is *not* final and there is eternal life after death, then *no temporal suffering* can be too great for eternity. However bad a day, a year, or a lifetime, there are more days, years, lifetimes in eternity to resolve our pain if we will allow God to do so.

Christ is victor: pain conquered in pain, death by death.

> By raising Lazarus from the dead before Thy passion, Thou didst confirm the universal resurrection, O Christ God! Like the children with the branches of victory, we cry out to Thee, O Vanquisher of Death: Hosanna in the highest! Blessed is he that comes in the name of the Lord! (Troparion).

The Passion of the Savior might overwhelm the reader of the Gospel, if he did not first read the story of Lazarus. The raising of the dead man, a stinking corpse, to full life is a promise that the story need not end on the Holy Cross. The rules of storytelling have changed: death need not be final.

What will happen when you kill the God-man? He will go where dead men go, but he will bring with him the Divine Nature. Modern skeptics often say of the resurrection of Jesus: extraordinary claims require extraordinary evidence.

How extraordinary was the resurrection of Jesus? Given what the Lord Jesus did in his lifetime, not so extraordinary at all. He was singular, so the rules changed. He could heal sick people, cast out devils, and raise the dead. Why would we be shocked that Jesus did not stay dead?

We have good evidence that Jesus was raised from the dead, as my colleagues at Houston Baptist University, Mike Licona, Jeremiah Johnston, and Jerry Walls argue in print, debates, and transmedia. His disciples did not *need* extraordinary evidence, because they knew his nature and his life. If we accept the description of his life in the Gospels, then his trampling down death with death is *natural*.

THE KINGDOM WAS, IS, AND IS TO COME

> Christ—the Joy, the Truth and the Light of All, the Life of the world and its Resurrection—has appeared in his goodness to those on earth. He has become the Image of our Resurrection, granting divine forgiveness to all (Kontakion).

The liturgy of Lazarus Saturday makes plain: I can experience the truth of John 11 *today*. Like Pentecost, this is a great day for *baptism* in the Church and this outer sign of an inner work is another key to understanding the Lazarus story. When I was dunked under the waters of the Little Sandy

River in West Virginia, I died to the old life, was buried, and raised to new life. This implies that I can experience the entire Gospel *today*.

I *experienced* and *experience* what Lazarus experienced: right down to stinking in my sin. My being raised up in the river was an image of what happened to Lazarus, just as Lazarus coming from the tomb is an image of what happened to me. The Kontakion takes this reflection to the ultimate conclusion, the Resurrection of the Christ *has become the image of our Resurrection*.

The positioning of Lazarus Saturday at the end of Lent reminds me of my humanity, but also of the Divine Life that not only *is coming, but also is present in the world now*. I will be raised with Christ, but I am now raised with him mystically to heavenly places.

I am as Lazarus was. I too will die (again!), but having died once, death has no more power over me. I have been called forth from the grave of the waters of baptism and so live *now*. Just as Lazarus was dead, resurrected, died again, and will live again, so it is for me. The message of John 11 is that victory has been won, is being won, and will be won. The faithful experience all of these conditions *now: an eternal now*.

A BRIEF PHILOSOPHICAL REFLECTION ON TIME AND ETERNITY

This is not mere rhetoric, but a theology that has philosophical implications. Any story about Jesus takes place in two times: God's time and human history. I *am not* saying this philosophical idea was fully worked out in the mind of Saint John, but is suggested to readers by the details of the Gospel and the teachings of the Old Testament. Professor George and the rest of us should recall that the events of the Incarnation are the intersection of time and eternity.

The liturgical understanding of John 11 suggests the view of Divine timelessness like that found in Boethius *Consolation of Philosophy*: "God is eternal; in this judgment all rational beings agree. Let us, then, consider what eternity is. For this word carries with it a revelation alike of the Divine nature and of the Divine knowledge. Now, eternity is the possession of endless life whole and perfect at a single moment."[4] While some philosophers have attacked the coherence of Boethius idea, philosophers such as Norman Kretzmann and Eleonore Stump[5] have ably defended it.

---

4. Boethius, *Consolation of Philosophy*, Book V.VI.
5. Stump and Kretzmann "Eternity," 429–58.

The traditional Christian view that God exists in an eternity ("timelessly"), possessing life in a single moment, makes sense of the raising of Lazarus and theological meaning. From the perspective of God: Christ is coming, Christ is come, Christ will come again is how God experiences. God never waits, never grows impatient. There is only one day for God: the Day of the Lord and it is *now*.

What is the relationship of God's eternal present to human time? We must unpack the ways "in time" is used, because with one way of using the phrase God "is in time" and in other usages he is not!

First, God is "in time" using one common use of the phrase "in time." Second, the story of Lazarus sometimes speaks of time differently and in this sense God is not in time.

I believe biblical writers usually view time as "the moment of action." Time is the medium in which events can take place. *When* does Isaiah see the Lord? Isaiah sees the Lord in the year that King Uzziah dies. Time is important as the "location" of an event. Something exists or a state of affairs is actualized in time. This is a commonsense way of thinking about time and since God exists he is in time (in this sense of time.)

Many later Christian philosophers had a different use of the term "time" and what it means to be "in time." These philosophers were influenced by Platonism and Neo-Platonism, but also by hints in Scripture such as those in the story of the raising of Lazarus or phrases like the "day of the Lord." For these thinkers "time" is a term for the "medium of change" and so God must be timeless. Augustine in the *City of God* XI and Chapter 6 sums up the case for divine timelessness when he states that there is no time in eternity, because eternity admits no change. God admits no change; therefore, he cannot be "in time" in this sense. He is in "eternity."

God's time (GT) is when God has his full existence if we use the commonsense usage of time. According to the Augustinian view; however, GT is not time at all, because there is only one instant of GT. GT admits no change: it is "eternity."

GT[6] is the "moment" or single time in which the state of affairs capturing God's existence is actualized. It is the moment of I AM. It is not like our own "time" in which our changing state of affairs is actualized.

GT is "time-like" in that an action takes place there: God has his eternal will in GT. It thus meets the common or early notion of what time is: the "place" where one thinks and wills. GT is "timeless" in that the state of

---

6. I prefer using GT to the term "eternity," because eternity has the unfortunate secondary usage—eternal duration. I AM does not "endure," He is.

affairs actualized at GT never changes. All of God's willing and thinking occur simultaneously: they are one.

Our time, containing past, present and presumably future states of affairs (change) is best pictured as a line. There is one instant, and only one instant, of GT because GT admits no change. This moment of GT is not a set of identical moments occurring in parallel to each individual moment of T. GT is distinct from T. This combines the Boethius's insight with more usual understanding of what it means to be "in time."

When a state of affairs comes to pass in T, a man can ask the concurrent state of affairs in eternity. The answer is always the same, since eternity never changes. The "time" in eternity (in the Biblical sense of when a state of affairs occurs) is always the same. We might call that GT moment "X." From our vantage point it is always X in GT. Since God created T with the cosmos, on the view of Boethius, the starting point of T, before the first change had occurred that brought forth the creation was also X.

T is a "ray" running from GT at a point X. It is not a time segment, because humankind and our cosmos are recreated and not destroyed in the Christian apocalypse, but we are never "god." To admit us to eternity (GT) would be to admit change to GT. We have never lived in eternity and never shall: mere eternal duration is not GT.

GT's X is the starting point for T. (This picture captures the Augustinian notion that time begins "out of" eternity.) Though T is distinct from GT, "a point," it interacts with GT. This separates my picture from that of C. S. Lewis.[7]

It is possible that there are other time "rays" and creations that would begin out of GT. The whole picture is like a great wheel with GT forming the hub of the wheel and various possible time "spokes" or states of affairs extending from that one hub.

There is at least one such actual "time" ray, namely the time "ray" we live in at present: T. At any point along the "ray" if one asked what the time was in GT, the answer would always be X. Events can occur in either "spokes" or at the "hub." Simple use of language, like that found in the Bible, might refer to both as "time." Later Christian philosophers would only call the ray "time" and would refer to the hub (GT) as "eternity."

GT is also unique from T in that God only exists in his fullness in GT. God exists only at X (as a subset of GT). The cosmos exists from (or through) X during T and contains everything in our cosmos except for God (strictly speaking). God interacts with T, but does not exist in T.

---

7. Lewis, *Mere Christianity*, 145–49.

GT is not merely part of "ray" T (unlike other unique moments of time in "ray" T), because other potential time lines stretch from GT. God as creator has (or had) the ability to create other possible time "rays" from the moment X (even if he has not or does not in fact do so). Since God exists eternally at X and not (strictly speaking) at any moment of T, there are no possible "rays" of time stretching from any moment of T. GT's point X (its only point) is potentially the starting point for an infinite number of created times.

GT, the eternity of Boethius, becomes a subset of a broader term called "time" by biblical writers. T, (the sequential moments of our cosmos: past, present, and future) is a second subset of this broad notion of time: the medium of change in some sequence.

Applied to the raising of Lazarus, we can see the different uses of time. Jesus "waits" during some duration of T, but in eternity (GT) Lazarus is raised already. In T sin and death exist, but in GT the Lamb slain from the foundation of the world has defeated sin and death. Jesus weeps from the perspective of T and has faith based on his knowledge of GT.

The "sickness is not unto death" from the eternal perspective: Lazarus is alive, because there is no death at GT. Lazarus dies in T and remains dead for some duration of T. There is no contradiction.

How can Jesus say we shall "never die" if we believe in him? If our life is hidden in God, then it is in a place where no change can take place. We might experience death in this life (some moment of T), but where God is we are alive. A man cannot be alive and dead at the same time, but he can be alive and dead at two different times.

To endure change and pass through to the victory that already is in Heaven (GT) must have been almost unendurable for Jesus. Lazarus is alive (GT), but Lazarus is dead (in T) and Jesus must endure T. We ask that God's will be done in this age (T) as it is already *is* in Heaven (GT). Our own time, human history, is transformed whenever any man or woman allows his or her vision to clear and see God in his time.

Looking at an icon on my wall of my house, I see two reactions to the great miracle picture on it. Some followers worship the Lord of Life, but others turn to plot his death. The God revealed in Jesus is the Jewish Messiah and in the raising of Lazarus is shown to be the very Son of God: equal to God. Surprisingly to moderns, not all embrace life when they see it.

The story of Lazarus ends with the opponents of Jesus expanding their hit list from Jesus to Lazarus. They saw life and embraced death. As Christians we too have two natures: the inheritance of Adam and the inheritance of Jesus Christ.

Much evil that exists is best explained by our perverse desire to embrace death and turn away from Life. It is also foolish, because Life exists in a time where no human can ever touch it: GT (eternity).

Professor George speaks of duality in his paper, but his insights gain greater force if we utilize the Christian idea of the duality of the experiences of the God-man. Jesus is in history, but (except perhaps when forsaken on the Cross) also alive in GT. The Word became flesh and dwelt among us. We could see him, but he also could see the Father and do what he was (eternally) doing.

We will die in this time, but if we believe in him then our true life will be hidden in a place where death and change are impossible. Christians never die: it is always Easter Sunday.

George Final Response

JAMES MCCLENDON TAUGHT US to think of theology as biography, and this is especially appropriate at a conference where we seek to engage one another and the text of Holy Scripture across confessions and across time. Thus I was grateful that Professor John Mark Reynolds shared something of his own personal background and pilgrimage of faith. A member of the Antiochian Orthodox Church, he is the provost of a Baptist university who has been shaped by the *Book of Common Prayer*, has studied Wesleyan theology, and has attended a charismatic Bible college. While he was not asked to tell the story of his life in this paper, I would like to know how he now evaluates these earlier phases in his spiritual journey. To what extent does he appropriate them in the context of the ecclesial space he inhabits now as a Western-rite, evangelical, and Orthodox believer in Jesus Christ? Later in his paper, he does recall the time when he "was dunked under the waters of the Little Sandy River in West Virginia" as marking a momentous transition from death to spiritual life.

Professor Reynolds makes a valuable point about the common textual data that Orthodox, Catholic, and Evangelical readers share in common. Of course, it is possible to deconstruct the biblical text in various ways. This strategy has been pursued copiously by many postmodern scholars and others who look for hidden layers and secret sources behind the text as we have it in John 11. One common way of doing this is to transpose the story Jesus told about the rich man and Lazarus in Luke 16 into background for the Johannine account. The evidence for this and for even more far-fetched scenarios is flimsy to non-existent. While anyone can speculate about the editorial process that resulted in John 11 as we have it in our Bibles today, I prefer to deal with the text in its present canonical shape. However this text was originally composed, it is inspired by the Holy Spirit, intended for the good of the church, and meant—like all of this Gospel—to lead persons to true faith in the living Christ (see John 20:31).

Professor Reynolds makes a major contribution to our discussion of John 11 by pointing to its unique liturgical placement in the life of the church. He notes that Orthodox worshipers remember the raising of Lazarus at a precise junction in the church year, namely, at the end of Lent and the beginning of Holy Week. It is well known that John 11 serves as a hinge in the structure of John's Gospel, bringing to conclusion the Book of Signs and opening to the Book of the Passion. Reynolds deepens this point by showing how the Lazarus account is also a hinge text for the entire church year. It is thus a moment of transition between the penitential disciplines of Lent and the focused journey of Holy Week toward Maundy Thursday, Good Friday, Silent Saturday, and Victory Sunday on Easter. In this way, Lazarus Saturday anticipates (and participates in) the following day, which marks Jesus's entry into Jerusalem on his way to the cross. As Reynolds puts it, "the church makes Lazarus Saturday a liturgical Sunday and Palm Sunday a liturgical Sunday: back-to-back. Saturday is the first day, and the first day has become the seventh day." One of the great gifts of the Orthodox tradition is to read the Bible in the light of the liturgy. This is a gift evangelical Christians can gratefully receive.

Professor Reynolds balks slightly at my somewhat rhetorical question, "Can God get mad?" My focus on the three decisive actions of the God-man in John 11—he "waited," "wailed," and "wept"—raises the further question of whether such actions can be attributed to God *tout court* or should instead be assigned solely to the human nature of the incarnate Son. As one who embraces without reservation the Christology of the Council of Chalcedon (451), I realize that the early church struggled over the precise definition of the two natures and one person of Jesus Christ. And, unlike many New Testament scholars who regard such later theological construals as irrelevant to the meaning of John, I believe it is quite appropriate to read the New Testament in light of the later dogmatic tradition which, in its central Christological affirmations, is a proper development therefrom. At the same time, I am a bit wary of making too precise a division of labor between divinity and humanity in Jesus.

To say that "each nature works together so synergistically that the duality is hard to see in most of the life of Christ" is exactly right. At one point, Reynolds accuses me of coming dangerously close to the Monophysite position. I plead "not guilty"—but I can see where he might have gotten such an idea. In the long history of Christian doctrine, it seems to me that theologians usually lean one way or the other on controverted matters of the faith—freewill and predestination, real presence or spiritual presence in the Lord's Supper, Alexandrian or Antiochene exegesis, Nestorian or Monophysite Christology. Thus in the debates of the Reformation, it can be (and has been) argued that Luther leaned slightly toward the Monophysite view (especially in his doctrine of the *communicatio idomatum*) whereas Calvin tilted in the direction of greater distinction of the two natures.

While I would never accuse an Orthodox thinker of being a crypto-Calvinist(!), I myself will confess to an anti-Nestorian bias. It was one of the great themes in Athanasius's doctrine of the incarnation that God—and only God—can redeem fallen human beings from sin and death. In the biblical language of St. Paul, "God was in Christ reconciling the world unto himself" (2 Cor 5:19). To avoid leaning so far (either way) into heresy, we need to stay within the bounds of the four famous Chalcedonian adverbs: "unconfusedly, unchangeably, indivisibly, inseparably." I intended to do no less in my paper. But I do want to say that the waiting, wailing, and weeping of Jesus Christ in the Lazarus event is not mere prolegomenon to the real event of the grave-bursting. Professor Reynolds imagines the tears drying on the face of Jesus as Lazarus comes forth, but I am not so sure. That same Jesus will soon be anointed for his own burial in the very home of Lazarus (John 12:1–8), he will soon declare his heart deeply troubled (John 12:27), and he will soon—we know from Luke—pray in the Garden of Gethsemane with such intensity that his perspiration turns to blood. In no way does this diminish the great victory that Easter Sunday represents: *Christus Victor!* Yet, even in his glorified state in heaven, the risen Jesus still bears in his body the marks of his passion and, in that sense, God still waits, wails, and weeps.

Professor Michael Waldstein and I met for the first time at the Paradosis conference, and for me it was an altogether delightful encounter. We discovered that we had both studied at Harvard during approximately the same time. I also learned that Professor Waldstein had worked closely with His Eminence Cardinal Christoph Schönborn of Vienna, one of the ablest Catholic theologians I have met and from whose work I have learned so much. It was a pleasure to share this assignment with a fellow believer in Jesus Christ, one so deeply rooted in the common patrimony we share in the Holy Scriptures and the life of faith.

Professor Waldstein's response to my talk on John 11 is a major paper in its own right, richly textured and worthy of more than the few comments I can make here. I shall comment briefly on five themes in Waldstein's engaging response: tone, truth, intratextuality, ecclesiology, and presence.

1. TONE

Waldstein begins by reminding us that theology in the age of the Reformation often included the language of invective, violence, and recrimination. It will not do simply to reply that Luther, Calvin, and the other reformers had the same kind of abuse leveled against them, though that was certainly true. Nor is it possible, I think, to divorce completely the bloody religious wars of the age from the violent language used by both sides against one another. I addressed this issue in the preface to my book, *Theology of the Reformers* (first edition, 1988) in this way: "Luther's invective against the Jews, Zwingli's complicity in the drowning of Anabaptists, and Calvin's in the burning of Servetus are all the more tragic because one senses that these, of all people, should have known better." Jaroslav Pelikan once spoke about the "tragic necessity" of the Reformation. It is not hard to find champions on one side of this antinomy or the other. The tragic side of the Reformation is obvious to those who care deeply about the unity of the church and who feel keenly the *dis*-evangelical impact of a fractured Christian community. On the other hand, the necessity of the Reformation is evident to those who hear in the teaching of the reformers the good news of God's free and unfettered grace and the message of justification by faith alone. But Pelikan was right. The legacy of the Reformation involves both dimensions. Perhaps *simul iustus et peccator* applies not only to individuals, as Luther taught, but also to particular epochs and episodes in the history of the church. As Catholics and evangelicals look forward to the Reformation commemorations of 2017, we can celebrate together many aspects of the spiritual and ecclesial renewal that took place in the sixteenth century, but we also need to repent together of other aspects that are less than worthy of Jesus Christ and his gospel.

2. TRUTH

Waldstein approaches his task as an interpreter of the Bible and a faithful member of the Catholic Church aware both of the common unity we share in Christ and also of the serious differences that remain to be resolved between our two traditions. He is right to emphasize the priority of truth in our theological exchange. This principle is too often forgotten by those who practice what I have called an ecumenism of accommodation rather than an ecumenism of conviction. Unity apart from truth is not real unity. All of us at this conference, Catholics, Orthodox, and evangelicals alike can resonate with these words from Cardinal Joseph Ratzinger, now Pope

Emeritus Benedict XVI, who wrote that "our quarrelling ancestors were in reality much closer to each other when in all their disputes they still knew that they could only be servants of one truth which must be acknowledged as being as great and as pure as it has been intended for us by God."

3. INTRATEXTUALITY

Waldstein commends me for interpreting John 11 in the wider context of the entire gospel. He pursues such intratextuality himself by linking together the miracle of the wine at Cana (John 2) with the scene of the mother of Jesus beneath the cross (John 19). The leitmotif that links these two Johannine episodes with the raising of Lazarus in John 11 is the theme of glory. As I pointed out in my paper, glory frames the resurrection of Lazarus in John 11—but for John it is precisely at the cross that the glory of God is most fully displayed. This does not mitigate the literal truth of the amazing event of Jesus bringing back to life a man who had been dead for four days, but it does cast this entire story in the wider context of redemptive history. It points (as Luther noted) to a profound *theologia crucis* at the heart of the Christian gospel.

4. MARY AND ECCLESIOLOGY.

As Waldstein points out, another link between John 2 and John 19 is Mary, the mother of Jesus. She appears in both narratives with water and wine (John 2) and water and blood (John 19). Here is a place where evangelicals can learn from their Catholic brothers and sisters. For many evangelicals, Mary is a marginal figure, left on the sidelines, too often neglected altogether. Evangelicals disagree with Catholics about the later Marian dogmas of the Immaculate Conception and the Assumption and do not embrace (what even some Catholics call) the excesses of Marian piety, but we do share much common ground about Mary. Mary was a model of discipleship, a proclaimer of the gospel, and, as the Evangelicals and Catholics Together statement "Do Whatever He Tells You: The Blessed Virgin Mary in Christian Faith and Life" (2009) boldly declares, the Mother of God. As the early church realized at the councils of Ephesus and Chalcedon, to say less than this about Mary is to deny the incarnation itself. I see no reason why Bible-believing evangelicals should not recognize Mary as the New Eve in the sense that Irenaeus used that term in the second century. Ecclesiology remains the most difficult issue in our quest for full visible unity as followers of Jesus. On this front, Mary is at once a bridge across troubled waters and a barrier yet to be transcended.

5. PRESENCE

Professor Waldstein revealed a piece of autobiography that I find fascinating: He himself is a lineal descendant of the Swiss Protestant reformer Huldrych Zwingli! Zwingli is my least favorite reformer, I must confess. To be sure, Zwingli was a bold witness for the gospel in many respects, but he needs the correction of Luther and Calvin, especially in his doctrine of the Lord's Supper. For many low-church and free-church Protestants, the celebration of Holy Communion too much resembles a mournful funeral service—a solemn observance dutifully performed in memory of an absent Lord. Catholics and evangelicals understand differently the *how* of Christ's presence in the Lord's Supper, and this is only one of several issues (another being ministerial orders) that keep us separated at the Table of the Lord. But evangelicals too need to reclaim a theology of presence, one that emphasizes the role of the Holy Spirit in eucharistic worship. In doing so, evangelicals are not departing from but digging more deeply into our own tradition. For example, the 1549 *Book of Common Prayer* speaks of the Lord's Supper as "feeding on Christ in thy heart by faith," and the 1677 (Baptist) *Second London Confession* declares that in receiving the Lord's Supper we "spiritually receive and feed upon Christ crucified and all of the benefits of his death: the body and blood of Christ being not corporately or carnally but spiritually present to the faith of believers."

CHAPTER 4

John 17
A Theological Reading for an Ecumenical Audience

R. R. Reno (Catholic)

For more than a century, the seventeenth chapter of the Gospel of John has served a popular scriptural warrant for the ecumenical movement. Jesus's prayer to the Father in verse 21—"That they may all be one"—echoes through many ecumenical documents, from early Faith and Order statements, through the Second Vatican Council's Decree on Ecumenism, to contemporary calls for Christian unity. However, John 17 provides us with much more than a proof text for a commitment to ecumenism. The ancient and medieval traditions of commentary do not draw attention to the ecumenical implications of John 17. Instead, the unity—the at-oneness—so prominent in this chapter of the Gospel of John is read in a Trinitarian and soteriological way. The incarnate Son is one with the Father, and in faith we are one with him, and through him with the Father.

I see it as my task to deepen the modern ecumenical reading of John 17 along the lines suggested by the earlier traditions of commentary. I plan to argue that this remarkable and extended prayer serves as an outline or précis for an ecclesiology organized around a central emphasis of the Gospel of John: that we can overcome the distance that separates the sinner from God by becoming at-one with Christ, and in him with the Father. I begin, therefore, with a quick survey of the larger context of the at-one-ment theology we find in the chapters leading up to John 17.

John 17 brings Jesus's so-called "farewell discourse" to an end, and thus it is this extended section of the Gospel of John that provides the immediate context for interpretation. The discourse begins with chapter 13. The Passover festival is at hand; his hour has come. He washes the feet of his disciples and prophesies his betrayal. After Judas departs, Jesus pronounces himself glorified, and his gives his disciples a new commandment: "That you love one another, even as I have loved you, that you also love one another. By this all men will know that you are my disciples, if you have love for one another" (13:33–35). This new commandment of love serves as the leitmotif for the farewell discourses, for love seeks union with the beloved. Love wishes to abide in the beloved, to be at-one with the beloved. The main thrust of the farewell discourse is therefore to be found in Jesus's instructions to his disciples about how they can be with him, even as he goes away; be at-one, even as he departs. Love can transcend separation and distance.

Immediately before issuing his new commandment, Jesus has announced something seemingly strange and paradoxical. The one who so loves his friends is going away. He is separating himself from his disciples: "Where I am going you cannot come" (13:33). Peter doesn't like this idea at all. He understands quite well, it seems, that love seeks to be with the beloved, and therefore he wished to continue to be at-one with Jesus. So he announces there's no place he won't go with Jesus. He'll even go to the point of death itself if that's what it takes to remain in union with him. But Jesus tells him, no, dear friend, you won't. Quite the contrary, you'll run the other direction, denying me three times.

It is this tension—a love the wishes to draw near and a savior who is going away—that characterizes the farewell discourse as a whole and provides the background for Jesus's extended prayer in John 17. On the one hand we are to love as he has loved, which means drawing close to him and each other. We are to abide in him and by imitating his love also abide in the fellowship of the disciples. And yet it seems we can't do this, because he is going somewhere we cannot go. This "somewhere" is left deliberately vague. The farewell discourse is conveyed in "figures" (16:25). But one doesn't need an advanced degree in theology to spell out reasons why Jesus is going somewhere we can't. Jesus is divine, the one who was with the Father "from the beginning," while we are finite creatures. There is an infinite metaphysical distance between divinity and humanity, between Creator and creature. We are also sinners enclosed in upon ourselves, largely incapable of going any place that involves sacrificing our self-love. By contrast, Jesus is spotless and without sin and able to give of himself without reserve. There is a fundamental moral difference between our captivity to sin and his freedom for love.

But Jesus is not interested in a theological digression to explain why Peter (and by implication all of us) cannot go with him. Instead, he wishes to reassure: "Do not let your hearts be troubled." There is a way a spiritual way of "going with" Jesus. It allows us to abide in him even as he departs from us to go to the cross: "Believe in God, believe also in me" (14:1). This spiritual way of "going with" in faith constitutes one of the main teachings of the farewell discourse—it is the way of atonement.

It is very telling that the same "where I am going you cannot come" and "do not let your hearts be troubled" sequence of distance and enduring intimacy gets repeated immediately with Thomas. Jesus tells his disciples, "In my Father's house there are many rooms" (14:2). In essence, he's reassuring them that although he must go away he will return and bring them to the Father to dwell with him. He is leaving, but for the sake of a future, deeper, and permanent unity or at-oneness in love.

But, again, Thomas, like Peter, understands the imperatives of love and seeks to be united to those whom he loves. He is not satisfied with waiting for Jesus to return. He is eager to get going right away. He wants to be reunited with Jesus as soon as possible, and so he presses him: "How can we know the way?" Again, Jesus teaches that, paradoxically, we can go with him even as he goes where we cannot go. He states: "I am the way, and the truth, and the life" (14:6). We can abide in him by *knowing* him, a protean word that connotes union with and participation in that which we know. We can be with him in faith even as he goes where we cannot go. And in knowing him, we know the Father. Put in St. Paul's terms, faith is the spirit of adoption that conforms us to the image of the incarnate Son (Romans 8).

The tension between distance and intimacy gets recapitulated yet again, this time by Philip, and again the lesson is that faith unites us with Christ even as he goes where we cannot. In this instance, Philip shifts the key, as it were. Instead of the paschal "going to the cross" that echoes in Peter's insistence that he will remain at-one with Jesus, or the eschatological pathway from present to future consummation that's in the background of Thomas's question, Philip evokes the desire to overcome the metaphysical distance between God and man: "Lord, show us the Father, and we will be satisfied" (14:8). Satisfied indeed! But what could be farther from finite human flesh that the Godhead? Jesus's answer is a rebuke. Perhaps the Lord tires of teaching the same lesson! Has Philip failed to understand? "Do you not believe that I am in the Father and the Father is in me?" (14:10). Faith in Jesus as the incarnate Son of God brings the Father to us, because in the

Son we find the fullness God. The Son is always at-one with the Father, and the Father with the Son, and so if we abide in the Son, we abide in the Father.

Not surprisingly, therefore, Jesus suddenly and significantly shifts the direction of his own travel. He is no longer going away but instead preparing to come still closer. On the day of his glorification on the cross, he will reveal himself as the one who lives—the One who is Life—and "in that day you will know that I am in my Father, and you in me, and I in you" (14:20). He is going away to the cross for the sake of coming to us (14:28). The distance of the cross, the distance none of the disciples can traverse, is for the sake of love's closer embrace. The atoning sacrifice that only Jesus can make—his going where we cannot—is at the same time his coming to us in love, making us at-one with him.

To this Jesus adds a crucial teaching that reinforces his words about believing in him. It's his love for his disciples (and for us) that takes him away from them and to the cross: "Greater love has no man than this, that a man lay down his life for his friends: (15:13). Therefore if we abide in his love—if we who keep his word and obey his command to love as he loves—we abide in him. In our conformity to his commandment, we actively participate in the reason for his departure from us, and thus in a spiritual sense go with him even as we're left behind. Yes, Jesus goes where we cannot go. He alone is our savior. He alone can redeem the world. He alone is consubstantial with the Father. But we need not be troubled in our hearts. We need neither fear his departure, nor weep over the infinite distance between God who dwells in holiness and human beings who live in sin. For if we love as he has commanded us to love, we abide in him.

In chapter 15, as if to reinforce the point, Jesus reiterates his new commandment: "This is my commandment, that you love one another as I have loved you" (15:12). He then restates the power of this commandment to secure an enduring union with him: "You are my friends if you do what I command you" (15:14). To do as he does—to love as he loves—is to conform ourselves to him. In obedience to his commandment we become Christ-like and thus unite ourselves with him. In love we become a branch of the true vine, a vivid image of abiding in Christ.

Branches of the true vine bear good fruit, and we will be known by our fruit. It is at this point that Jesus warns his disciples that abiding in him will put them at odds with the world. The world hates him, and as he is in us and we are in him, we too are hated (15:18). "If they persecuted me, they will persecute you" (15:20). In this sense, Jesus foresees that his disciples will accompany him to the cross, not on Good Friday but eventually. Abiding in him, they will go with him.

The teaching here is clear. Friendship with Christ overcomes the distance between God and man, between self-love and love of neighbor—but in so doing it opens up a new distance, this time between those who believe in Christ and those who live according to "the world," which in this context does not mean creation but instead the regime of life governed by sin and death. This distance between discipleship and worldliness will become extreme: "They will put you out of the synagogues; indeed, the hour is coming when whoever kills you will think he is offering service to God" (16:2). Jesus's offer of friendship forces a choice. Will we be friends with Christ or friends with the ruler of this world? Will we abide in him or abide in "the world"? And once again, as is the case throughout the farewell discourse, going away is for the sake of love. We must cleave to Christ and go with him out of the "the world" in order in order to bear witness to him "that the world might be saved through him" (John 3:17).

In another recapitulation of this theme—going away is for the sake of drawing near—Jesus reassures his disciples. "I tell you the truth: it is to your advantage that I go away, for if I do not go away the Counselor will not come to you; but if I go, I will send him to you" (16:7). Here we see a shift from an anthropocentric to theocentric perspective. Up to this point Jesus has been teaching about the spiritual union made possible by his commandment to love one another. In faith in him and obedience to his commandments we can abide in him, which means we can go with him to the Father, for whomever abides in him, abides in the Father. Or put differently, in love and friendship with him we can go with him to the cross. In fellowship with him we can bear witness to his love, even amidst the persecutions of this world. Now he speaks of the way in which *he* will continue to abide in us, even as he goes away. He will send the Holy Spirit who will bind the disciples even more closely to him. By the power of the Holy Spirit, those who believe in Jesus will speak his words, not their own. Their lives will glorify him. The Holy Spirit will "take what is mine and declare it to you" (16:15), which means to clarify and give assurance to the faithful that they are indeed branches of the vine, beloved by the vinedresser.

The final section of Jesus's address to his disciples recapitulates for a final time the central theme of distance for the sake of intimacy: "A little while, and you will see me no more; again a little while, and you will see me" (16:16). The disciples wonder what he is talking about, but the reader knows. Jesus is going down into the tomb. The world will rejoice, imagining its regime of sin and death triumphant. The disciples will sorrow, imagining their beloved teacher taken from them forever. But the Lord's going away is for the sake of a joyful return. The crucified Son of God will rise from the dead. "I will see you again," Jesus tells his disciples, who are confused by all this talk of going away that somehow involves drawing nearer still, "your hearts will rejoice, and no one will take your joy from you" (16:22). Like a woman whose joy in new life after delivering her child overcomes the anguish of childbirth, the coming intimacy with the risen Son—and in him with the Father—will eclipse the dark distance of the cross. "I have overcome the world," Jesus concludes. This triumphant declaration serves as the Gospel of John's form of Jesus's statement at the end of the Gospel of Matthew, "I am with you always, to the close of the age" (28:20). Both assert the same truth: "I am sure that neither death, nor life, nor angels, nor principalities, nor things present, nor things to come, nor powers, nor height, nor depth, nor anything else in all creation, will be able to separate us from the love of God in Christ Jesus our Lord" (Rom 8:38–39).

This has been, no doubt, a too superficial sketch of some of the most profound chapters of the New Testament. The Johannine literature opens out in countless different directions. The Church Fathers read these chapters as invitations to Trinitarian reflection, and rightly so, while I've read them in a soteriological way, focusing on our participation in Christ, our at-one-ment with him and through him with the Father. I've done so because it provides the most helpful background for an ecumenically-oriented reading of John 17. Ecumenism has to do with the unity of the church—abiding with each other as friends in and of Christ. Obviously, then, ecumenism implicates the church. By my reading, John 17 is such an important ecumenical text because it teaches us about unity—the at-one-ment or abiding that love seeks—in such a theologically fundamental way that it illuminates aspects of our common life together that we might not otherwise see as relevant to ecumenism.

John 17 is an extended prayer. This is important in this context, because prayer seeks to abide in God. The very act of prayer presumes the presence of God. It can be perfunctory and rote. But even when we address God without much in the way of inner intention, we are speaking as if he were near, as if he can hear us, and in that sense there's always a spiritual "drawing near" even in the most mechanical and routine prayers. And if by God's grace we are truly present in prayer, our hearts are open to communion with God. We converse with our Lord; we bring before him our concerns and share our lives with him. Prayer aspires to spiritual union with the divine.

The same holds for the role of prayer in our common life together as Christians. When we pray for others, we join ourselves to them, making their concerns ours, sharing in their lives as we bring them before God. The corporate prayer of the church is also an act of unity. At certain moments in the liturgy, the priest or leader of the congregation prays on behalf of the entire community, making his voice the voice of the community. In the Catholic Church this union in prayer is most poignant during the sacrifice of the Mass. He speaks on behalf of the gathered faithful as he offers up the bread and wine. At the same time, his voice is Christ's own as he repeats the words of institution. In the Eucharistic prayer, therefore, the priest becomes the focal point of at-one-ment: the congregations seeking God and God seeking his elect.

Jesus begins his prayer by petitioning the Father: "Glorify thy Son that the Son may glorify thee" (17:1). Jesus is asking his Father to accept the sacrifice he desires to offer on our behalf. He wishes for the Father to call him to the cross, which is his glorification. For on the cross the Son will demonstrate his "power of over all flesh" (17:2), and he will use that power, not for his own sake, but for the sake of those whom he loves—or perhaps more precisely, he'll use that power for the sake of his mission precisely by using it for the sake of others. Thus, the glory of God is not found in his power, but instead his mercy. "Father, glorify me in thy own presence with the glory with thee before the world was made" (17:5). And what is the source of this eternal glory? It is the inner life of the Godhead, which John elsewhere teaches is love: "God is love" (1 John 4:8).

If we keep in mind the tensions between distance and unity that so predominate in the farewell discourse, we can see how this passage of scripture is pregnant with the Trinitarian theology that would eventually be formulated by the Church. Jesus is praying, in his human nature, that he and the Father should be one in will and purpose. He has been sent; the Father has sent him. He has his own mission; he has accomplished the work the Father has given him (17:4). But they share in the same eternal glory (17:5). The Godhead is united through all eternity, and this union of divinity can obtain even as there is a distinction of persons, even when the Son leaves the Father for the sake of their unity in love.

Jesus then shifts the focus of his prayer, now speaking to the Father on behalf of his disciples whom he must now leave, also for the sake of his unity with them in love. It is in this part of John 17 that we find a tacit theology of the church that the larger context union in love invites us to unpack as (1) apostolic continuity, (2) a counter-sign to the world's modes of unity, (3) a mode of sanctification, and (4) a foretaste of the wedding banquet of the Lamb.

1. APOSTOLIC CONTINUITY

The Father has given the disciples into the care and love of the Son. Discharging this love is the "work" Jesus does, a work that has glorified both him and the Father. In prayer, Jesus specifies the nature of this work. He has "manifested thy name" and "given them the words which thou gavest me" (17:6–7). This teaching has been effective: "they have kept thy word" (17:6). In short, the disciples have abided in Jesus's teaching, which is the Father's teaching, for he and the Father are one.

In the past Jesus himself kept his disciples true to the words he has taught. He teaches with authority (Matt 7:28). His authority guides his disciples, bringing them into a communion with his mind and purpose. In a real sense, Jesus personally oversees the continuity of his teaching. But he is leaving them to go to be glorified, and so Jesus petitions the Father: "Keep them in thy name, which thou hast given me, that they may be one, even as we are one" (17:11).

We can readily see the importance of this petition. Union in doctrine is a very important kind of unity. If we are at-one with the word Jesus has given us, then we will speak in one voice—his voice. This is a crucial feature of a united church. It is also important to have unity through time. To say that our churches today teach in continuity with the church of the apostles is to say that we are in unity with their teaching—Jesus's teaching. This continuity—unity through time—is what makes the church apostolic.

It is in both senses that I interpret Jesus's petition: he asks the Father to make the disciples at-one in their teaching. This means having them abide in what he has given them, just as the Son abides in the Father, and the Father in the Son. Jesus is petitioning the Father to oversee the apostolic faithfulness (continuity) of the church's teaching. He is saying, "Just as I am eternally faithful to your truth—at-one with your word—keep my followers faithful."

It is also important to see that the Father must *do something* in order to respond to Jesus's petition. And so he does. As we learn in the Acts of the Apostles, the Father sends the Counselor, the Holy Spirit, to inspire in the leaders of the church a spirit of unity, the spirit of abiding in. Guided by the Spirit, they will teach with one voice—and in accord with the word that has been given them. Thus, we read of the conflicts over divergent teachings about the early church's mission to the Gentiles (Acts 15). Then, to ensure unity, the Jerusalem council comes to a common decision. It is prefaced in a way that reflects that fact that the Father has answered Jesus's petition: "It has seemed good to the Holy Spirit and to us. . ." (15:28).

Christians are divided about how to ensure that we are at-one in a Spirit-guided way with the word that Christ has given us. We're divided about how God ensures we abide in his truth. Catholics have a robust and precise doctrine of apostolic continuity that specifies the role of the bishops as successors to the apostles, and the bishop of Rome as final arbiter. By contrast, Protestants rely on a Spirit-guided reading of Holy Scripture to ensure unity in apostolic teaching, with confessional statements serving at tests or guides, but not final authorities. It's tempting for a Catholic like me to point out that the Protestant approach hasn't been very effective. But I will refrain. Instead, I want to focus on a typical Protestant objection to Catholic views of the Church's authority, which is that the magisterial apparatus is not in scripture. True, but consider Jesus's petition: "Keep them in thy name." Surely the Father, who loves the Son and seeks to glorify him, will ensure the efficacy of that petition. Thus, whatever one thinks of the Catholic ecclesiological excess of Vatican I's the doctrine of papal primacy and infallibility, one must allow the integrity of the spiritual ambition. The doctrine presumes the superabundant love that the Father has for the Son. It's a love that will go as far as it takes to ensure continuity and unity—at-one-ment—in the Lord's name, even so far as to guide the development of a doctrine of apostolic authority that goes beyond the bare specifics we find in the New Testament.

2. A COUNTER-SIGN

"I have given them thy word; and the world has hated them because they are not of the world, even as I am not of the world." Unity with and in Christ is a *counter-sign* or offense to the world. The world has its own principles of unity, its own empires and regimes, its own common loves. Rome and her many successors are the authors of a worldly peace. Mammon reigns over many hearts and organizes our lives. We are beckoned to abide in the marketplace or in the nation state, in the Republic of Letters or in the Halls of Science. Each has a proper, finite, and limited claim on our souls. But all seduce us to give them our supreme loyalty. Each furthers subordinate goods, tempting us to consider them as providing our supreme and final good.

St. Augustine envisioned the company of the faithful as a city united in a common love of God. This unity provides a powerful guard against the seductions and temptations of the world. For a city is a place organized to promote its common love. Thus the Church has apostles, prophets, teachers, workers of miracles, healers, helpers, administrators, and speakers in different tongues (1 Cor 12:28). These many members of the one body are organized in a hierarchy so that they can be coordinated toward their common end, which is friendship with Christ. The Church is a countersign, therefore, because she makes a claim on the loyalty of her members: a creed to believe in, a constitution to govern affairs, and a way of life to be loyal to. We do not abide in Christ in a merely spiritual or intellectual way. He has a body, a dwelling place that has many rooms.

Catholic legalism, bureaucracy, and hierarchy are sometimes thought to be liabilities. But given Jesus's teaching that we must be a counter-sign, I think the opposite is true (at least most of the time). In the modern era that Catholic Church has reorganized itself as a city that seeks to be as independent as possible from the modern nation state. She has her own laws, her own diplomats, and even her own tiny plot of land in the middle of Rome. In this sense, the Catholic Church is the only significant, large-scale, and visible counter-regime in modernity, the only substantial form of life not organized by the economic, therapeutic, and political principles that reign in the West, and increasingly around the globe.

3. A MODE OF SANCTIFICATION

Unity is a mode of *sanctification*. It is important to avoid seeing Christian unity simply as a goal to be achieved and ideal sought, as if it existed as a discrete ecclesial or institutional reality. Jesus prays to the Father, "Sanctify them in the truth" (17:17). The truth to which he refers is that he and the Father are one. This Trinitarian truth is the essence of the Gospel. Here the logic of sanctification is tightly wound, as is so much of Jesus's farewell discourse. To confess Jesus as the eternally begotten Son of God is to abide in him and acknowledging him to be one with the Father. To abide in Jesus is to abide in the Father as well. Therefore, in effect, when petitioning God to sanctify us in the truth, Jesus is asking the Father to impress upon us ever more deeply the truth of what we believe. For as he has taught in the farewell discourse, to believe in him is to go with him, and thus to go to the Father—to be at-one with the Father.

Here, the object is not Christian unity, at least not primarily, but instead the unity of Christians with Christ in faith, and through Christ with the Father. The world does not come to believe because it sees divided Christians united; instead, it is because they see human beings united with the living God, at-one with the Eternal. This does not mean Christian unity has no role to play. One cannot abide in Christ—and thus be sanctified in the truth—if one does not obey his commandment of love, and love seeks unity. Thus, to venture a restatement of Jesus's prayer, he petitions the Father to bring us to believe in him more deeply, and in believing to seek unity in love, just as he and his Father enjoy an eternal unity in love.

If we think about unity and sanctification in this way, we can avoid a false chicken-and-egg dilemma. Must we seek unity in order to deepen our faith, or do we need first to become more faithful so that we can do what needs to be done to achieve Christian unity? This way of thinking is not fruitful, because it encourages an ecumenical works righteousness. It also may be unique to the divided Christian West. The rest of Christendom sees unity as something to be preserved or deepened rather than achieved. Unity is something one seeks within the already existing unity of the Church; it is not something that is established or created. There's something right about this circular logic: one needs unity to seek unity. We must be sanctified in the truth if we are to have any hope of practicing genuine Christian unity in the truth. But those who are sanctified in the truth abide in Christ's love, and thus already participate in the unity his love seeks. And so, we must abide in unity—abide in Christ—in order to seek unity in an effective way.

There are lessons to be drawn from the close relation between sanctification in the truth and abiding in the unity of Christ's truth. One is that our ecumenical hopes are in vain if we do not first attend to the unity of our own communities. We need to practice unity locally, as it were, if we are to achieve it globally.

The other lesson is descriptive. The modern ecumenical movement is not rooted in good will, and certainly not in a quasi-Pelagian commitment to our ecumenical duty to seek Christian unity. Instead, it flows from the ways in which Christians of different denominations have already tacitly and informally and haltingly found themselves one in Christ. This has happened in many ways. The late nineteenth-century missionary movement was a seminal instance of "found unity." In our time, shoulder-to-shoulder efforts in the pro life movement and other cultural struggles has played a similar role. There are many other latent unities as well, more subtle but no less important. For example, modern theology, especially biblical studies, has been greatly influenced by the modern academic culture we all share. By my reckoning, the Lutheran-Catholic Joint Declaration on the Doctrine of Justification was made possible because modern biblical studies has formed Catholic and Protestant biblical scholars to read St. Paul in pretty much the same way.

4. A FORETASTE OF THE WEDDING BANQUET OF THE LAMB

Unity is a *foretaste* of love's eschatological triumph. Jesus's final prayer for unity leans toward future consummation. He no longer prays for his disciples, but instead addresses the Father on behalf of "those who believe in me through their word" (17:20). Jesus continues by reiterating the logic of faith. To believe in him is to be united with him in faith, and through him with the Father. In his words: "That they may all be one; even as thou, Father, art in me, and I in thee, that they also may be in us" (17:21). In this at-one-ment with God in Christ, and in him with one another, the world will see God's truth. This truth—God is love—is what we see in the crucified Son who gave his life for his friends and in the Father who sent him and raised him from the dead. "So that the world may believe that thou hast sent me" (17:21).

Jesus recapitulates and expands this hymn to the power of love in 17:23–24. "The glory I have thou hast given me I have given them." The glory referred to is that of the cross and resurrection. It is the glory of election going back to Abraham, the glory of God's indomitable love that overcomes all obstacles, even sin and death. The Son has received this glory from all eternity. He has now given it to his disciples, and through them to all who believe in him. Earlier in the farewell discourse we've seen exactly how that gift is given to us. It comes in the form of a new commandment: love one another as he has loved us.

Thus the next step of the prayer: "that they may be one even as we are one." He has given us the commandment of love so that we might become God-like, which means firmly united in love, as he is united with the Father. He goes on to pray, "I in them and thou in me," reinforcing the at-one unity that God's love brings to the world, and then continues, "that they may become perfectly one, so that the world may know that thou hast sent me and hast loved them even as thou hast loved me" (17:23). In effect, Jesus is praying that we might participate in the love that makes the Holy Trinity eternally One (17:24). Of course, in this life we are never perfectly one—neither perfectly at-one with God in Christ, nor with each other in the Gospel. However, insofar as we are at-one—united with God in Christ and with each other—we participate in the Triune life of God, and in so doing we abide in and enjoy a foretaste love's triumph in the last days.

In this effort to read John 17 I have deliberately equated unity with at-one-ment. In so doing I have conjured a connection between the ecumenical goal of Christian unity with the doctrine of the atonement, which I think justified. As I hope this exercise in theological exegesis has made clear, in the Gospel of John our union with God is intimately connected to our unity in Christ. The doctrine of the atonement is the theological locus where we analyze how that we are taken over the great chasm of sin to enter into union with God. Therefore, with the guidance of our Lord's own words in John 17, I'm quite sure we could mine that the traditions of atonement theology that are so richly developed in the West for powerful insights into just how we might overcome the chasms that continue to separate our churches. I am reinforced in this conviction by the fact that St. Paul *does* make the connection between classical themes of atonement theology and unity in Christ (Eph 2:11–22). I fear I have not said anything very clear about that connection, at least not in the usual way in which our theologies conceive of atonement as a discrete doctrine. I encourage those more learned than I am to formulate a theology of Christian unity that does so.

Response to Dr. Reno
Richard Mouw (Evangelical)

In his insightful discussion of John 17, Rusty Reno rightly encourages us not to move too quickly to discussions of unity among Christians without first of all attending to the unity—the "at-one-ment"—within the Godhead. And in doing so he reminds us of some excellent explorations along these lines that took place among medieval commentators on this passage. Then, after drawing out some of those lessons from the medievals, he gives us some excellent thoughts of his own about the relationship between intra-Trinitarian unity and unity within the Body of Christ. And then he concludes by expressing the hope that "those more learned" than himself will work at "a theology of Christian unity" that looks more deeply into the connection to the doctrine of the atonement.

I am not the one to take up that important assignment. If Rusty lacks the necessary learning to move that discussion forward—something that I doubt—he has at the very least demonstrated in the wisdom that he has offered us that he is much closer to the "more learned" on the subject than I am. Not only, for example, have I not read the medieval commentators to whom he refers, but I would have a hard time finding them without Rusty's help. Nor, speaking with much candor, am I likely to ask for that help. I certainly would like a deeper grasp of the important matters he has discussed in his paper. But, like Rusty, I will hope for others to take up the task. And in my case I will hope specifically for evangelicals to follow through on these all-important concerns.

An official from the World Council of Churches once visited my presidential office at Fuller Seminary. He had been attending meetings on our Pasadena campus for a couple of days, and he dropped by to tell me how impressed he had been with the quality of the theological discussion. "I only wish," he said, "that you folks would try to be more ecumenical!"

I responded to his comment by pointing out that our student body represented over one hundred denominations, as well as large churches that claimed no denominational identity, and that these students came from over seventy nations. What more would we need to be and do," I asked him, to become more ecumenical?

My visitor found some way to change the topic, but I was sure that his honest answer would have been that we, as evangelicals, should be more active in the "conciliar" manifestations of ecumenism. And while that would have been an expression of a rather narrow understanding of ecumenism, there was a point implicit in his comment that is important to make explicit.

Evangelicals are in fact very ecumenical, if we understand the term to refer to the forming of energetic patterns of interdenominational cooperation. The Council of Christian Colleges and Universities is in fact an impressively ecumenical association, as have been the broadly sponsored evangelistic efforts of the Billy Graham Association—to say nothing of the large "Lausanne" gatherings of global evangelicals.

Again, evangelicals have formed cooperative arrangements that surely deserve to be called "ecumenical." But while these arrangements have been manifestations of Christian unity, they have not fostered much talk about the theology of Christian unity. It is not insignificant that when the National Association of Evangelicals was formed in 1942, after several decades dominated by a separatistic spirit in the fundamentalist world, the newly formed association named its magazine *United Evangelical Action*—where the need for united "action" grew out of, for example, the very practical concern in that war era for working together in sponsoring military chaplains.

This is not to say that no attention has been paid to the theology of Christian unity. In my own spiritual journey, I discovered the topic as a matter of theological interest in my college undergraduate years, especially as an avid reader of *Christianity Today*. I read the first issue as a high school student when it arrived at our home—my father was a pastor, and the magazine was sent free to a large number of evangelical clergy. *Christianity Today* began with a strong emphasis on the need for a new evangelical theological engagement; the theologians who wrote in its pages included, among others, Anglicans, Lutherans, Dutch Calvinists, Presbyterians, dispensationalists and Wesleyans. In its own way, this was an important ecumenical endeavor and it was inevitable that the magazine would address the challenges posed by the conciliar ecumenical movement.

Stimulated by what I was reading in *Christianity Today*, I chose to write a paper for one of my college religion courses on the subject of ecumenism. I long ago lost the paper, but I clearly remember relying heavily on a lengthy treatment of the subject in book by Marcellus Kik, *Ecumenism and the Evangelical*, published in 1958. Kik was a Reformed pastor-theologian who had begun his seminary studies at Princeton, but then transferred to Westminister Theological Seminary when J. Gresham Machen left the Princeton faculty in 1929 to establish the new school in Philadelphia.

Kik's arguments against an inclusive structural unity made good sense to me at the time, and indeed they have had a lasting influence on my thinking on the subject. When I re-read his book several years ago, I was surprised how well I have remembered over the years the actual formulation of his key argument, which focused on both the organizational efficiency and missional effectiveness of small denominations. Here he is on the subject:

> Often the smaller denominations evidence greater activity in casting out devils prevalent in the world, than do the larger denominations. In Christian work quality counts far more than quantity.
>
> For more effective organization and efficiency the Lord divided the small nation of Israel into 12 tribes, each having its own government. But did they not have one king who molded them into an organized kingdom? Yes, but that desire to have a visible king was against the will of God and finally caused division into two kingdoms. The Israelites rebelled against the theocratical government and wanted a visible head. One wonders how much of the nature of the ancient Israelite is in the ecumenical movement with its passion for a visible central government.[1]

Kik accompanies this argument, however, with an equally strong acknowledgement that there is indeed a biblical mandate for working toward Christian unity. On this matter he gives considerable attention to Christ's high priestly prayer in John 17. It cannot be denied, he argues, that the Savior is praying for some sort of visible manifestation of unity:

> Without a visible oneness how could the burden of the petition be effected, "that the world may believe that thou hast sent me"? The world cannot behold the invisible. Surely the world would be more inclined to believe the divine mission of Christ if unity among professing Christians were perceptible.[2]

---

1. Kik, *Ecumenism and the Evangelical*, 23.
2. Ibid., 42.

Kik then goes on to argue at length that true unity must mirror, in accordance with Christ's prayer, the unity between the Father and the Son, which is a unity, he says, of doctrine, of purpose, and of love.[3] Unless these conditions are met, we will only have a false unity.

While Rusty Reno does not use exactly the same language as Marcellus Kik, his helpful observations about the John 17 prayer comport well with Kik's three conditions. We might say, taking Rusty's "atonement" motif seriously, that any Christian unity that we presently display, if it is to be God-honoring, must be grounded in a proper theological understanding of Christ's atoning mission; it must be guided by a commitment to the atoning purposes of the Triune God's redemptive purposes; and it must be expressive of the atoning love that took the Savior to Calvary.

Like Rusty, I am convinced that we ought to work for more visible manifestations of this unity. But also—and I am confident Rusty agrees with me on this—the "visible unity" schemes that have often been set forth in the mainline ecumenical movement are deficient precisely because they fail to acknowledge the kind of "atonement" grounding that Rusty sees as essential to understanding the John 17 prayer.

The three traditions represented at this conference—Catholic, Orthodox, and Evangelical Protestantism—have typically resisted the kinds of "visible unity" schemes that have often been set forth in the mainline ecumenical movement. And my informed guess is that those of us representing those traditions here in this present discussion would locate the deficiencies of those schemes precisely in their failure to acknowledge the "atonement" grounding that Rusty has rightly pointed to as essential to understanding the John 17 prayer.

Let me say that our agreement on that important concern is itself a sign of the unity that Christ prayed for. Just the fact that we are here is an acknowledgement that there are important matters that we must discuss together. It is also a fact, however, that our own differences—about authority, ecclesial structures, the sacraments, and the like—pose serious obstacles to agreeing together about anything beyond our shared dissatisfaction with what has often been trumpeted in the calls for Christian unity coming from "conciliar" circles.

What can we do about these issues—our desire to work for unity in a context in which our own differences loom so large? I will offer a few recommendations here about some steps we can take.

For starters, it is an important step in the right direction simply to *want* to do something about it. In this regard I offer an account of a profound

---

3. Ibid., 42–44.

experience dealing with unity matters that began for me during one summer in the late 1970s at the Institute for Ecumenical and Cultural Research in Collegeville, Minnesota. I was on the faculty at Calvin College at the time and had represented the Christian Reformed denomination for five years on the Faith and Order Commission of the National Council of Churches, as one of the representatives of non-member denominations. I had approached that involvement with some cynicism, and my experience on the Commission did not completely cure me of that attitude. So it was with some trepidation that I journeyed to Collegeville for a weeklong discussion of "The Meaning of Ecumenism."

I was pleasantly surprised by the tone of the Collegeville discussion, but I also experienced some initial discomfort. Two people in particular frustrated me. One was a very serious Catholic theologian who regularly expressed her amazement—even her shock—at some of my theological formulations. The other was a Russian Orthodox layman, later to become a priest, who seemed to be coming from a totally different religious universe than the one that I inhabited. I can still remember feeling eager to get back to Grand Rapids where I could tell my fellow Dutch Calvinists about all of the strange things I had heard from these two individuals.

A funny thing happened to me over the next several months, however. From time to time, one of my fellow Calvinists—a faculty colleague, or a preacher—would refer to something related to either Catholicism or Orthodoxy that I knew was not a fair representation of the views I had heard from these two individuals in Collegeville. When I agreed to return to the Institute the next summer for another round of discussions, it was with a new kind of eagerness: I could not wait to tell my two new-found friends about the misinformed things I had heard some Grand Rapids people say about their two traditions. Those two Collegeville participants, Margaret O'Gara and Anthony Ugolnik, were to become close Christian friends from whom I have learned much. Over the years I have been able to build on this and other Collegeville experiences, engaging very freely and extensively in both intra-Christian and inter-religious dialogues.

This account that I have given of my ecumenical formation displays some key evangelical themes. For one thing, I have represented it as a kind of "conversion" experience, which is a favorite evangelical motif. But I also linked the emergence of my ecumenical consciousness to very personal encounters. What this means, I suggest, is that the presence of *desire* is of the utmost importance. We may not know exactly where our conversations will lead us, but we have to *want* to keep at it.

A second step, closely related, is to acknowledge the tensions between our desire for unity and the obstacles presented by our respective theologies. An excellent case in point for this kind of acknowledgment can be seen in remarks made by the Orthodox theologian Peter Bouteneff in a World Council of Churches exchange he had with Anna Marie Aagaard, a Lutheran theologian.[4] Boutenoff observed that while ecumenical declarations about the nature of the church typically give the impression that their formulations are neutral, they actually exclude the basic convictions embodied in Orthodox ecclesiology. The drafters of these declarations seem to have no difficulty, said Bouteneff, affirming the existence of a variety of genuine Christian churches, each of them possessing—to one degree or another—legitimacy as an ecclesial entity.

That widely shared perspective, Bouteneff argued, does not sit well with the Orthodox. Orthodoxy unapologetically "identifies *itself* with the one, holy, catholic and apostolic Church." On this self-understanding there cannot really be any divisions *within* the true church—all other groups claiming churchly identity in fact exist in separation from the one true church. The very notion, then, of a council of diverse "churches" is problematic from an Orthodox perspective, according to which Christian unity can only occur when all of these separated individuals and groups to return to the Orthodox fold.[5]

In her response to Bouteneff, Aagaard, the Lutheran theologian, complained about Orthodoxy's inability to give any precise account of the positive ecclesial status of Christian groups outside of Orthodoxy. But she also found some glimmers of hope on the subject in several of Bouteneff's comments, especially in his insistence that Orthodoxy has to find a "space" in its ecclesiology for those non-Orthodox who, while not belonging to churches, properly understood, still obviously "share in the life of Christ."[6]

Bouteneff responded to her challenges by acknowledging that there is more work to be done in developing an Orthodox ecclesiology that takes ecumenical realities into account, while at the same time continuing to insist that "we Orthodox . . . are clear and unapologetic about the content of our theology." For the Orthodox to engage in dialogue on these matters, he said, it will require that others "stop being surprised and offended" every time the Orthodox state their understanding of the church.[7]

The tension in Bouteneff's case for Orthodoxy is evident in his strong affirmation of the "one true church" perspective while also acknowledging

---

4. Aagaard and Bouteneff, *Beyond the East-West Divide*.
5. Ibid., 35.
6. Ibid., 108.
7. Ibid., 116.

the need to search for ecclesiological "space" for others who, in his straightforward affirmation, "share in the life of Christ."

We can find the same kind of tension in my own Reformed tradition—very clearly in fact in John Calvin himself. Calvin certainly made no secret of his verdict that the Roman Catholic authorities had done much to destroy the proper patterns of the church's life and mission. Nonetheless, the Genevan Reformer confessed that he could not bring himself to "deprive the papists of those traces of the church which the Lord willed should among them survive the destruction." Thus "the Lord wonderfully preserves" within the Catholic church, he argues, "a remnant of his people, however woefully dispersed and scattered." This remnant preserves "those marks whose effectiveness neither the devil's wiles nor human depravity can destroy." But these marks are not enough to grant legitimate churchly status to the Roman church as such. Since some of the most important marks of proper church-ness "have been erased" in that body, Calvin is forced to conclude "that every one of their congregations and their whole body lack the lawful form of the church."[8]

Calvin is also acknowledging the tension. On the one hand he wants to draw some clear boundaries between churches that remain faithful to the Gospel and those that are Christian churches only in name. But he is not prepared simply to write off all members of the latter category as infidels. So he is left with a distinction not unlike the one drawn by Bouteneff: there are Christians who belong to that body which is properly thought of as being *church*, and there are others who, while belonging to entities that lack legitimate ecclesial status, must nonetheless be viewed as a preserved "remnant" (Calvin) who still "share in the life of Christ" (Bouteneff).

The Catholic Church's Second Vatican Council also recognized the tension, addressing the issues directly in its 1964 Decree on Ecumenism: *Unitatis Redintegratio*. The various "separated Churches and Communities," the bishops declared, are "deficient in some respects," since "it is only through Christ's Catholic Church, which is 'the all-embracing means of salvation,' that they can benefit fully from the means of salvation." Yet these "separated" communities "have been by no means deprived of significance and importance in the mystery of salvation. For the Spirit of Christ has not refrained from using them as means of salvation which derive their efficacy from the very fullness of grace and truth entrusted to the Church."[9]

---

8. Calvin, *Institutes of the Christian Religion*, 2.4.11 and 12 (1051–52).

9 See more online: http://www.vatican.va/archive/hist_councils/ii_vatican_council/documents/vat-ii_decree_19641121_unitatis-redintegratio_en.html.

A third step requires that we not be content simply to live with our respective tensions, but to do the ecclesiological work necessary, if not to eliminate them, at least to reduce them. Our mutual recognition of the reality of those in other communities who "share in the life of Christ" makes more work on the subject a mandate.

For the three traditions represented here, this certainly means that the Bouteneff request is profoundly important. We must agree to "stop being surprised and offended" when we each state our ecclesiological starting points.

This work must be in good part dialogical. And dialogue can be especially difficult when the convictions in play are both strongly held and not popular in the surrounding culture.

I mentioned earlier that I spent five years as a member of the National Council of Churches' Faith and Order Commission, representing the Christian Reformed Church, which was itself not a denominational member of the Council. At one session, I took a seat next to a good friend, Father Robert Stephanopoulos, at the time the Dean of the Greek Orthodox Cathedral in Cleveland. As I looked down the row, I noticed that each of us in that row represented non-member ecclesial communities: Christian Reformed, Greek Orthodox, Missouri Synod Lutheran, and Roman Catholic. I whispered to Bob, "Look at this row of people. We could leave and have our own discussion about Christian unity." He responded: "Maybe we should. It would be a more heated discussion. But at least we would be dealing with the right question: What does it mean to represent communions where it makes good sense to talk about being 'the one true Church'?"

A "heated discussion" indeed. But an important one. But a conversation that could be productive if we genuinely accepted each other as dialogue partners with whom we would not act—to use Bouteneff's formulation again—"surprised and offended" by our strong theological claims.

Once again, the personal dimension of trust is crucial for doing the necessary dialogue work. My Collegeville experience forced me to stick with a conversation with folks—Catholics and Orthodox—whom evangelicals have typically not seriously engaged in theological discussion. Our evangelical selectivity of conversation partners allows us to maintain our caricatures and stereotypes. By resisting engagement with others in more inclusive settings for dialogue, we miss out on opportunities for better understanding of other Christians—and even worse, we promote the conditions in which we continually commit the sin of bearing false witness against our Christian neighbors. What my Collegeville experience also exemplifies, of course, is that more intimate face-to-face sustained discussions accomplish more in correcting these sinful tendencies than do large "official" discussions among church leaders. A healthier quest for Christian unity will foster this more sustained face-to-face mode of exchange.

I turn now to specific concern that I believe must be named on behalf of evangelicals in pursuing the kind of dialogue—actually trialogue—we are fostering at this conference. Truth be told, we are at a serious disadvantage when discussing ecclesiological topics with our Catholic and Orthodox friends. The Anglican evangelical Alister McGrath has observed that evangelicalism's critics often accuse us of "having an 'under-developed ecclesiology.'" To which he responds: "[P]erhaps it might be suggested that it is others who have over-developed ecclesiologies?"[10]

McGrath's point is an important one to put on the table here. Many evangelicals approach ecclesiological discussions with clear memories of harsh voices from our collective past—and for those of us in mainline denominations, in our collective present!—that seeks to silence our pleas for renewal by calling us to "respect the structures," "follow due process," and "submit to the Body." If we evangelicals are suspicious of "strong" ecclesiologies, then, it is due at least in part to our experiences at the hands of those who have used ecclesiology as an instrument of control.

But none of this excuses inattention to ecclesiological topics in interaction with Catholicism and Orthodoxy. In reviewing Marcellus Kik's 1958 book for this occasion, I wished that I could quiz him about what he had in mind when he talked about the need for "visible unity." Given his argument about organizational efficiency, he clearly was not thinking of the disappearance of a plurality of denominational structures. Nor does he seem to operate with a very expansive view about who should be included in a quest for visible unity. He certainly shows no interest in finding common ground with liberal Protestants, Roman Catholics, or Orthodoxy. My educated guess is that he had in mind something like active cooperation and dialogue among denominational groups who agreed—with reference to criteria that relied heavily on the formulations of Calvinist orthodoxy—on the basic requirements regarding the three factors that he explicates on the basis of John 17: doctrine, purpose, and love.

As Christians who claim to take the Bible as our supreme auhtority for faith and practice, we evangelicals would be hard put, given the fact that Christ's prayer "that they all be one" is in the Bible, to deny the importance of unity as such. Nor can we easily make the case that the unity that we are called to has to remain highly "invisible" until the eschaton.

---

10. McGrath, "Evangelical Anglicanism," 14.

We evangelicals need more attention to "visible" unity. This can happen best if we are honest about the historical exprences that have given rise to evangelical nervousness about structural unity, and to think clearly about what kinds of visible structures we ought to be searching for. There are structures and there are structures. Evangelicals have certainly been skilled at forming trans-denominational networks and affiliations. Rather than rejecting the call for structural unity as such, then, evangelicals would do well to think about how a consideration of their own experiments in reaching across denominational and other organizational boundaries might make a contribution to a new stage of ecumenical dialogue concerning the visible unity of the Body of Jesus Christ I have been referring here to "steps" that we can take in pursuing together the unity mandated by the John 17 prayer. The image here is intentional and important. We evangelicals like to talk about our "stands" on this or that subject. Standing, of course, does not allow for much forward motion. To be sure, there are times when we need to pause and see what we are standing upon. But those are pausings—and not meant to be permanent postures.

"Steps" are also important. Motion is essential to our earthly pilgrimages, and stepping together is what we need right now in our three communities. To walk side by side is to treat each other as companions on a journey. And as we walk, it is crucial to talk together about the destination at which we long finally to arrive. In such a traveling-together conversation is to urgent to seek the guidance of the Spirit about how we might find new ways of configuring—yes, even "structuring"—the patterns of our shared pilgrimage.

Perichoretic Ecumenism Inspired by John 17
A Response to Prof. R. R. Reno

PAUL GAVRILYUK (ORTHODOX)

IN HIS PRESENTATION PROFESSOR Reno has offered many insightful points that considerably enrich biblically inspired reflection on the problem of Christian disunity and the path to unity. In my response I will highlight two of Reno's points and develop them in a manner congenial to my tradition. I will close by offering brief remarks on what one could call a perichoretic model of ecumenism inspired by John 17.

As Professor Reno noted in the beginning of his talk, in contrast to the twentieth-century readings of John 17 in light of ecumenical concerns, the pre-modern interpretations of this text explored its Trinitarian and soteriological implications. According to John 17:21, the foundation of church unity is nothing less than the unity enjoyed by the persons of the Trinity: the Father is in the Son and the Son is in the Father. In the language of later patristic theology, the persons of the Trinity enjoy a perichoresis, which, on one reading at least, is a relationship of mutual indwelling or interpenetration. One is at a loss to find a suitable spatial analogy for such a relationship, unless one is prepared to do rather intricate work on the metaphysics of relative identity (something that I will spare you for the time being). Perhaps a more accessible analogy is suggested by the genre of John 17, which is a prayer. When two people, Peter and Paul, pray for each other, it could be said that Peter is in Paul's mind and Paul is in Peter's mind, they are in each other's prayers, as their prayers are lifted up to God. To be sure, this is only an analogy, since it is only a mental image of Peter, not the flesh-and-blood Peter that, properly speaking, is in Paul's mind, and it is only a mental image of Paul, not the flesh-and-blood Paul that, properly speaking, is in Peter's mind. In contrast, the Son of God is entirely in the divine Father and the Father is entirely in the Son. Besides, the union of Peter's and Paul's wills is far from the perfect oneness of will enjoyed by the Father, Son and Holy Spirit. For these and other reasons, I am personally not inclined to stake as much on the so-called social model of the Trinity as some contemporary theologians tend to do. Any union of human thoughts, prayers, souls, or minds always falls short of the perfect love that unites the three persons of the Trinity.

While the unity of the three persons of the Trinity is enjoyed by them alone and is not humanly attainable, the divine Incarnation uniquely bridges the infinite ontological gap that exists between the Trinity and humankind. In the Incarnation, the Son of God assumes human nature and redeems it by making it his own. The hypostatic union of the two natures in Christ is different in kind from the union of the three divine persons in the Trinity. The Trinitarian union involves three ontologically equal entities, the divine persons, sharing one essence and one will. The hypostatic union is a bridge between God and humanity, as it involves two ontologically distinct natures and two ontologically distinct natural wills, divine and human. The hypostatic union is the foundation of human salvation and of the church, which is a divine-human institution, the body of Christ. Through the church each believer has communion with Christ and through Christ with the triune God. Although no creature can attain the union enjoyed by the persons of the Trinity by nature, the believers enjoy the benefits of this union by participation in the body of Christ, to the extent to which this is humanly possible. I submit, therefore, that any consideration of the "horizontal" unity between Christian communions—the consideration that dominates ecumenical discussions—must be firmly grounded in the "vertical" aspect of the union, which connects these communities with Christ and through Christ and the Holy Spirit with the life of the triune God. Ecumenical theology needs a biblically grounded ontology of participation, according to which the believers sacramentally participate in the mystery of Christ's Incarnation, and through the Incarnation have access to the unity shared by the persons of the Trinity.

Professor Reno also points out that Christ's "farewell discourse," including the intercessory prayer of John 17, is punctuated by a tension between Christ's drawing near to his disciples and his going away. Christ bids his disciples to be close to each other precisely at the time when he announces that he is going to leave them. Here Professor Reno insightfully comments that the disciples cannot follow Jesus to Golgotha because the cross marks a point of the Son's utter self-giving for the sake of humanity and for the sake of love, something that sinful humanity, locked as it is in self-love, is incapable of doing. Reno beautifully connects Jesus's going away with the extent of Christ's self-sacrifice, rather than with his spatial separation from his disciples in the Ascension. Christ grows distant from his disciples in order to pour out God's love for humanity from the cross, by his death and resurrection completing the work of humanity's at-onement with God. In the words of John 15:13, "Greater love has no one than this, than to lay down one's life for his friends." In a fine paradox, precisely by going away Christ grows even closer to his disciples in love. The cross measures the extent of human rebellion against God and at the same time manifests the immensity of God's self-giving love. According to John 16:7, Christ's departure is the condition of the sending of the Comforter, who continues to guide the church until Christ's return. In and through the Holy Spirit, the Word of God makes himself present in the sacramental life of the church, in her prayers, and in her missionary work for the salvation of the world. Christ's departure provides a way of drawing his followers, through the work of the Holy Spirit, into the life of the triune God.

At the same time, Christ's departure from his apostles acutely posed the problem of leadership and of the unity of his disciples as well as the early Christian communities founded by them. Christ is and will forever remain the head of the church, but after his departure his presence in the church takes a form different from that of his earthly ministry. How precisely is Christ's authority mediated in the church after his Ascension?

Orthodox, Catholics, and Evangelicals agree that the structures of authority in the church must be the vehicles of Christ's continuing Lordship over the church and must ensure the continuity of the faith. We disagree on the specific forms that the structures of authority must take and we typically use arguments from scripture and tradition to cement our disagreements. To rehearse these arguments would be to open Pandora's box. If I were to argue from Scripture alone, then the Congregationalist structure defended by the Evangelicals and the episcopal and conciliar structure defended by the Orthodox appear to me to be more plausible historically and exegetically than the papal structure defended by the Catholics (that's not to say that there is no plausible argument for a papal authority of sorts; but such argument can rest on scripture only when some of its Petrine passages are applied to considerably different authority structures). But I have no intention of arguing from Scripture alone. In fact, the principle of *sola scriptura*, quite contrary to the intention of those who had originally proposed it, has been a major, if not the greatest source of disunity among Christians since the time of the Reformation.

Equally, I have very little stake in engaging in confessional apologetics in defense of the episcopal structure that resembles that of the Orthodox Church. The tragic fact of our present situation is that there is an acute crisis of the episcopal leadership in the Orthodox Church. In the western world, this crisis manifests itself in the number of bishops who have "retired" or even been deposed, because they were unfit to serve. In the Orthodox Church of America alone, we have just gone through a period when two consecutive primates of our church were forced to resign amidst accusations of moral and canonical character. In the historically Orthodox lands, such as Greece, Russia, and Ukraine, we see the leaders that succumb to the nationalist passions divide the church by their petty quarrels or fail to act when the circumstances demand their action. I have just returned from Ukraine, where numerous priests of the largest Orthodox body—the Ukrainian Orthodox Church, Moscow Patriarchate—have stopped commemorating the head of their church, patriarch Kiril, during the liturgy, as an expression of their distrust in his leadership, especially his handling of Russia's invasion of their country. In Ukraine and elsewhere the public discourse about the structure of church authority is strongly politicized and often obfuscates the message of Christ instead of proclaiming this message to the world.

A perpetual optimist might reasonably object that despite their rhetorical power, these considerations are merely arguments from abuse. The principle of *sola scriptura* leads to disunity only when it is *mis*applied; however, the principle of *sola scriptura* ensures the unity of the church, when it is properly applied. Similarly, it is the dysfunctional episcopal leadership that causes divisions and scandals. However, the episcopal authority properly exercised is the surest guarantor of the continuity of the faith and the unity of the church. Throughout the centuries, there have been sinners and criminals among the bishops, just as there have been martyrs and saints. In this respect the bishops are simply no different from the rest of the faithful (and why should they be expected to be different?). Despite the seriousness of the present troubles, we should not lose heart. The episcopal structure may be imperfect, but it is the best assurance of continuity of the Christian tradition that we have available this side of the eschaton.

While I concede the force of the perpetual optimist's objection, I nevertheless fear that the problems that I have mentioned are so deeply entrenched in the lives of our respective communions that *in practice* it is very difficult to separate an authoritative vehicle that is meant to serve church unity from its concrete historical manifestations. For this reason, I suggest that future forms of ecumenism should engage in binding each other's wounds, rather than looking for specks in each other's eyes. The spirit of ecumenical generosity, in my interpretation at least, has nothing to do with doctrinal apathy or compromises vis-à-vis the moral aspirations of our age. Rather, the spirit of ecumenical generosity includes an acceptance that the charisms that we find better exercised in other Christian communions, if recovered, could revitalize and heal our internal wounds. Thus, the perfect sharing of being and love that exists among the persons of the Trinity and to which we have access through the Incarnation and the sacrifice of the Son of God, could serve as an ideal type of sharing that could be encouraged among different Christian communions. Such a perichoretic model of ecumenism, understood as an exchange of gifts, would differ dramatically from the more traditional models of ecumenical engagement, which normally range from outright confrontation to diplomatic avoidance of the hard issues that continue to separate us. The perichoretic model would emphasize mutual enrichment without ignoring the differences and would recognize that such enrichment can happen precisely because Christian communions continue to differ considerably. Much of such sharing is already happening on a theological level in our academic institutions and in our private scholarly engagements with the theological ideas of each other. Our own scholarly assembly serves as a good example of such an exchange. Perichoretic ecumenism could also happen in the sphere of Christian evangelism, mission and catechumenate. Still more could happen as we face together the challenges of contemporary world.

Reno Final Response

PAUL GAVRILYUK COMMENDS TO us a spirit of ecumenical generosity. We're to bind each other wounds rather than pointing out the theological and ecclesiological defects of our ecumenical partners. He exemplifies that generosity, overlooking the flaws in my essay and drawing attention to the core teaching of John 17.

Paul is surely right that *perichoresis*, participation, must serve as the crucial concept for an ecumenical theology based on John 17. The "in" or "abide" language, which is so prominent throughout the Gospel of John, plays a central role. The Father is *in* Jesus. His disciples believe *in* him, and thus they too are *in* the Father. This is not a static *in*. The language of giving and sending mobilizes the indwelling. Jesus has been sent to give us the Father's word. The Father has given us to Jesus to be sent in to the world to bear witness to his truth. It is no wonder that the Church Father's read these verses in order to enter into the mystery of the Trinity, a union of giving and sending!

As I understand Paul, the ecumenical generosity he commends is not based in a general spirit of kindness, nor even the Christian virtue of charity, generally applied. Instead, he grounds it in the participatory character of faith. We are given to and sent by Jesus. We are at once drawing near to him and are on our way to do his will, a sending that includes binding the wounds of our brothers in Christ, no matter how far they have wandered from what we regard as the Christian true home, the one, catholic, and apostolic Church.

I find this a compelling vision. It allows for a plastic intransigence, if you will. What I mean by that is honesty about our ecclesiological convictions. After Vatican II, many were hopeful that a synthesis or consensus about church dividing doctrines might be achieved. This has proven elusive. We feel quite strongly (and with intellectual conviction) that we abide must fully in Christ at the center of our traditions, and we won't forsake the doctrines so central to our traditions. And yet, this intransigence is consistent with going forth, being sent, not to correct our brothers at the peripheries, but to build them up and strengthen their traditions so that they too might come to us in our failures and strengthen our traditions. This is a beautiful view of ecumenical relations. It does not hold out the false hope of convergence based on doctrinal harmonization. Instead, it proposes serious theological engagement for the sake of a mutual service of Orthodox, Catholics, and Evangelicals to each other.

I'm very grateful for Richard Mouw's thoughtful response to my theological reading of John 17. A great deal resonates with my own thinking about ecumenism, and I appreciate the generous spirit Rich also brings to this ecumenical discussion.

"Over-developed ecclesiologies." Rich draws this arresting notion from Alister McGrath's impatient riposte to the standard Catholic and magisterial Protestant criticisms of evangelical, low-church ecclesiologies. Rich goes on to offer some evangelical self-criticism, reminding his brethren that attention must be paid to the need for "visible unity." How can the world see that the Father and the Son are one if they can't *see* Christian as one?

In the same Matthew 7 spirit, I want to point out that there's something to McGrath's remark, and Catholics like me neglect it at our peril. Catholicism enjoys a remarkable hierarchical unity, centered on the Vatican and the bishop of Rome. We also have an (almost) universal liturgy. Although the Mass is no longer in Latin throughout the world, even when I'm in countries where I don't know the language, I am at home in the worship service. The Catholic Mass has a set shape and rhythm. You know where you are even when you don't know the words.

That said, I'm more and more convinced evangelicals *experience* the unity of the church more frequently and profoundly. Their missionary commitments provide an obvious example. Many evangelicals *live* with their faraway brothers in faith, and those who stay at home are often very involved, providing support in prayer and donations. Evangelical leaders are also more likely to have face-to-face international contacts. And as Rich points out, evangelical seminaries such as Fuller are hubs with many spokes. Catholicism's institutional bulk allows us to take our unity for granted. Evangelicals have to work at it, and in my experience they are constantly expanding and renewing their networks of informal unity, sometimes for the sake of common mission, sometimes in order to hammer out the theological consensus necessary for a deeper union in Spirit and truth.

I'm not in favor of "under-developed ecclesiologies." As does Rich, I believe we need "visible unity," which requires theological commitments about the visible church. Moreover, the regime that St. Paul calls "the world" coaxes, seduces, threatens, and punishes us. If we are to dwell more fully in Christ, we need to be surrounded by a sacred counter-regime, which is the church. This need not require Catholic ecclesiologies, or Orthodox ones. But if we really believe that the Gospel gives us a place to stand against the world, then we all need to work on *developing* our ecclesiologies. I encourage evangelicals to do exactly that, perhaps most urgently in an institutional direction. And I encourage my Catholic brethren to do so as well, perhaps most importantly in a relational direction.

The reality of unity among evangelicals, a reality often underdeveloped conceptually in evangelical theologies of our common life in Christ, even as it is lived out in practice, points toward another important point Rich makes. He observes that there's a tension between our desire for unity and the obstacles presented by the divergent theological convictions we hold dear. He's surely right about that tension. We all feel it.

He reflects on this tension, discussing ways in which different traditions moderate it as best they can. Calvin has a way of recognizing the Christian reality of Catholicism, even as he denied its claims. Rich recounts Peter Bouteneff's observations about the need to find "space" in Orthodox ecclesiology for the non-Orthodox. And he points out the novel formulations of Vatican II that create "space" for non-Catholics.

The desire to find "space" for the Christian Other has become very powerful over the last two generations. It no longer seems possible to sustain our "one true Church" affirmations without, somehow, accounting for the fact that we see Christ in those whom our ecclesiologies teach us cannot abide in him, because they do not abide in the one true church. What I have called Paul Gavrilyuk's "plastic intransigence," underwritten by a Trinitarian theology of participation, reflects yet another way of dealing with this tension.

As I thought about this tension between desired unity and obstacles to it, I found myself formulating it differently. It is not so much a tension as a conundrum. Evangelicals, Catholics, and Orthodox have engaged each other more deeply over the last two or more generations. As Rich notes, this face-to-face encounter, often growing into cherished friendships, allows us to see something we share—the most important thing we share—which is faith in Christ. And so we are perplexed. How is that disunity does not destroy unity?

Let me rephrase the conundrum: How is it that, even as we fail to abide with each other (to be at-one with each other, if you'll permit me to return to the idiosyncratic ecumenical theology of my essay), we continue to abide in Christ, so much so that in an imperfect but real way we *do* abide with each other? The answer, I think, is in John 17, and it's the essence of the Gospel: The love by which the Son abides in the Father, and the Father in him, is stronger than the spirit of division, just as it is stronger than sin and death.

In my paper I spoke of this surprising discovery that we are at-one with each other in spite of our disunity as "found unity." Rich's reflections have helped me see the issue more clearly. There's a grief and joy in ecumenism: a grief over our division and joy over our "found unity." Both should be cultivated.

Chapter 5

John 18:28—19:16
Witnessing Truth

Fr. John Behr (Orthodox)

Isaiah 41:21–24

> ²¹Your judgment draws near, says the Lord God
>   your counsels have drawn near, says the King of Jacob.
> ²²Let them draw near and declare to you the things that will happen
>   or speak of the former things, what they were,
>   and we will apply our mind
>   and know what the last things will be—
>   and tell us the things that are coming.
> ²³Declare the things that are coming at the end,
>   and we will know that you are gods;
>   (ἀναγγείλατε τὰ ἐπερχόμενα ἐπ' ἐσχάτου καὶ γνωσόμεθα ὅτι θεοί ἐστε)
>   do good and do harm,
>   and we will wonder as well as see.
> ²⁴For whence are you,
>   and whence is your works?[1]
>   (ὅτι πόθεν ἐστὲ ὑμεῖς καὶ πόθεν ἡ ἐργασία ὑμῶν;)

---

1. Isa, LXX.

Isaiah 46:8–11

⁸Remember these things and groan,
  repent, you who have gone astray,
  turn in your heart,
⁹and remember the former things of old,
  because I am God, and there is no other beside me,
¹⁰declaring the last things first, before they happen,
  and at once they came to pass,
and I said, "My whole plan shall stand,
  and I will do all the things I have planned,
  (ἀναγγέλλων πρότερον τὰ ἔσχατα πρὶν αὐτὰ γενέσθαι, καὶ ἅμα συνετελέσθη· καὶ εἶπα Πᾶσά μου ἡ βουλὴ στήσεται, καὶ πάντα, ὅσα βεβούλευμαι, ποιήσω)
¹¹calling a bird from the east,
  and from a far country those concerning whom I have planned,
I have spoken and brought it;
  I have created and made it."[2]
  (ἐλάλησα καὶ ἤγαγον, ἔκτισα καὶ ἐποίησα)

Isaiah 44:6–8

⁶Thus says God, the King of Israel,
  who delivered him, God Sabbaoth;
I am first, and I am after these things;
  besides me there is no god.
⁷Who is like me? Let him stand; let him call,
  and let him make ready for me,
  inasmuch as I have made the human being for ever,
  (ἀφ᾿ οὗ ἐποίησα ἄνθρωπον εἰς τὸν αἰῶνα)
and let them declare to you,
  the thing that are coming
  before they come.
  (καὶ τὰ ἐπερχόμενα πρὸ τοῦ ἐλθεῖν ἀναγγειλάτωσαν ὑμῖν.)
⁸Do not cover yourselves,
  did you not give ear from the beginning,
  and I declared it to you?
You are witnesses (μάρτυρες ὑμεῖς ἐστε),
  whether there is a god besides me,
  and they were not formerly.[3]

---

2. Isa, LXX.
3. Isa, LXX.

Isaiah 43:10–13

> ¹⁰Be my witnesses;
>> I too am a witness, says the Lord God,
>> and the servant whom I have chosen,
> so that you may know and believe,
>> and understand that I am.
> (γένεσθέ μοι μάρτυρες, κἀγὼ μάρτυς, λέγει κύριος ὁ θεός,
> καὶ ὁ παῖς, ὃν ἐξελεξάμην, ἵνα γνῶτε καὶ πιστεύσητε καὶ συνῆτε
> ὅτι ἐγώ εἰμι)
> Before me there was no other god,
>> nor shall there be any after me.
> ¹¹I am God,
>> and besides me there is none who saves.
> ¹²I declared and saved; I reproached,
>> and there was no stranger among you.
> You are my witnesses;
>> I too am a witness, says the Lord God.
> ¹³Even from the beginning
>> there is also no one who rescues from my hands;
> I will do it and who will turn it back?[4]

Thus speaks the Lord God through the prophet Isaiah, in the part of the work known as the Book of Consolation (Isaiah 40–55, "Deutero-Isaiah"). In the face of the apparent catastrophe and adversity of the exile, God comforts his people. But he does so by calling them to a cosmic lawsuit, in which the Lord and his witnesses are placed on one side, and the gods of the nations and their followers are on the other side, with the Lord as both the prosecuting witness and the judge. The nations and their gods are challenged to make their case: Let them tell of the things to come, the things which the Lord has spoken from the beginning; let them say whence they come and what their works are; let them show that they have indeed spoken previously of what is now happening, and in these ways show that they are gods.

But, as it turns out, despite all appearances, they have no case to make; they can give no answer; they are not gods. "I am the first and I am the last: besides me there is no god"[5] the Lord asserts through Isaiah. Truth is at stake in this trial, the correspondence between the word of the Lord and his action, and the ability to perceive this correspondence is what makes Israel a witness to the Lord. This correspondence, this truth, which lies in the future, demonstrates that the Lord alone is the God of the whole world, and all creation and history are in his hands.

---

4. Isa, LXX.
5. Isa, LXX.

He alone *is*. Several times, through the words of Isaiah, the Lord proclaims, in the absolute, "I AM"—the very name of God:

Isaiah 41:4

> Who has wrought and done these things?
> The one calling her from the beginning of generations, has called her.
> I, God, am first, and for the things that are coming, I AM.[6]
> (ἐγὼ θεὸς πρῶτος, καὶ εἰς τὰ ἐπερχόμενα ἐγώ εἰμι)

Isaiah 43:25

> I am, I am, the one who blots out your acts of lawlessness and
> I will not remember them at all.[7] (ἐγώ εἰμι ἐγώ εἰμι ὁ ἐξαλείφων
> τὰς ἀνομίας σου καὶ οὐ μὴ μνησθήσομαι)

Isaiah 45:19

> I am, and there is no other.
> I have not spoken in secret, nor in a dark place of the earth...
> I am, I am the Lord, speaking righteousness and declaring truth.[8]
> (ἐγώ εἰμι ἐγώ εἰμι κύριος λαλῶν δικαιοσύνη καὶ ἀναγγέλων ἀλήθειαν)

At stake, then, in this trial of truth, is the very identity of the Lord God as the one and only God, known by his name, and known in his glory:

> I am the Lord God; this is my name;
> my glory I will not give to another;
> nor my excellences to the graven image.[9]

If God is moved to act, to redeem Israel, it is for the sake of his name and to vindicate his glory:

> For my own sake will I do this for you,
> because my name is being profaned,
> and my glory I will not give to another.[10]

---

6. Isa 41:4, LXX.
7. Isa 43:25, LXX.
8. Isa 45:19, LXX.
9. Isa 42:8, LXX.
10. Isa 48:11, LXX.

Yet in doing this, God will bring Israel to share in his glory, thereby glorying himself in them: "You are my servant, Israel, and in you will I be glorified."[11] It is, specifically, by being lifted up that the servant shall be glorified:

> See, my servant shall understand
>   and he shall be exalted and glorified exceedingly
>   (ὑψωθήσεται καὶ δοξασθήσεται σφόδρα).
> Just as many shall be astonished at you—
>   so shall your appearance be without glory from men,
>   and your glory be absent from the men—
> so shall many nations be astonished at him,
>   and kings shall shut their mouth,
> because those who were not informed about him shall see
> and those who did not hear shall understand.[12]

The one who had "no form or glory," whose "life is taken up from the earth," "led to death on account of the lawlessness of the people" is the one "who shall inherit many and divide the spoils of the earth" so that the "barren one" will give birth to more children than the one who has a husband (Isa 53:1—54:1). In this way, sons and daughters are called from the ends of the earth: "All who have been called by my name, whom I created for my glory, whom I formed and made."[13]

No one has seen this more clearly than the apostle John that Isaiah spoke of Christ: that they did not believe Christ, despite his having done so many signs before them, was to fulfill the word of Isaiah: "Lord, who has believed our report and to whom has the arm of the Lord been revealed."[14] And as Isaiah also says, "He has blinded their eyes and hardened their heart, lest they should see with their eyes and perceive with their heart and turn to me to heal them"[15] and, John adds, "Isaiah said this because he saw his glory and spoke of him."[16]

The glory of God revealed in Christ is, according to John, the very moment of judgment, of *krisis*, in which the world is judged and the truth of God established. As Andrew Lincoln has persuasively argued, in his book *Truth on Trial: The Lawsuit Motif in the Fourth Gospel*, the cosmic lawsuit

---

11. Isa 49:3; c.f. 44:23; 45:25; 49:5; 55:5, LXX.
12. Isa 52:13–15, LXX.
13. Isa 43:7, LXX.
14. Isa 53:1, LXX, John 12:38, ESV.
15. Isa 6:10, LXX.
16. John 12:41, ESV.

laid out in Isaiah's book of consolation forms the framework, and even the most characteristic vocabulary of the Gospel of John:[17]

- The word "witness" appears fourteen times in John compared to four times the rest the Synoptics combined.
- The verb "to witness" appears forty-four times in John; only twice in the rest of the Synoptics combined.
- "Judgment" appears nineteen times in John; six in Matthew, six in Luke.
- "To judge" appears eleven times in John; four in Luke and twelve in Matthew.

Likewise with the word "truth," and its cognates:

- ἀλήθεια — twenty-five times in John; seven times in the synoptics.
- ἀληθής — fourteen times in John; once in Mark, once in Matthew.
- ἀληθινός — nine times in John; once in Luke.
- ἀληθῶς — seven times; eight times in the synoptics.

Clearly John is more concerned with the issues we have seen in Isaiah than the authors of the other Gospels. But it is not only the vocabulary—this theme dominates the plot and the discourses of the narrative of this Gospel quite unlike the others. In the first part of John, the prologue (whether it was originally an independent hymn or not, whether it has been reworked to suit its present context or not—the text is as it is) specifically introduces John the Baptist as a witness, saying "He came for testimony (εἰς μαρτυρίαν), to bear witness (μαρτυρήσῃ) to the light, that all might believe through him."[18] The one who became flesh, such that we all saw his glory, the glory of the only Son of the Father[19]—this is the one of whom John bore witness (μαρτυρεῖ).[20]

The second main part of the Gospel of John, the public ministry of Christ, begins again with John bearing witness. It opens with the words: "This is the testimony (μαρτυρία) of John."[21] It then speaks of John's testimony about himself, as one crying in the wilderness, preparing the way of the Lord (quoting directly from the opening of Isaiah's book of consolation[22]),

---

17. Lincoln, *Truth on Trial*, 20–23.
18. John 1:6, ESV.
19. John 1:14, ESV.
20. John 1:15, ESV.
21. John 1:19, ESV.
22. Isa 1:23, LXX.

and then gives John's testimony of the Lamb of God in his report of the baptism of Jesus.[23] During the course of his public ministry, Christ provides seven signs[24] that manifest his glory, often followed by controversy with the Jews over the nature of his authority, in which the question of judgment and testimony looms large.[25]

His opponents take their lead from Deut 13:1-11, which stipulates that if there should arise a prophet performing signs or wonders, calling people to follow him, and worship other gods, it should be taken as God testing the people, to know whether they love him with their whole heart. Such a prophet speaks rebellion against the God who has brought them up from Egypt and redeemed them from bondage, trying to make them "leave the way in which the Lord God has commanded you to walk." Such a prophet should, according to Deut 18:20-22 and Lev 24:16, be put to death. While his opponents seek to interpret Jesus in the terms of the law, to determine whether he is a true or a false prophet, John, on the other hand, though occasionally depicting Jesus as a prophet like Moses[26] draws upon Isaiah's lawsuit to depict Jesus as one greater than Moses, one to whom, Moses in fact bears witness.[27]

During the course of Jesus's public ministry, seven witnesses are specifically named:

1. The Baptist: In John 1:19, 32, 34; 3:26, 28; called upon by Jesus in 5:33.

2. Jesus himself: "My testimony is true" he says in John 8:14, c.f. 3:11, 32, 33; 7:7; 8:18.

3. Jesus's works: "These very works which I am doing bear witness that the Father has sent me," in John 5:36, c.f. 10:25.

4. God: "The Father who sent me bears witness to me," in John 8:18, c.f. 5:32, 37.

5. The Scriptures: "You search the Scriptures because you think that in them you have eternal life, yet it is they that bear witness to me," in John 5:39; c.f. 2:17, 3:14, 6:31-33; 7:39.

And, in bearing witness to Christ, they witness against the people, fulfilling Moses's prophecy in Deut 31:26, 32:46: "Take this book of the law and put

---

23. John 1:29-34, ESV.
24. John 2:1-11; 4:46-54; 5:1-18; 6:1-15; 6:16-21; 9:1-41; 11:1-53, ESV.
25. E.g., John 5:19-47; 8:12-59, ESV.
26. C.f., John 12:49, ESV.
27. John 5:46, ESV.

it by the side of the ark of the covenant of the Lord your God, that it may be there for a witness against you."

1. The Samaritan woman: By whose witness many believed in Jesus in John 4:39.
2. The crowd: Those who bore witness to the raising of Lazarus in John 12:17.

And, then, at the end of his public ministry, as Jesus specifies that for this purpose he has come to this hour, that he might glorify the Father's name and declares, "Now is the judgment of the world" in John 12:27, 31, the narrative concludes by appealing to the words of Isaiah (mentioned above), and emphasizes that Jesus's words, which are in fact the Father's words, are the judge on the last day in John 12:48.

Then, in the next main block, the "farewell discourse," the theme is again present, this time in terms of the other paraclete—the advocate— whom Christ will send and who will bring to mind[28] all things pertaining to Christ, that is, who will lead them into the truth.[29] This advocate "will bear witness to me; and you also are witnesses, because you have been with me from the beginning"[30]

As we move into the fourth main block of text, it is important to note that John, unlike the Synoptics, has no trial of Christ before the Sanhedrin. As Lincoln suggests, "throughout his public ministry, Jesus can be viewed as on trial before Israel and its leaders."[31] What happens, during the days of Christ's Passion, in the Synoptics, is seen to have been the dynamic of the whole ministry of Christ—one cosmic lawsuit. Between the arrest and interrogation in John 18:1–27, and the crucifixion and burial in 19:16b–42, there lies the trial scene in 18:28—19:16a. But before we finally turn to this scene, it should be briefly noted that the theme of testimony is at the heart of John's account of the Crucifixion. For John, as has often been noted, the suffering and death of Christ is the very moment of the "lifting up and glorification" of the servant.[32] It is the moment at which his very identity as the divine I AM, is revealed: "When you have lifted up (exalted) the Son of Man, then you will know that I AM"[33] (ὅταν ὑψώσητε τὸν υἱὸν τοῦ ἀνθρώπου, τότε γνώσεσθε ὅτι ἐγώ εἰμι,). Immediately after recounting what happened, John

---

28. Throughout the Scriptures, c.f. John 12:16, ESV.
29. John 16:13, ESV.
30. John 15:26–27, ESV.
31. Lincoln, *Truth on Trial*, 23.
32. Isa 53, LXX; John 3:14, 8:28, 12:32–34, ESV.
33. John 8:28, ESV.

adds: "He who saw it has borne witness, and his testimony is true, and he knows that he tells the truth, that you also might believe."³⁴ Finally, after the resurrection accounts (which reflect extensively on the nature of seeing and believing), the Gospel concludes by reiterating the all-pervading theme: "This is the disciple who is bearing witness to these things, and who has written these things; and we know that his testimony is true."³⁵

It is clear, then, that John has creatively and pervasively drawn upon Isaiah's book of consolation, to demonstrate that, despite all appearances, the Lord is indeed God and is indeed in control—that what takes place in Christ is the work of God, spoken of from the beginning yet accomplished only at the end: τετέλεσται³⁶—it is finished, completed, perfected. As the true servant of God, spoken of by Isaiah, Jesus seeks only the glory of the one who sent him,³⁷ and so asks his Father to glorify his name³⁸ such that he can say, "Now the Son of Man has been glorified and God has been glorified in him."³⁹ His exaltation in glory establishes the glory of God upon the earth, and this glory bathes everything he does: the signs done throughout his ministry reveal this glory⁴⁰ and his whole life is oriented towards this glory, in his death and departure to the Father.⁴¹

Unlike the Synoptics, John's depiction of Christ is always as the Lord of glory, always in control—especially in his arrest, trial before Pilate, and his death—and always sure and confident in and of his Father's will. If he says, "now is my soul troubled,"⁴² he does not sweat great drops of blood in anguish,⁴³ nor does he ask that this cup might be taken from him⁴⁴ but he says, rather: "What shall I say? "Father save me from this hour"? No! "For this purpose I have come to this hour: Father glorify your name."⁴⁵

This is not a naively docetic Christology (contra Käsemann), but theology; for, from the earliest times, John has been recognized as *the* theologian. It is theology in the sense that his proclamation of Christ is in accordance

---

34. John 19:35, ESV.
35. John 21:24, ESV.
36. John 19:30, ESV.
37. John 7:18, ESV.
38. John 12:28, ESV.
39. John 13:31–32, ESV.
40. Cf. John 2:11, 11:4, ESV.
41. Cf. John 12:23, 27, 28; 13:1; 17:1–5, 13, etc., ESV.
42. Cf. John 2:11, 11:4, ESV.
43. Cf. Luke 22:44, ESV.
44. John 22:42, ESV.
45. John 12:27, ESV.

with the Scriptures throughout his narrative; for unlike the synoptics, where the books are not opened until the end,[46] in John, the Scriptures are opened from the beginning of his account: as Philip tells Nathanael at the beginning, "we have found the one of whom Moses in the law and also the prophets wrote."[47] And it is such theology by drawing especially upon Isaiah, in the proclamation that the glory of God is revealed in the exaltation of the Servant, an exaltation identified by John with the lifting up of Christ on the Cross, revealing his divine identity, his divine name—I AM—*the* moment in which the world is judged, and those who believe on his name become witnesses, exiles in this world, called to follow him to his Father.

This cosmic trial of truth, writ large throughout John, is recapitulated or brought into clear focus in the trial of Jesus before Pilate in John 18:28–19:16a. As with many other complexly drawn episodes in John (such the healing of the blind man), this episode with Pilate is composed of seven subtly depicted scenes, alternating between dialogues between Pilate and Jesus within the praetorium and Pilate and the Jews outside the praetorium:

1. John 18:28–32. The trial begins with Pilate going to the Jews to ask what charge they are bringing against Jesus, but receives no clear answer.

2. John 18:33–38a. Returning within, Pilate questions Jesus in private about the nature of his alleged kingship, a kingship not of this world, but one which defines the identity of Christ, who says, "You say that I am a king. For this I was born and for this I have come into the world, to bear witness to the truth. Everyone who is of the truth hears my voice."[48] To which Pilate responds sardonically, "What is truth?" Perhaps he should have asked, as is often said, "*Who* is the truth?"—emphasizing that truth is not merely an abstract idea, but a person. But to leave it at this misses the significance of the identity of the person *of Christ*, for there is more to Christ's self-identification as "The Way, the Truth, and the Life,"[49] as we have seen from Isaiah and will see again.

3. John 18:38b–40. Going outside again, Pilate declares that he finds Jesus innocent, and invokes the practice of releasing a prisoner at Passover.

4. John 19:1–3. Back inside, Pilate has Jesus scourged, and the Roman soldiers mock him by investing him with royal insignia, the plait of thorns and purple robe, hailing him as the King of the Jews.

---

46. Cf. Luke 24, ESV.
47. John 1:45, ESV.
48. John 18:37, ESV.
49. John 14:6, ESV.

5. John 19:4–7. Going out again, Pilate brings Jesus, thus adorned, and introduces him to the crowd: "Behold the man."[50] The chief priests and officers reply with calls for his crucifixion. When Pilate tells them to do it themselves, they call out all the more—he ought to die because he made himself out to be the son of God.

6. John 19:8–1. Going back inside, Pilate again engages Jesus in a dialogue about the nature of power and authority, and hears from Jesus that any power that Pilate might have over him he has only because it has been given from above.

7. John 19:12–16a. Finally, outside again, when Pilate tries to release him, the Jews imply that Pilate is acting in treason against Caesar for tolerating Jesus's act of proclaiming himself to be a king. Jesus is brought out, and, although the Greek is ambiguous, it is most likely to mean that Pilate sits Jesus upon the judgment seat (rather than sitting upon it himself). Pilate then says to the Jews, "Behold your King," to which they cry out. "Away with him; crucify him." When Pilate attempts, a third time, to avoid this action, saying, "Shall I crucify your king?" the chief priests answer, "we have no king but Caesar." At this astounding assertion, the only conclusion is the final words: "Then he handed him over to them to be crucified."

In this masterfully drawn drama, John gives flesh to the cosmic lawsuit between God and the world, making it visible for all to see. It is for this that Christ has been born and come into the world: to bear witness to the truth. And, after the proceedings have taken place, with the various parties bringing their cases, it is Christ, with the marks of a divine sovereignty—the crown of thorns and purple (bloodied) robe—who sits, as King, upon the judgment seat. It is the Jews, in particular the chief priests, who affirm that they have no king but Caesar. This abandonment of the God proclaimed by Isaiah and brought to focus in Christ by John, means that what appears to be the judgment of Jesus and his condemnation to death, turns out to be *the* judgment of this world, putting it in crisis and demanding our response. The cosmic trial, enacted throughout the narrative of John, culminates in this point, so that there is nothing left to do but for Jesus to be handed over to be crucified. The case is closed: the world, both Jew and Gentile, have been shown to be hostile to God, abandoning his ways. And yet the very lifting up of Christ upon the cross is his glorification, in the glory which he had with the Father outside of time, in eternity, so that now the glory of God is established upon the earth, and, as he hands over the Spirit, a new means

---

50. John 19:5, ESV.

of life and being comes to be, for those who are now prepared to witness to this truth.

Clearly, John has made a tremendously effective use of the cosmic lawsuit spoken of in Isaiah's book of consolation. However, to understand the profundity of this, we must also hear further scriptural allusions. When God speaks through Isaiah, he does not simply foretell things which are to come (Isaiah speaking of Christ), but also harkens back to things which have been spoken from of old. There is no other God besides the one who "declares the last things first, before they happen, and at once they come to pass" (or "they come to pass all together"); who said, "My whole plan (βουλή) shall stand, and I shall do all the things I have planned."[51]

Isaiah harkens back to things spoken from the beginning, and so too does John. As is often observed, the opening verse of the Gospel explicitly echoes of the opening verse of Genesis. When we return to these opening verses of Scripture, we find a striking difference in the way that God's creative activity is described. Scripture begins with God issuing commands:

> Let there be light—and there was light.
> Let there be a firmament...
> Let the waters under the heavens be gathered...
> Let the earth put forth vegetation...
> Let there be light in the firmament...
> Let water bring forth swarms of living creatures...
> Let the earth bring forth living creatures...[52]

This divine "fiat"—"let it be"—is sufficient to bring all these creatures into existence, "and it was so... and it was good." But, then, having declared all these things into existence by a word alone, God announces his own project—not with an injunction but in the subjunctive: "Let us make the human being (ποιήσωμν ἄνθρωπον) in our image, after our likeness."[53] This is the work of God; this is what he has set his mind to; this is what he specifically deliberates about: this is the divine purpose and resolve. Yet it is the only thing not issued by a divine fiat; it depends rather upon the fiat of Christ. Scripture opens by declaring God's purpose, to make a human being in his image and concludes with Christ's exaltation in glory upon the Cross as proclaimed by the theologian, for only here do we hear that the work of God is complete: τετέλεσται:[54] and confirmed, though unwittingly, by no

---

51. Isa 46:10, LXX.
52. Gen 1:3–24, LXX.
53. Gen 1:26, LXX.
54. John 19:30, ESV.

less than Pilate: "Behold the man"[55] (ἰδοὺ ὁ ἄνθρωπος). Echoes of this can be heard in the literature of the second century (and thereafter), especially in the martyrdom literature and those figures, such as Irenaeus of Lyons who trace their lineage back to John (through Polycarp, the martyr), giving a further dimension to the witness to which God calls us. For example, when Ignatius of Antioch journeys slowly but surely towards his impending martyrdom in Rome, he nevertheless embraces his fate with joy, urging the Roman Christians not to try to impede his martyrdom:

> It is better for me to die in Christ Jesus than to be king over the ends of the earth. I seek him who died for our sake. I desire him who rose for us. Birth-pangs are upon me. Suffer me, my brethren; hinder me not from living, do not wish me to die.... Suffer me to receive the pure light; when I shall have arrived there, I shall become a human being (ἄνθρωπος ἔσομαι). Suffer me to follow the example of the passion of my God. (*Rom.* 6)

Only by being a witness, a martyr, will Ignatius be born into life, receive the pure light, and become a human being, a human being in the stature of Christ, the "perfect human being" or the "new human being," as the martyr refers to "the faithful martyr, the firstborn of the dead."[56] His hope to write a second book, describing the "plan that leads to the new human being" (*Eph.* 20), was, as far as we know, never fulfilled by Ignatius, but is expounded most fully by Irenaeus of Lyons. When Irenaeus asserts (in one of his most often-quoted, but much misunderstood, lines) that "the glory of God is the living human being" (*Haer.* 4.20.7), he is speaking specifically of the martyr, flesh no longer animated by a breath of life, but vivified by the Spirit.[57] God's purpose, spoken of old and reiterated by Isaiah, to make the human being for ever[58] (ἐποίησα ἄνθρωπον εἰς τὸν αἰῶνα) is thus completed when we give our fiat to God's purpose: for the only work said to be God's own are the ones who must give the fiat! And we do this by following Christ, as Ignatius did, so becoming witnesses, martyrs, no longer trying to secure our lives, but rather taking up the Cross. Having come into this world, with no freedom and into an existence which necessarily culminates in death, we are now given the possibility to use our death through our free witness, giving our fiat, and so grounding our being in the free, self-sacrificial love that Christ has shown to be the very identity, the being and life of God, becoming human beings in his image and likeness. The cosmic lawsuit in which

55. John 19:5, ESV.
56. Rev 1:5, ESV.
57. Cf. Behr, *Irenaeus of Lyons*, 162–203.
58. Isa 44:7, LXX.

God is engaged with the world, as described by Isaiah and given flesh in John, turns out to be not merely a lawsuit (subservient, as Lincoln supposes, to John's theme of Christ's ascent/descent, incarnation and return[59]) but the completion of God's creative activity (completed "all together"[60]), brought to completion in, or even *by*, his witnesses, his martyrs, living human beings, and living forever. One cannot create beings already living the life of voluntary and loving self-sacrifice that Christ has shown to be God's own life, but one can create those—men and women—who can do this through giving their own fiat. "Be my witnesses; I too am a witness, says the Lord God, and the servant whom I have chosen."[61]

---

59. C.f. Lincoln, *Truth on Trial*, 13
60. Isa 46:10, LXX.
61. Isa 43:10, LXX.

You Shall Judge Angels
A Response to Fr. Behr

PETER LEITHART (EVANGELICAL)

INTRODUCTION

WHEN I READ FR. John's paper, my reaction was not unlike that of the Queen of Sheba when she visited Solomon: "How blessed are your servants who stand before you continually and hear your wisdom" (1 Kgs 10:8). I do not know if St. Vladimir's provides servants, but students are a pretty close substitute. If your students hear teaching of this depth and beauty and are being trained to teach so, the churches your graduates lead will be vibrantly, luminously biblical communities of faith.

I have differences here and there with Fr. John's presentation, but it would be churlish to spend my time on quibbles. Instead, I want to offer some harmonization of the themes he initiated, looking at variations in how the cosmic lawsuit is presented, with particular attention to the book of Revelation.

Let me begin by schematizing the arrangement of the courtroom in Isaiah and John. Isaiah's court is set up like this:
Judge: Yahweh
Prosecutor/witness: Yahweh
Defendants: Gods of Nations, Idolaters

Israel is also a witness on Yahweh's behalf, but *not* because she is reliable. In the very passage that Yahweh declares Israel to be His witnesses, they are disqualified because they are "blind, even though they have eyes" and "deaf, even though they have ears" (43:8–13). Israel is a witness because in her history as a people, Yahweh's word has overridden Israel's unfaithfulness. God has proven true, though every Israelite is a liar. Blinded, deafened, and hardened by her idols, Israel stands as witness in spite of herself.

There are at least two transformations of this scene in Isaiah. Among the deaf, there is *one* with an open ear (50:5), but that obedient Servant is rejected, accused, assaulted, and set in the dock. The Servant is certain he will be exonerated because someone stands "as one" with him (50:8). He trash-talks his opponents: Who has a case? Bring it on! (50:8). Here the scheme is:

Judge: Yahweh?
Prosecutor/witness: Unfaithful Israel
Defendants: Servant, with Yahweh

Elsewhere, the scene shifts more radically, as Yahweh assembles the court and submits to a trial (Isaiah 41):

Judge: Yahweh
Prosecutor/witness: Coastlands, nations
Defendants: Yahweh

Isaiah the Barthian prophesies of a Judge judged in our place.[1]

John presents Jesus's trial in two different registers. Empirically, it looks like this:

Judge: Pilate
Prosecutor/witness: Jews
Defendants: Jesus

Jesus sees it differently: "Now is the judgment *of this world*." As in Isaiah, the same person serves as both prosecutor and judge, with Jesus now taking the place of Yahweh:

Judge: Jesus
Prosecutor/witness: Jesus[2]

---

1. In reality, of course, Barth is Isaianic.

2. As Fr. John points out, the synoptic gospels use "witness" and "testify" (the μαρτυρ- word group) very seldom. Many of the uses in the synoptics are in the trial narratives. Mark tells us that the Sanhedrin attempted to gather testimony against Jesus, and were content to hear false witnesses. Violating Torah's requirements, the high priest tore his robes at Jesus's testimony, and cried, "What more need do we have of witnesses. By contrast, despite the wide use of "witness" and "testify" and "testimony" in John's gospel, these terms are almost completely absent during the trial. No witnesses are called, not even lying ones. Jesus *alone* gives testimony, rebuking the officer who beat him with "If I have spoken wrongly, bear witness of the wrong" (18:23) and telling Pilate, "for this have I come into the world, to witness to the truth" (19:37). As in Isaiah, Jesus is both witness and judge. He testifies to truth because He is Truth, the one in

Defendants: Word of Israel and Gentiles

Pilate puts Jesus in the seat of judgment to ridicule Him and the Jews. But God is not mocked, and Pilate's mockery unveils the truth of this trial. The Jews are on trial, and they ultimately stand condemned, for they reject their King in favor Caesar. Standing on the "pavement" (cf. 2 Chron 7:3; John 19:13) they do not fall in worship, but demand the blood of God incarnate. Meanwhile, Pilate the governor stands before the Judge, and not all great Neptune's ocean can wash this blood clean from his hands. This second arrangement applies not merely to the trial scene but to the entire gospel, where Jesus is continuously chief witness, prosecutor and judge.

It would be fruitful to pursue the implications of these shifting configurations, but I want to extend Fr. John's discussion first by backing up to look at the creation patterns in John's gospel and then returning to the courtroom scene, now in Revelation rather than in John's gospel.

WHAT IS FINISHED?

At his death, Jesus announces "It is finished." But *what* is finished when "It is finished"? Not John's gospel, which moves on to tell of Jesus's burial and resurrection. Not the story of the disciples, which continues on into Acts and for the next two millennia and beyond. The answer is the one that Fr. John gives: "what takes place in Christ is the work of God, spoken of from the beginning yet accomplished only at the end." When Jesus says, "It is finished," he declares the work of creation completed in the fashioning of a new creation.[3]

The crucifixion scene is less clearly organized than the trial scene, but it too is laid out in seven scenes: 1) Jesus bears his cross to the place of the skull; 2) He is crucified between two men; 3) Pilate fastens a mocking-true inscription to the cross, announcing Jesus the Nazarene as king of the Jews; 4) the soldiers divide his garments; 5) Jesus delivers his mother into the care of the Beloved Disciple; 6) Jesus drinks some wine and 7) cries out with a loud voice, It is finished! Like the trial scene, this is a series of new-creation actions.

---

whom, as Fr. John has so profoundly expresses it, the Word of God and the action of God correspond, the One in whom all the promises of God are Yes and Amen.

3. Fr. John's claim reflects a typically "Eastern" orientation, according to which Jesus's death does not merely rectify the damage done by sin, but brings humanity to maturity and perfection. I agree that this is simply a biblical teaching, and it is an "Eastern" emphasis that needs to be more fully incorporated into "Western" theology.

To get the full impact of John's creation theology, we have to discern an additional pattern in John's typological tapestry. From the outset, John presents Jesus as God's dwelling place, the tabernacle. The Word that was in the beginning with God and was God took flesh and pitched his tent (σκηνοω) among us, so that we saw the glory of the Only-begotten. That is the whole gospel in miniature. Throughout the gospel, Jesus acts as a new Moses assembling and furnishing the new tabernacle that he is. Jesus offers living water to the woman at the well, reminiscent of the laver of water in the tabernacle court, and then heals a man who has been waiting by a pool for thirty-eight years. Jesus is heavenly bread, the manna that was kept in a jar in the ark and the bread of the face that lay on the golden table in the earthly heaven of the sanctuary. Jesus is the light of the world, the true lampstand. He stands at the altar as priest to offer the incense of prayer before his Father on behalf of the disciples. Tabernacled in flesh, the Word draws near to his people, and in drawing near the Word becomes all that the tabernacle was to Israel—cleansing and refreshing water, the bread of life, the light of the world, the incense that ascends to the Father.

In this sequence, the cross might seem to be one of the butcher blocks where priests kill and carve sacrificial animals, but that is *not* how John arranges his tour of the tabernacle. Rather, John's gospel moves from the outer courts to the holy place, so that, by the time we arrive at the crucifixion, we are in the inner sanctuary, the most holy place. When the tabernacle was completed, Yahweh's glory descended from the mountain to take the throne above the cherubim. At the end of John's gospel, the glory of God announced in the Prologue is finally revealed in all its radiance. Broken and bleeding, Jesus crucified is Yahweh enthroned on the ark, hanging between two criminals who serve as cherubic throne-guardians. Later, the empty tomb will replicate the tableau of the cross, with two angels sitting at either end of the stone where Jesus lay (20:12). Cross and tomb are shocking places for divine glory to be revealed, scandalous, macabre arks, the polar opposite of holy spaces. (Can Yahweh dwell in Sheol!?) For John, they constitute the inner sanctuary where the glory of God is most fully displayed: In the mangled flesh of the crucified Word, in the emptiness of the tomb of the Risen Lord, *that* is where glory shines. Had Aaron been able to pull back the veil, had Moses seen Yahweh's face instead of his back, had they gotten a clear view of the light of the knowledge of the glory of God, they would have seen the face of Jesus the Christ, crucified and risen.

When Yahweh came to the seventh day of the creation week, "the heavens and earth were completed" (Gen 2:1). When Moses had assembled the microcosmic tabernacle, "all the work of the tabernacle and the tent of meeting was finished" because "Moses finished the work" (Exod 39:32;

40:33). Having spent his ministry as the living tabernacle, Jesus puts the capstone on the edifice by ascending the cross to take his throne. When that is done, Jesus repeats the creation and tabernacle announcement, It is finished!

The one hanging on this new ark is the Word *made flesh*. The cross reveals the glory of God because it elevates the *image* of God to Yahweh's throne above the cherubim. In Jesus, Israel finally enters behind the veil into the most holy place. God takes his throne when he shares it with the God-man. Only *then* is creation complete. Only then can Jesus say of God's house, "It is finished!" because only then and there has one man become fully human.

And yet there is more to come. It is finished, yet it continues, because God is determined not merely to share his glory with *Jesus* but to enthrone a people. The book of Revelation tells of this continuation after completion.

MAKING JUDGES[4]

Even more obviously than John's gospel, Revelation is patterned by creation-week sevens: Seven letters are sent to the angels of seven churches, seven seals close the book that the Lamb takes from the hand of the Father, seven angels blow seven trumpets, seven bowls of wrath-blood are poured out on the earth and especially on the city that is mystically Sodom and Egypt and Babylon. "Seven Spirits" glow as lamps before the throne, which become the seven burning eyes of the Son of Man.

John's begins "in the beginning" and ends with an "It is finished!" But this creation story is continued in Revelation, as various themes and

---

4. Modern scholars are skeptical that John and Revelation come from the same John, but most recognize the overlap of terminology and theology. The internal evidence that they are mutually interpreting, not to mention the ancient tradition that they come from the same author, is overwhelming. Outside John, Revelation is the only book that identifies Jesus as the Word of God (John 1:1–3; Rev 19:13). John and Revelation are the only two books that use the verb σκηνοω, and both use the verb to describe God's dwelling among men. The Word becomes flesh and pitches a tent among us, and as the Bridal city descends at the end of Revelation, a loud voice announces that the "tabernacle of God is among men and He will pitch His tent among them" (21:3). John the Baptist introduces Jesus with "Behold the Lamb of God!" (John 1:19, 36), and when John ascends into the heavenly liturgy Jesus appears as a Lamb (Rev 5:6–8). Some of these are positioned to bind the two books into a single overall framework. Jesus is the Word in John 1, and again called the Word of God in Revelation 19. He tabernacles among us in John 1, and the Bride is the tabernacling of God in Revelation 21. The most complete and creative work on the structural connections between John and Revelation is that of Warren Gage.

story-lines that begin in John's gospel are concluded in the Apocalypse.[5] John the Baptist introduces Jesus as the Bridegroom of the bride who brings joy to His friends (John 3:29), and Jesus's first sign is to supply wine at a wedding feast (2:1–12). During his life on earth, Jesus encounters women who might take the role of Bride: the Samaritan woman at the well, the woman taken in adultery, Mary and Martha, Mary Magdalene in the garden. They *might* be the bride, but they are not, and Jesus explicitly tells Mary Magdalene that she cannot touch him because he is going to the Father. When we arrive at the end of John's gospel, we have a Bridegroom who has given his life for the Bride, waiting for the wedding feast to begin. He might as well be a jilted Groom, because there is no Bride.

She finally shows up in Revelation. As soon as the harlot city is burned, the wedding announcements go out: "The marriage of the Lamb has come and His bride has made herself ready" (Rev 19:7). At the close of Revelation, she is unveiled: "I saw the holy city, new Jerusalem, coming down out of heaven from God, made ready as a bride adorned for her husband" (Rev 21:2). At the end of the gospel, Jesus is risen king, but he has no queen. Only when John and Revelation are read together do we have a complete Johannine royal romance.

The cosmic lawsuit is no more finished at the end of the gospel than the romance is. As Fr. John has said, the gospel of John is a series of episodes in a long trial. It appears that Jesus is put in the dock, but it gradually becomes clear that Israel and the Gentiles are accused and finally condemned. Revelation is even more obviously a trial. Witness terminology is nearly as common in Revelation as in John's gospel.[6] John enters a temple when he

---

5. This is partly a matter of vocabulary: Until the seventh angel trumpets, the "mystery of God" is not yet complete (10:7). The wrath of God is "finished" when the bowl angels pour out their bowls (15:1, 8). God's words are not "complete" until the beast strips the harlot city, consumes her flesh, and burns her with fire (17:17).

6. The verb "bear witness" or "testify" (μαρτυρεω) occurs four times (1:2; 22:16, 18; 20); the noun that describes a person as a "witness" (μαρτυς) is found five times (1:5; 2:13; 3:14; 11:3; 17:6); the noun that describes the testimony (μαρτυρια) of witnesses is used eight times (1:2, 9; 6:9; 11:7; 12:11, 17; 19:10; 20:4). G. B. Caird noted that "the repeated use of the words 'witness' and 'testimony' is one of the many points of resemblance between the Revelation and the Fourth Gospel," and argues that in both texts they should be understood in their primary "forensic" sense: "The author of the Fourth Gospel, perhaps inspired by the example of Second Isaiah, presents his argument in the form of a lawcourt debate, in which one witness after another is summoned, until God's advocate, the Paraclete, has all the evidence he needs to convince the world that Jesus is the Son of God, and so to win his case. In the Revelation the courtroom setting is even more realistic; for Jesus had borne his testimony before Pilate's tribunal, and the martyrs must face a Roman judge. What they have to remember as they give their evidence is that that evidence is being heart in a court of more ultimate authority, where judgments which are just and true issue from the great white throne" (*The Revelation of*

ascends to heaven in Revelation 4, and he begins his sky journey among the constellations. But the combination of *a* throne and throne*s* indicates another setting: Swept up to heaven, John enters a *courtroom*.[7]

In Revelation 4, the trial is aborted. No case is presented, no witnesses called, no judgment passed. The officers abandon the process mid-stream, piling their crowns before the throne, resigning from the bench. No one can open the book (5:4), and if the court is going to make a decision, it needs the evidence that the book provides (cf. Dan 7:9). But if the book were the only obstacle, the trial could proceed as soon as the Lamb appears. He is qualified to take and look into the book. As the True Witness (Rev 1:5), Jesus presents the evidence. The Lamb seems ready enough to declare a verdict and pass the sentence. When the firmament is rolled back, men scurry under rocks to escape exposure before the Lamb and the One on the throne (Rev 6:12–17).

Installing the Lamb on the throne of heaven, however, is *not* enough to finish off the trial. The Lamb serves as Witness and Judge only when he has been joined by others. The Lamb is in the midst of the throne, but he has promised to leave room for victors to share the throne with Him (Rev 3:21). Eventually, John sees thrones set up again (20:4) and *then* books are opened so that the dragon, living and the dead can be judged (20:12). The Lamb is a qualified Witness and judge because he was slain to purchase a kingdom and priests (5:9). He is Judge insofar as he gathers witnesses and puts together a judicial *panel*.

Revelation is a forensic drama, a long series of trial scenes. It shows how God qualifies the witnesses and judges who will finally complete the lawsuit that began in the gospel. In John's gospel, Jesus calls seven witnesses: the Baptist, Jesus, the works of Jesus, the Father, the Scriptures, the Samarian woman, and the crowd that witnesses the raising of Lazarus. In Revelation, the witnesses are nearly all human beings. Jesus himself is the "faithful witness" (Rev 1:5), the Amen and true witness (3:14) who sends an angel to bear witness (21:16). Others bear witness *to* Jesus. Antipas of Pergamum is, like Jesus, a witness and a "faithful one" (2:13), two witnesses appear in the great city (11:3), and there are scattered references to multiple witnesses of Jesus (17:6) who hold to the testimony of Jesus (1:2, 9; 12:17; 19:10; 20:4).

Because as they bear witness to Lamb who was slain, their witness conforms to his, and that means that their witness, their μαρτυρια, edges toward what we mean by "martyrdom." Bearing faithful witness to the crucified and risen One, they face threats and dangers. John testifies about Jesus,

---

St. John the Divine, 17–18).

7. Elsewhere in Scripture, scenes with thrones are court scenes (Ps 122:5; Dan 7:9), and this is most especially evident in Rev 20:4.

and for that reason suffers on the island called Patmos (1:9). The dragon carries on a war against the children of the heavenly mother who hold to the testimony of Jesus (12:17), and the harlot city is drunk with the blood of the witnesses of Jesus (17:6). The life-history of the two witnesses replays the life of Jesus: After a ministry of signs and wonders in the great city, they are slaughtered and their bodies thrown in the street for three and a half days, until the Lord breathes new life into them and catches them up to heaven (11:3–12).

The incarnation produced the first fully human human being—Jesus. Revelation unveils the formation of a fully human church as it describes the cruciformization of witness: To be a witness is to be a witness to death, a witness in death. Jesus handed over his Spirit from the cross to accomplish just this: So that his Spirt might hover over the world to form new witnesses conformed to his image. These witnesses become, like Jesus in his suffering, fully human as they bear witness to God's glory in the face of Christ.

Literally, the trials of the martyrs look like the trial of Jesus:
Judge: (Roman authorities)[8]
Prosecutor/witness: Enemies of the Church
Defendants: Christian martyrs

In Revelation as in the gospel, what appears is not identical to what is:[9]
Judge: Lamb
Prosecutor/witness: Martyrs
Defendants: Persecutors

The world that was placed on trial in the trial of Jesus is accused and condemned again in Revelation. The world is condemned on the testimony of multiple witnesses: Not only Jesus, but faithful witnesses like Antipas who follow Jesus even to the cross.

---

8. The Jews handed Jesus over to Pilate, in whose court Jesus gave literal testimony, witnessing to the truth about himself, his kingdom, and his Father. The saints of Revelation face the very same combination of enemies. That they have enemies among the Jews is evident from the letters to the churches (2:9; 3:9), and that they will have to stand before Roman authorities is evident from the fact that the beast who attacks them is a Gentile beast who emerges, like the beasts of Daniel 7, from the sea. On this, see Trites, *New Testament Concept*, 160–61.

9. Several lines of consideration justify this rearrangement. The Lamb's enemies in Revelation are voluble and active. The dragon attacks again and again, the beast from the sea speaks arrogant words and blasphemies (13:6) and the land beast adds his sales pitch to deceive the land-dwellers to worship the beast from the sea (13:14). Before the Judge, they have nothing to say. There are *no* witnesses but those who hold to the witness of Jesus. Like the gods in Isaiah, the Lamb's enemies fall into abashed silence.

If Revelation draws on Isaiah, we expect another transformation. In Isaiah and John, the positions of witness and judge are occupied by the same person, and the same is true in Revelation. Revelation 4 shows a heavenly temple that is also a courtroom, but the court does not pass judgment until chapter 20, when the martyrs take up the thrones given up by the twenty-four Ancient Ones and play a part in the proceedings. By that point in Revelation, the beasts have already been thrown into the lake of fire and the harlot city is smoldering ruins, but the Lord does not pass *final* judgment on the dragon or on the living and dead until the saints are enthroned to judge alongside him. The lawsuit is well and truly finished when it reaches this climactic arrangement:

Judge: Martyrs
Prosecutor/witness: Martyrs
Defendants: Persecuting beasts; dragon

"You shall judge angels," Paul says to the Corinthians. Contrary to Corinthian expectations, the saints are qualified to judge angels not by spectacular charismata but by enduring tribulation faithfully, and winning through to victory.[10]

CONCLUSION

Already in Eden, Adam was destined to rise above angels. A newborn, he was not prepared to eat from the tree of knowledge of good and evil, with its fruit of judgment and rule.[11] The martyrs constitute a new-Adamic humanity, conformed to the glory of God revealed in the suffering Christ, and so qualified to judge angels. When all the martyrs have been made, *then* the tabernacle of God is with men (Rev 21:3), for then the martyrs share the ark-throne that is the cross of Jesus. Then and there, they have become fully human and God has been glorified in the sharing of his glory. John is incomplete without Revelation, and the new creation is not fully realized

---

10. Here is patience. "How long, O Lord?" the Psalmist cries. "Rise up, Judge of the Earth," but he does not. He seems to let the wicked flourish for decades, even centuries. What is he waiting for? Before the court assembles to pass judgment, there must be qualified witnesses and judges, and the only qualified ones are those who have kept the testimony of Jesus, who have not loved life even to death, who have been beheaded because of the word of God. Those who overcome by the blood of the Lamb and the word of their testimony are elevated to the status of judge. In the meantime, God is at work purifying members of the court in the fire of affliction.

11. This characterization is based on the use of the phrase elsewhere in the Bible, especially in 1 Kings 3, where Solomon requests "knowledge of good and evil" to judge Israel.

until the saints come to their thrones, sharing not only in the suffering witness but in the glory of Jesus, sharing also his work of bringing the world into judgment, and so participating also in the vindication of God the Creator as the Truth, as the One whose word and actions correspond without remainder.

Advocacy and Justification
Christ, the Paraclete and Ecclesial Scripture

Fr. Thomas Joseph White, OP (Catholic)

In the course of his apostolic life, Jesus is revealed to be one with the Father, the eternal Logos. The Son who is himself God makes manifest his identity by giving testimony to the Father in words and signs, as well as in his trial, passion and death. "When you have lifted up the Son of Man, then you will know that I am." (John 8:28) Here the language of Exod 3:14-15 and Isa 45:5,18 (in the Septuagint version) are recapitulated and applied to Jesus himself. He is YHWH, the God of Israel, revealed at Golgotha as the crucified God.

The Son who is crucified is placed on trial before Pilate and through him, in a sense, before all humanity. And at the same time it is the Son himself who is the judge of the world. "Now is the judgment of this world, now shall the ruler of this world be cast out; and I, when I am lifted up from the earth, will draw all men to myself." (John 12:31-32) The judgment in question is accomplished by God, the Father and by the sending of the Holy Spirit, who convicts the world of its sin. (John 16:8-11) However, it is also accomplished by the Son made man. That is to say, Christ carries out the judgment of God upon this world, for he is himself God, with the Father and the Holy Spirit.

At the same time, Christ is the one who comes before the Father and who is judged as a representative of Adam, "Behold the man." (John 19:5) By his moral impetration on our behalf it is Jesus who assists us as an advocate or "paraclete" so as to render us just, so as to "justify" us. This is, after all, the express teaching of the First Epistle of John 2:1-2: ". . . if any one does sin, we have an advocate (*paracletus*) with the Father, Jesus Christ the just (*dikaios*), and he is the expiation for our sins, and not for ours only but also for the sins of the whole world." In this "trial" that is simultaneously both of Christ and of humanity, it is *he* our advocate or defense lawyer, who stands before God as righteous in our stead, releasing us from condemnation and rendering us righteous before God.

In this brief essay I would like to consider four interrelated points that all converge around this truth about Christ and his "advocacy" on our behalf. First I will discuss his *human* knowledge, and how it contributes to his divine mission. Second, I will argue that there is a deep congruency or fitting harmony between the way Christ redeems us as man (rendering us just by his merits in charity) and the way that the grace of God renders us just by grace, through the intrinsic transformation of our intellectual and voluntary powers, by faith, hope and love. Third, I wish to note the congruency between Christ's mission as advocate on our behalf, and the mission of the Spirit as advocate or "paraclete," according to the teaching of John's Gospel. The two ideas are clearly intended to be interrelated. Last, I will note the way that Scripture as the word of God is given to us to justify us, in the Spirit, but also therefore in the Church, as the visible apostolic structure instituted by Christ. Potential ecumenical repercussions of these claims will be evident at each juncture.

JESUS'S HUMAN KNOWLEDGE OF HIS OWN MISSION AS OUR ADVOCATE

The Chalcedonian creed that unites Christians in a common scriptural confession of Jesus as the Lord, as true God and as true man, was formulated in AD 451. As each one knows, an important component of this teaching was the famous *Tome* of Leo, incorporated into the official documentation of the council. The council had confessed that Christ is one person or *hypostasis*, subsisting in two natures, united and distinct, without separation or confusion. Chalcedon was complemented, however, two centuries later, by the sixth ecumenical council of AD 680–81, the Third Council of Constantinople. The latter text confessed that Christ, the one person of the Word made man, acts simultaneously by two operations and wills, as both God and man.[1] In this way, Constantinople III sought to safeguard a Christologically orthodox interpretation of the Tome of Leo with respect to its controversial

---

1. Constantinople III: ". . . *each nature wills and performs the things that are proper to it* in a communion with the other; [and] in accord with this reasoning we hold that two natural wills and principles of action meet in correspondence for the salvation of the human race"; Tanner, *Decrees of the Ecumenical Councils*, 1:129–30.

and disputed affirmation that "each of the natures acts," in the Incarnation.[2] In the words of John Damascene, a defender of Constantinople III: "The power of miracles is the energy of His divinity, while the work of His hands and the willing and the saying 'I will, be clean,' are the energy of his humanity. And as to the effect, the breaking of the loaves, and the fact that the leper heard the 'I will,' belong to His humanity, while the multiplication of the loaves and the purification of the leper belong to his divinity."[3]

There are, then, two operations that stem from the two natures of Christ. Yet both natures operate in concord and harmony as the expression of the one person of the Word incarnate:

> For we hold that the two operations are not divided and that the natures do not act separately, but that each conjointly in complete community with the other acts with its own proper activity.... We speak sometimes of His two natures and sometimes of His one person: and the one or the two is referred to one conception. For the two natures are one Christ and the one Christ is two natures. Wherefore it is all the same whether we say "Christ acts according to either of His natures," or "either nature acts in Christ in communion with the other."[4]

This teaching has an evident basis in the Gospel of John. It is in virtue of his personal operation as man that the Logos incarnate weeps for Lazarus when he dies, and calls forth aloud in his tomb, "come out." It is principally in virtue of his personal operation as God that the eternal Logos raises Lazarus from the dead. (John 11:35, 43–44) However, the action of the Logos incarnate is both divine and human. When Christ raises Lazarus from the dead, he does so by virtue of his divine wisdom and power in which he is one with the Father. But he also conceives of doing so with a human mind and wills to do so with a human heart. The two operations are harmonious but distinct, and allied within a hierarchical subordination, in which Christ knows and wills humanly that which he also knows and wills as God, just as his human nature is the instrument of his divine person.

Western scholastic theologians were sensitive to this crucial symmetry of thought derived from the Gospels, the reflection of the Councils and developed by eastern theologians like Sophronius of Jerusalem and Maximus the Confessor.[5] They derived their most immediate knowledge of it

---

2. On the controversy surrounding Leo's tome in the aftermath of Chalcedon, see Chesnut, *Three Monophysite Christologies*.

3. John Damascene, *The Orthodox Faith* III, c. 15.

4. Ibid., III, c. 19.

5. See von Schönborn, *Sophrone de Jerusalem*, esp. 199–224; Bathrellos, *Byzantine*

from John Damascene, through the medieval Latin interpretation of *The Orthodox Faith*, which served as a focal point for reflection on the mystery of Christ in the university of Paris in the thirteenth century.[6]

However, they also contributed to this same tradition by prolonging it, especially in reflecting upon the mystery of the human knowledge of Jesus. In effect, it is not enough simply to affirm that Christ reveals to us the truth that he is one with the Father, and is himself the uncreated Logos. For Christ does this *precisely as one who is human*, who has human understanding of his mission from the Father which he articulates in the language and concepts of our nature, as the definitive *human* interpreter of the prophecies of the old covenant. Consequently, in order to think out the ontological implications of the soteriology of Chalcedon, Aquinas posits the existence of infused habitual prophetic knowledge in Christ, co-existing with what he calls our ordinary "experiential knowledge."[7] As a human being in time, Christ can and does learn from his environment as we do, but as one whose humanity is the instrument of his divine person, he is also suffused with a habitual capacity to grasp supernaturally what God is doing in the divine economy, to interpret correctly the fulfilling of the scriptures, and to speak truly of that which the Father has given him to reveal.

In addition, and even more significantly, Aquinas posits that Christ as man did not possess supernatural faith. The main reason given by Aquinas is soteriological. A person who lives in faith inevitably awaits the fulfillment of salvation in grace that is to come from another. Christ, however, is not saved by another but is himself the Savior. Consequently, he was not himself subject to receiving salvation from another through the medium of revelation received in faith and trust, but is himself the Source of revelation, the emissary of the truth, truth incarnate.[8] Instead of the theological virtue of faith, Christ possessed in his human intellect the immediate vision of the essence of God even in his earthly life, precisely so that he might be our savior in his human understanding, willing, actions and words. This teaching is grounded firmly in the Gospel of John: Jesus sees the Father, knows him, and reveals him to us. As he says in John 5:19: "the Son can do nothing of his own accord, but only what he sees the Father doing; for whatever he does, that the Son does likewise."[9]

Christ, esp. 176–85.

6. See Barnes, *Christ's Two Wills*; Morard, "Thomas d'Aquin," 211–365, and "Une source de saint Thomas d'Aquin," 21–56.

7. Thomas Aquinas, ST III, q. 9, a. 3; q. 11.

8. Ibid., ST III, q. 9, a. 2.

9. Traditional Catholic theology asserts that Christ can possess the immediate knowledge of God in his human intellect and still suffer grievously in the passion,

Here, then, the medieval Latin theologians developed what they received from the Greek eastern fathers, regarding both the instrumentality of the sacred humanity of Christ, and the dual operations of Christ as God and man. There is a deep connection between the knowledge of Christ as man, and his human action in the mystery of his trial, passion and death. For as is evident in the Gospel of John, Christ assents freely *as man* to the mystery of his death, *for our sake*. John 10:17 ". . . I lay down my life that I may take it up again."[10]

In fact, the Son will be raised from the dead by the Father's power, by his own power, and by the power of the Holy Spirit, not only due to the intention of God to refashion the human race in the resurrection, but also due to a kind of inward moral fittingness of justice. Just as Christ gave his life for us freely as man, in the fullness of charity and in perfect obedience to the Father, so also he is fittingly raised from the dead, glorified in soul and body, in just or proportionate compensation to the righteousness of his self-offering.[11]

Why is this significant for our purposes? It follows from what we have been saying that Christ makes expiation for human sin, that he justifies us, not first and foremost by what he suffers, though his suffering does add to the merit of his action, but from what he *offers* to the Father. The atonement occurs by means of a reparative charity and obedience in the human heart of Christ, who offers himself to God for our sake, so as to make satisfaction to God for all human sin, and so as to restore the human race "from within" to friendship with God.[12] Christ as man knows that he is sent into the world to do the Father's will, and wills to do so freely so as to refashion and divinize our human condition in and through his own sinless obedience and love.

I am restating succinctly the famous atonement theory of Anselm of Canterbury which is adopted by Aquinas. On the reading I am offering of it, this theology clearly has its organic roots in eastern Chalcedonian theology and dyotheletism. There exists a profound continuity between the Christological ontology of the eastern fathers and the progressive elaboration of western medieval atonement theory. Man should not divide what God has united. If we wish to understand how God has saved us (by both atonement and divinization) we would do well to keep together both the Byzantine century theology of dyotheletism and the thirteenth theology of *satisfactio*

---

enduring even more intense suffering, in some respects, due to the acuity of his knowledge. See on this question White, *Incarnate Lord*, chapter 6.

10. See the study of this theme in Aquinas and its patristic roots in White, "Voluntary Action," 497–534; "Kenoticism and the Divinity of Christ Crucified," 1–41.

11. Thomas Aquinas, ST III, q. 53, a. 4.

12. Ibid., ST III, q. 48, a. 2.

theory.[13] The profound point of continuity here, between the Byzantine fathers and the western scholastics, is found in the medieval development of thinking about the human understanding of Christ, the principle of his human engagement to live out freely the will of the Father in all his human actions and sufferings.

THE RIGHTEOUSNESS OF CHRIST AND OUR JUSTIFICATION

We have noted above that 1 John 2:1–2 calls Jesus our advocate or *paracletus* precisely because he has made expiation for all human sin through his meritorious death. However, this raises the traditional question about the nature of this advocacy and its effects. In what way is it something wholly extrinsic to our life as human beings, and to what extent is it something that we are assimilated to by an intrinsic transformation of the spiritual powers of the human intellect and will?

In one sense, the Johannine witness clearly suggests that we are dependent entirely upon a righteousness that is alien to our fallen human condition. The "world" in the Johannine sense of the term "does not know" the truth about Christ (1 John 3:1) and this truth is one that is "coming into the world" (John 11:27) so that we might receive it gratuitously as an unmerited gift. In another sense, however, faith in this truth alone does not suffice to render us just before God. The saving truth of Christ is only "in us" if we confess our sins and ask Christ to purify us, so that we may with the help of his grace, "keep [his] commandments." "If we confess our sins, he is faithful and just, and will forgive our sins and cleanse us from all unrighteousness." (1 John 1:9) "All who keep his commandments abide in him, and he in them. And by this we know that he abides in us, by the Spirit which he has given us." (1 John 3:24)

All of this mitigates against a purely extrinsic account of the work of justification by grace in the soul of the Christian believer. Not only are we transformed noetically by faith in Christ's own righteousness, but we are given a progressive participation in his own mystery of charity and love, his grace of obedience, so that we might also walk in the light of Christ, and inwardly conformed to the mysterious justice of his love.

Curiously, both Calvin and Aquinas perceive parallels here, but in an inverse sense. Calvin portrays the expiation of Christ for our sins in primarily ontologically extrinsic terms, as Christ who is truly innocent is

---

13. For a similar point of view to the one I am arguing, see Hart, *Beauty of the Infinite*, 360–73.

denominated objectively guilty for our sake through a saving prerogative of the divine will.[14] Christ is even subject to the pains of damnation in the crucifixion so as to bear the punishment of spiritual separation from God that is due to us.[15] Meanwhile we are denominated just for the sake of Christ by the imputation of righteousness that is forensic and extrinsic, independently of and prior to all work of sanctification that may take place (subsequently) in the soul of the redeemed Christian.[16]

Aquinas understands the righteousness of Christ to stem above all from his internal human act of charity that moves his will toward God for our sake.[17] His sufferings bear witness to the gravity of human sin, since he is subject passively to the human refusal of divine truth. Furthermore, the sufferings of Christ show forth the depths of the divine love of the Son, and the extent Christ is willing to go to in order to effectuate our salvation.[18] However, these sufferings are not revelations of guilt attributed extrinsically to Christ. Likewise, for Aquinas, we are not denominated just merely for the sake of Christ, in faith, but are rendered just also through the infusion of a habitual disposition of the will.[19] Justification entails a turning of the will under grace toward God in theological hope and love.[20] The intellectual grace of faith has a causal precedence in the order of justification, because we cannot hope for and love what we do not know. But the knowledge of Christ is only confirmed in us as an effectively saving knowledge, rendering us intrinsically righteous *with the justice of Christ himself*, when we turn our hearts toward Christ in hope and charity.[21]

We should notice, then, that there is an ontological parallel (but not an identification!) between Jesus's way of saving us actively, as the God-man, and our way of being saved by his grace, through faith, hope and love. For Aquinas, Jesus is just before God not merely by extrinsic denomination, but by virtue of the intrinsic righteousness of his charity. In turn, he communicates this to us through the inner transformation of our minds and wills, by the illumination of faith *and* the principle of divine love poured into our hearts by grace. Here, I believe, both Aquinas and the Council of Trent have

---

14. Calvin, *Institutes of the Christian Religion*, II, 16, 1–6.
15. Ibid., II, 16, 10–11.
16. Ibid., III, 11, 4 and 23.
17. Thomas Aquinas, ST III, q. 48, aa. 1–2.
18. Ibid., ST III, q. 46, a. 6.
19. Ibid., ST I-II, q. 113, a. 4, ad 1.
20. Ibid., ST I-II, q. 113, aa. 3 and 5.
21. Ibid., ST I-II, q. 114, a. 3.

interpreted the Gospel of John correctly. In the act of justification, members of the Church are conformed inwardly to Christ by love.[22]

At the same time, we can rejoin certain profound intentions of Calvin if we state things in the following way. Jesus did not take upon himself our objective guilt in the passion, but he did take upon himself temporal punishments that stem from the original sin and from our human history of personal and collective sin. The intensive agony of Christ in the passion is, among other things, a reflection of a representational exchange, in which he takes upon himself our *punishments* (extrinsically, so to speak, out of love) so as to communicate to us his innocence.[23] Likewise, we may note that justification for Aquinas and for the Council of Trent is an sheer gift that is wholly unmerited.[24] It implies a gratuitous initiative of divine sanctification insofar as the will is rehabilitated (in an initial but firm way) by infused virtues, reordered away from sin and toward the preferential love for God in hope and charity.[25] This gift of renewal of the heart cleanses from within, and creates a foundation for subsequent "merit" and sanctification. Like Calvin, Aquinas believes that justification is a free gift of grace, and that it lays a foundation for a subsequent life of sanctification through cooperation with the grace of God.[26] However, the justification in question is a form of "gratuitous intrinsicism": the grace offered does affect and transform not only the intellect but also the heart of man, acting from within.

THE HOLY SPIRIT AS ADVOCATE FROM THE FATHER AND FROM JESUS

Christ promises in *John* to send the Holy Spirit. John 15:26: "But when the Advocate comes, whom I shall send to you from the Father, even the Spirit of truth, who proceeds from the Father, he will bear witness to me." This is our second defense lawyer. In court, when we stand before the accusations of the enemy who can rightly claim that we have fallen short of the law, the Spirit will convict us of our sins, but he will also allow us to keep the commandments of the Son. (1 John 3:24) This occurs when we live in the

---

22. Council of Trent, Sess. 6, Decree on Justification, chap. VII.

23. Eschatological innocence.

24. Thomas Aquinas, ST I-II, q. 113, a. 2; 114, a. 2; Council of Trent, Decree on Justification, chap. III and IV.

25. Ibid., ST I-II, q. 110, a. 3–4.

26. Ibid., ST I-II, q. 112, aa. 1–3; q. 111, a. 2; q. 113, prologue. See the important and nuanced comparison of the views of Aquinas and Calvin on justification of Charles Raith II in *Aquinas & Calvin on Romans*.

charity of Christ by grace. "This is my commandment, that you love one another, as I have loved you." (John 15:12) It is the charity of Christ poured into our hearts by the Holy Spirit, the Paraclete, who renders us just before God. This teaching accords profoundly with that of St. Paul in the Letter to the Romans: "There is therefore now no condemnation for those who are in Christ Jesus. For the law of the Spirit of life in Christ Jesus has set me free from the law of sin and death. . . . For those who live according to the flesh set their minds on the things of the flesh, but those who live according to the Spirit set their minds on the things of the Spirit. . ..for if you live according to the flesh you will die, but if by the Spirit you put to death the deeds of the body you will live." (Rom 8:1–2, 5, 13)

The Holy Spirit communicates to us a share in the righteousness of Christ, and does so by causing us to participate in the grace of Christ. Christ is the head and we are the members (Eph 5:23; Col 1:18), or to use the Johannine imagery, he is the "vine" and we are the "branches." (John 15:5) The Son, who originates eternally from the Father, sends the Spirit into the world so as to give to the Church a participation in his own life, engrafting fallen humanity into his own saving pattern of existence.

The Son cannot merely send the Holy Spirit upon the Church by virtue of his human nature, or through his human nature. Here we must retain the ancient Cappadocian principle, which is always valid in Trinitarian theology: the persons of the holy Trinity do all that they do *ad extra* in unity of nature, wisdom, power and will. That is to say, in all works of creation and redemption, the Father, Son and Holy Spirit, while personally distinct, also only ever act as one, just as they are each the one God, and each possess immutably the divine nature, wisdom, power and will. This is true also with regard to the grace of Christ, according to his human nature. Only the Son and Word is human, not the Father or the Spirit. But the Son possesses grace in his human mind and heart by the will of the Father, but also by that same will that he himself possesses as the Word, and that the Spirit possesses who issues forth from the Father eternally. If this is the case, then the Spirit is the author of the humanity of Christ and of the grace of Christ. He does not issue forth from Christ, as man, except insofar as he moves the human nature to be associated instrumentally in willing his (the Spirit's) own divine sending upon the Church.

Consequently, if Christ says that "I will send him to you," then the only fully realistic reading of the text must connote that the Son personally sends the Spirit upon the Church. This signifies a relation between the Son and the Spirit: that the Spirit comes forth from the Son *in time*, in the *economic missions of the persons*. However, need we conclude from this that the

Holy Spirit proceeds from the Son *eternally*, in the life of the Holy Trinity? Indeed, it would seem that we do need to affirm this.

The reason is that it is extremely problematic to say that new relations between persons of the Trinity come to be as a result of the creation or the divine economy. The person who has made this point most forcefully in recent theological literature is the Orthodox theologian David Bentley Hart. Hart has been critical of various theologies of modern derivation, basically inspired by Hegelian ontology, that Erich Przywara labeled with the term "theopanism."[27] Theopanism as so defined understands the being of God to undergo historical alteration, enrichment, diremption, or suffering as a result of the creation, incarnation or the passion of Christ. Various theologians in the Barthian tradition do not hesitate to attribute this form of alteration to the inner relations of the Trinity, at least in the sense that the eternal relation between the Father and the Son is characterized formally by the relation between Jesus in his human obedience and suffering, and God the Father.[28] However, traditional doctrine rightly insists that God is eternally impassible and immutable, in his life and essence as creator and redeemer, as Father, Son and Holy Spirit. If this is the case, then the temporal economy does not create the conditions that characterize the eternal relations between the persons of the Trinity. Rather the inverse is the case: it is the relational persons of the Holy Trinity who author our created history under grace.

It follows from this, however, that there should arise no new hypostatic relations between the Son and the Spirit in time than those that obtain between them eternally. So if Jesus knows as man that he is sending us the Holy Spirit who comes forth from him (and tells us so), this is also based on the fact that Jesus knows humanly who he is himself and who the Father are as the primal origin of the Spirit. One can only conclude, it seems to me, that Christ as man is aware and reveals to us that he is sending the Spirit upon us, because he is given from the Father and with the Father to be the principle of the Spirit from all eternity. If this is the case, then the ancient Alexandrian and western doctrine of the filioque is worthy of respectful consideration, and can be welcomed as a permissible theological interpretation of the revelation of the Gospel of John. We may say, following Maximus the Confessor, that the Father generates the Son eternally so as to give to the Son all that the Father has, including his potency as fontal

---

27. See in particular, Hart, "No Shadow of Turning," 184–206. On Przywara and "theopanism," see Betz, "After Barth," 35–86.

28. For example, Moltmann, *Crucified God*; Jüngel, *God as the Mystery of the World*; Jenson, *Systematic Theology*.

origin to spirate the Holy Spirit.[29] In this way, the Father spirates the Spirit eternally "through" or "from" the Son.[30] This perichoretic interpretation of the filioque is ecumenical in shape, and originated from Maximus's desire to delineate the profound unity between eastern and western theological traditions in the life of the Church. We would do well to imitate his example.

SCRIPTURAL JUSTIFICATION IN THE CHURCH

It would follow from this last point that Jesus did not intend first and foremost to justify us through a merely individual relationship with each of us in the Spirit, but by an active incorporation of all the elect into the apostolic community of the Church. The Paraclete or Advocate is not sent to individuals but to the apostolic community as a whole. "When the Spirit of truth comes, he will guide you into all the truth; for he will not speak on his own authority, but whatever he hears he will speak, and he will declare to you the things that are to come." (John 16:13) We can understand this most truly when we consider Christ's gift of the Spirit to the apostles in the wake of the passion and resurrection. Appearing to the apostles after rising from the dead, Christ associates them corporately with the mission of the Spirit, to reconcile the world to God through the forgiveness of sins. "Jesus said to them again, 'Peace be with you. As the Father has sent me, even so I send you.' And when he had said this, he breathed on them, and said to them, 'Receive the Holy Spirit. If you forgive the sins of any, they are forgiven; if you retain the sins of any, they are retained.'" (John 20:21–23) The forgiveness of sins is thus understood to occur through the mediation of the apostles. They have the power to bind and to loosen. By this power, (which they exercise only in Christ and from him, in the Spirit!) they *incorporate individuals into the visible communion of charity that the apostles themselves have with Christ.*

We must immediately add, however, that this forgiveness and justification in Christ are themselves based in the truth, for it is fundamentally the gift of faith that saves us, and faith has an essentially cognitive content. We believe in God the holy Trinity by the medium of the enunciations of the apostolic doctrine. This means in turn that the forgiveness of sins that incorporates us into a visible and apostolic Church also entails necessarily a corporate, public, apostolic *truth*. This is the message of the Gospel to which we adhere, given to us from Christ and the Sprit, through the apostolic

---

29. On St. Maximus and the contemporary ecumenical consideration of the Filioque, see Garrigues, *Le Saint-Esprit sceau de la Trinité*.

30. Thomas Aquinas, ST I, q. 36, a. 3.

revelation. Thus the apostle can rightfully say: "We are of God. Whoever knows God listens to us, and he who is not of God does not listen to us. By this we know the spirit of truth and the spirit of error." (1 John 4:6) We might say, then, not so much that justification is the article on which the Church stands, as that Christ and the Spirit working through the apostolic Church (in word and sacraments) are the foundations on which justification depends.

This way of thinking about the economy of salvation is reflected in the earliest ecclesial teachings of the post-apostolic Church, and which lend support to an ecclesiology of the episcopal monarchy. The Spirit of Truth is the Spirit of Christ received by the apostles, *and their successors*, the bishops of the one holy Catholic and Orthodox Church. As Ignatius of Antioch says, "Wherever the bishop shall appear, there let the multitude [of the people] also be; even as, wherever Jesus Christ is, there is the Catholic Church."[31] The fullness of communion with Christ is not merely reducible to communion with the episcopal hierarchy that stems from the apostles, but this latter communion is a sine qua non condition for the former.

If this is the case, are we obliged to abandon the notion that justification occurs in us through the instrumental role of holy scripture and the reading and preaching of the word of God? Of course not, nor could anyone rightly attempt to claim this. Scripture is essential to the life of the Church and has a primacy in and definitive authority over the life of the Church.[32] The Church only speaks in truth if and when she speaks in obedience to holy scripture. Here, however, we may speak rightly of *unica scriptura*, but not *sola scriptura*. The scriptures have a unique authority that the Church must heed and obey utterly, but they are also *only rightly heard and understood* from within the Eucharistic and episcopal communion of the Church, as the *divinely instituted locus* in which the Holy Spirit reveals his truth and in which that truth is safeguarded and transmitted.[33] The scriptures act upon us, to justify us, but they do so only because the Advocate acts through them and within us to communicate a saving faith that is truly ecclesial, as well as a hope and love that are catholic or universal. It is this inner advocacy of the Spirit from within that operates, justifies and transforms so as to save us, preparing the Church in infallible hope for the final judgment that we are to undergo, in Christ, before God. Salvation is from Christ alone. Salvation comes from the Holy Spirit alone. Salvation is essentially ecclesial in nature.

---

31. Ignatius of Antioch, *Letter to the Smyrnaeans*, para. 8.
32. Second Vatican Council, *Dei Verbum*, para. 9–12.
33. See on this issue, Congar, *Tradition and Traditions*.

CONCLUSION

The future of ecumenism among Christians must be based in an examination of holy scripture, but for this very reason, it must also be dogmatic in nature. Modern forms of convergence ecumenism that seek to identify similarities and likeness amidst diverse confessional traditions *presuppose* in truth that there are well defined interpretations of doctrine present in these confessional communities. In that sense the elaboration and clarification of doctrinal presuppositions is healthy and can facilitate not only dialectical modes of thought, but also the pursuit of common grounds of unity and a genuine respect for what are sometimes legitimately *distinct* modes of theological expression and articulation.

In this essay I have tried to suggest that the theme of Christ's righteousness in the trial metaphor that traverses the Gospel of John is one that has profound Christological, pneumenological and ecclesiological repercussions. One might even say that the mystery of justification is at the heart of this trial: the justice of Christ who is the God-man, the justification in Christ communicated to us by grace, the righteousness of the Spirit who infuses us with the charity of Jesus, and the inner communion of the visible Church that is the fruit of incorporation into Christ by faith, hope and love. Here Orthodox and Catholic Christians should find room to agree on profound truths about the mystery of the incarnate Logos, the mystery of divinization, and the visible, hierarchical nature of the Church. Catholics and Protestants may find room for convergence on truths related to the atonement of Christ, the mystery of the Holy Spirit as the Spirit of the Son, and the centrality of justification to a proper understanding of our relationship with God.

It is in the conversation among us that we should ask this same Spirit, the Paraclete, to lead us into a deeper unity of faith, hope and charity, and into the fullness of the apostolic truth. For the unity of Christians is itself a gift of grace willed by Jesus Christ, and authored by the Holy Spirit. It is his righteousness to give, and our judgment before God will depend in large part on whether we accept to receive it.

Behr Final Response

I AM VERY GRATEFUL to my two respondents, who have in their own ways contributed much to the discussion. Learning to read Scripture together is one of the most fundamental tasks of the ecumenical encounter and should be grounded in the ways in which Scripture was read by the disciples of Christ from the beginning: opening the books to see how Moses and all the prophets spoke of how the Christ should suffer and rise from the dead, so that repentance and forgiveness be preached in his name throughout the world, beginning from Jerusalem, such that we become "witnesses of these things" (Luke 24:46–8). The "hypothesis" for reading Scripture in this way certainly came to be articulated in terms of a "canon of truth" and then later the creeds and dogmatic reflection; but, I would suggest, the latter is in fact misunderstand when it becomes the starting point for the former, when, that is, having turned dogmatic reflection into a system, Scripture is then read for confirmation of that system. The separation between scriptural exegesis and theological reflection that has become entrenched over the last couple of centuries (such that they usually form different departments in universities and schools) requires reintegration if we are to be effective 'witnesses' today, and the best way to do so is to learn, again, the language of Christian theology as it developed, exegetically, in the early centuries.[1] And this is, at its heart, a true ecumenical encounter, encountering each other on the road to Emmaus as we are taught by another, by Christ himself, how the Scriptures speak of him.

I am especially grateful to Peter Leithart for his fascinating and stimulating response: the insights he offers both complement and supplement my own work. Alongside the lengthy trial motif throughout the Gospel of John, alongside its affirmation that the work of God "in the beginning" is now complete and perfected—"behold the human being"—is the further dimension, woven seamlessly together by John's theological artistry: the

---

1. Cf. Behr, "Reading the Fathers Today," 7–19.

preparation and completion of the dwelling place of God, the tabernacle that Christ is, now dwelling among or in human beings. By ascending the cross, Christ takes his place upon the throne above the cherubim, and his words, "It is finished," refer back not only to Gen 2:1 and God's completion of creation, but to Exod 40:33 and Moses's completion of the tabernacle. By bringing both to completion together, in one act, Christ shows the whole of creation—and not just the tent of meeting—to be the dwelling place of the Lord and so too each human being. According to Maximus the Confessor, the holy Church of God, bringing all things into unity in Christ, is seen in the whole of creation and each human being and can in turn be seen as a human being, as also can the whole of creation.[2]

But it is Peter's further suggestion that I find most fascinating: the connection between the drama unfolded in the Gospel of John and that unfolded in Revelation. If the Gospel of John, beginning "in the beginning" and ending with "it is finished," presents us with the Bridegroom, are we left waiting for the bride, for she is not any of the women that he has encountered to that point nor Mary Magdalene after the resurrection (although her question, "Are you the gardener?" is surely meant to cast her as Eve in her first approach to Adam). Although we now habitually read the Gospel of John as if it is meant to be followed by the book of Acts, it is not: in fact, the Gospel of John brings together the Crucifixion, the Ascension, and Pentecost: in this Gospel Christ ascends the cross in glory and from the cross bestows the Spirit.[3] Instead, the Gospel of John should be read together with Revelation, as Christians did for the first couple of centuries before doubts about the authorship of the latter began to be expressed.[4] It is here, in Revelation, that the bride is finally unveiled. Only read together, as Peter suggests, "do we have a complete Johannine royal romance." The themes that we have traced in the Gospel of John—the courtroom, the trial, and witnesses—are again present in Revelation, but even more clearly, and bringing out more fully the "martyric" dimension of witnessing. In the Gospel of John, then, we see the first fully human being; in Revelation, as Peter puts it, the unveiling of "the formation of a fully human church as it describes the cruciformization of witness.... These witnesses become, like Jesus in his suffering, fully human as they bear witness to God's glory in the face of Christ." Christ is indeed, as the Apostle puts it, "the first born of many brethren," and the whole of

---

2. Cf. Maximus the Confessor, *Mystagogy*, 1–5; and *Ambiguum*, 41.

3. John 19:30. See Ashton, *Understanding the Fourth Gospel*, 347–8: "Now the expression παραδιδόναι τὸ πνεῦμα allows him to fuse Easter and Pentecost as well, hinting that there is no need to think of the latter as a distinct and separate event."

4. For a full survey, see Hill, *Johannine Corpus in the Early Church*.

creation is groaning, awaiting the revelation, the apocalypse, the unveiling of the sons of God (Rom 8:18–30).

However, is it really the case that Revelation is, as it were, the second-part of this Johannine drama? Or does it point to the same mystery but in an unveiled way? As has been noted since at least the third century, to call this book "Revelation," "Apocalypse," which literally means "unveiling," is rather odd, for it is to all appearances the most "veiled" of all the New Testament writings. That revelation occurs through the interplay of veiling and unveiling was often reflected upon by the Fathers: the revelation of the mystery of Christ is an unveiling which takes place through a further veiling. Origen, for instance, points out that the Word of God takes flesh in the Scriptures, so that it can come to our comprehension. But if we remain at the level of the letters, that is all that we will see; yet if we, like the apostles, ascend the mountain, we will be able to see the transfigured Lord in every passage of Scripture.[5] Athanasius similarly points out that as our minds were held by things of sense perception, the Word of God had to come to us in the flesh, so that he could grab our attention. But again if that is all we see, we will never encounter the Word of God; rather, it is through the things that he does that, little by little, culminating at the Cross, we learn that he is not only human but God.[6] The book of Revelation unveils the mystery that is enacted and embodied by Christ, but, necessarily, uses veiled language to do so.

There is, however, one further word from the cross, in the Gospel of John, that intimates that something more is already going on within this crucial scene, rather than awaiting a second act: "Woman, behold your son," Christ says to his mother, and to this disciple, "Behold your mother" (John 10:26–27). Origen makes an intriguing comment on these words:

> We might dare say, then, that the Gospels are the firstfruits of all Scriptures, but that the firstfruits of the Gospels is that according to John, whose meaning no one can understand who has not leaned on Jesus's breast nor received Mary from Jesus to be his mother also. But he who would be another John must also become such as John, to be shown to be Jesus, so to speak. For if Mary had no son except Jesus, in accordance with those who hold a sound opinion of her, and Jesus says to his mother, "Behold your son," and not, "Behold, this man also is your son," he has said equally, "Behold, this is Jesus whom you bore." For indeed everyone who has been perfected "no longer lives, but

---

5. Origen, *Philokalia* 15; cf. Behr, *Way to Nicaea*, 169–84.
6. Athanasius, *On the Incarnation*, 16.

Christ lives in him," and since "Christ lives" in him, it is said of him to Mary, "Behold your son," the Christ.[7]

Not only has John brought together, in the crucifixion scene, Easter, Ascension, and Pentecost, as noted above, but, at least as Origen reads these words, there is an intimation or figuration of the bride, the Church, and those who, through her, put on the very identity of Christ.

This fertility of the Cross takes us back to Isaiah. Although what follows the "Fourth hymn of the Suffering Servant" is treated as a separate oracle by modern scholars (and is printed as such in modern Bibles), it was read, from the time of Paul, as the conclusion: "Sing, O barren on, who did not bear; break forth into singing and cry aloud, you have not been in travail. For the children of the desolate one will be more than the children of her that is married, says the Lord" (Isa 54:1). The Passion of Christ is catalyst for the barren woman to give birth to many children: she, the heavenly Jerusalem, "is our mother" (Gal 4:26). The Bride is already present at the crucifixion, and the tomb becomes the womb for those born into life as brethren of the firstborn of the dead. The Gospel of the Theologian, then, encompasses the beginning and end of all the work of God, as Christ's "It is finished" brings to completion creation, the temple, and the marriage feast.

---

7. Origen, *Commentary on John*, 1.23.

CHAPTER 6

John 21

Peter, John, and Jesus On the Beach

MICHAEL ROOT (CATHOLIC)

BIBLICAL TEXTS CAN INVITE interpretation in various ways. Some passages attract by their narrative skill in depicting the interaction of the divine and the all-too-human (e.g., the stories of Joseph in Genesis and of David in 1 and 2 Samuel). Some attract by the theological depths they uncover (e.g., the "I am" speeches of Jesus in John or Paul's reflections on God and Israel in Romans). The closing chapter of the Gospel of John, John 21, attracts interpretation by its sheer accumulation of oddities. If the disciples have already received a missionary commission in the previous chapter ("As the Father has sent me, even so I send you;"[1] 20:21), then why have they returned to fishing (v. 3)? If the risen Jesus has already appeared to the disciples two times, why can only the Beloved Disciple recognize him (v. 7)? Why does Jesus ask if the disciples have anything to eat if he already is cooking fish on the beach (v. 9)? Why are we told the precise number of fish the disciples catch—153—and what is that rather odd number supposed to mean (v. 11)? And so on, to the end of the chapter. Besides, what is this chapter doing here at all, since the ending of the previous chapter has every sign of being the end of the book?

These puzzles in John 21 have attracted attention since the earliest commentaries on the text and many remain without widely accepted

---

1. Unless otherwise indicated, all citations are to the Revised Standard Version.

solutions. A presentation on this passage can explore many things. In the ecumenical context of this conference, however, the focal point of interest is unavoidable: Jesus's thrice repeated command to Peter to feed or tend my sheep or lambs (vv. 15, 16, 17). This passage, along with Matt 16:18 ("you are Peter and on this rock I will build my church"), has been the most commonly cited biblical text in official Catholic texts asserting papal primacy. *Pastor aeternus*, the First Vatican Council's 1870 Constitution on the Church of Christ, states: "And after his Resurrection, Jesus conferred upon Simon Peter alone the jurisdiction of supreme shepherd and ruler over his whole flock with the words: 'Feed my lambs . . . Feed my sheep'" (Dz. 3053).[2] References to papal primacy in *Lumen gentium*, the Second Vatican Council's Constitution on the Church, cite John 21 similarly (sections 19 and 22; Dz. 4143, 4146).[3]

The Catholic interpreter thus has an aid to interpreting John 21, a magisterial teaching on a core sense of what the passage means. The magisterial teaching need not imply the anachronism of thinking that Jesus imposed upon the apostle Peter the office of pope as it came to be described by Vatican I, which Peter refrained from exercising out of modesty or prudence. It does imply, however, that Jesus here makes Peter the unique and authoritative shepherd of Christ's flock. The Catholic interpreter can agree that the papacy went through a long historical development. That development is complex. Some aspects (e.g., the Bishop of Rome as ruler of a state similar to other states) were historically accidental and in principle reversible. Some were simply sinful (e.g., the entanglement of the papacy with the rivalry of Roman noble families in the tenth century, the papacy's lowest point). But some developments the Catholic will see as the unfolding of essential elements in some sense implicit in what Jesus granted to Peter (e.g., the role of the Bishop of Rome as final court of appeal in the Church). Explicating such claims about the papacy and about the development of doctrine are

---

2. Citations marked 'Dz.' refer to texts by number in Heinrich Denzinger and Peter Hünermann, eds. *Enchiridion Symbolorum Definitionum et Declarationum de Rebus Fidei et Morum* (San Francisco: Ignatius Press, 2012). It may be of some significance that the canon attached to this statement (Dz. 3055) makes no mention of specific biblical texts. The canon does, however, refer explicitly to 'the blessed apostle Peter' being constituted "prince of all the apostles and the visible head of the whole Church militant," and states that Peter "received immediately and directly from Jesus Christ our Lord . . . a true and proper primacy of jurisdiction."

3. Denzinger's biblical index cites only one such use of John 21 in the first millennium: a letter of Pope Vigilius in 552 in the context of the Christological controversies of the time (Dz. 413). It also lists three medieval uses (Dz. 774, 872, 975) and the already cited references by the two Vatican Councils.

obviously tasks that go well beyond this presentation.[4] Something along such lines, however, seems to me an essential background to the Catholic's approach to this text.

How do these commitments shape the Catholic interpreter's participation in an ecumenical discussion of John 21? On the whole, they are in certain respects not far from what many, and perhaps most, interpreters find in this passage. That Peter is here made the unique shepherd of the flock is the most common reading of the text in the patristic and medieval periods, both East and West.[5] Later, Calvin read the dialogue between Jesus and Peter as describing only Peter's rehabilitation as an apostle, rather than the ascription to Peter of a special role,[6] but such a reading finds limited acceptance today. Especially when read in the light of the other two Petrine commissioning episodes in Matthew 16 and Luke 22:32 ("strengthen your brethren"), John 21 clearly indicates some unique role for Peter.

But what sort of role? Peter is to feed and tend the flock of Christ (which, as has been often noted, remains Christ's; they do not become Peter's sheep). Both Luther and Calvin insisted that the only true way to feed Christ's sheep is by the proclamation or (more broadly) ministry of the Word.[7] The question is how to interpret Jesus's command "tend" or "shepherd" (ποίμαινε). In the Septuagint, the verb ποιμαίνω has a strong sense of govern, as by the judges (2 Sam 7:7) or by a renewed "David" (Ez 34:23).[8]

---

4. John Henry Newman's discussion of these questions is still an excellent place to start: John Henry Newman, An Essay on the Development of Christian Doctrine (Notre Dame, Ind.: University of Notre Dame Press, 1989), 148–62.

5. Augustine, *Jo. ev. trac.* 124.5; Augustine. "Tractates on the Gospel of St. John," in *Nicene and Post-Nicene Fathers* (Peabody, MA: Hendrickson, 1888), 1.7.450; John Chrysostom, *Commentary on Saint John the Apostle and Evangelist: Homilies 48–88*, trans. Sister Thomas Aquinas Goggin, The Fathers of the Church, vol. 41. (New York: Fathers of the Church, 1960), 470, 473. Gregory the Great. *Forty Gospel Homilies*, trans. Dom David Hurst, Cistercian Studies Series (Kalamazoo, Mich.: Cistercian Publications, 1990), 182.

6. "The Evangelist now [v. 15] relates how Peter was restored to the rank of honor from which he had fallen. . . . And from the time he abandoned his post he had been deprived of the honor of apostleship. Now both the freedom and the authority of teach, which he had lost through his own fault, are restored to him"; John Calvin, *The Gospel According to St. John 11–21 and The First Epistle of John*, trans. T. H. L. Parker (Grand Rapids, MI: Eerdmans, 1961), 218.

7. See Luther's extensive discussion of 'feed' and 'tend' in these verses in Luther, Martin. "On the Papacy in Rome, Against the Most Celebrated Romanist in Leipzig," in *Luther's Works: Church and Ministry I* (Philadelphia: Fortress Press, 1970), 39, 95–100; Calvin, *John 11–21 and 1 John*, 219.

8. Urban van Wahlde notes: "The present passage [Jn 21:15] is so close to the Ezekiel passage that a first-century reader familiar with the Jewish scriptures would almost certainly recognize the Johannine text as an echo of the Ezekiel passage. Peter is to

The quotation of Micah 5:2 in Matt 2:6 prophecies a ruler who will "'shepherd" (ποιμανεῖ) Israel. Especially in light of Peter's predicted martyrdom (vv. 18-19), the echoes in John 21 of Jesus as the good shepherd (ποιμὴν) who lays down his life for the sheep (John 10:11) are unmistakable. As Philo said: "Those who feed [boskein] supply nourishment . . . but those who tend [poimainein] have the power of rulers and governors."[9] By calling upon Peter to "feed and tend," Jesus is calling him to a pastoral office with some sort of significant authority.[10]

So far, so good, and not so controversial. Peter does, after all, exercise a significant leadership role in the opening chapters of Acts, with considerable pastoral authority, as Ananias and Sapphira painfully discover (Acts 5:1-11). In his ecumenically important mid-twentieth-century study of Peter in the New Testament, the Lutheran scholar Oscar Cullmann found Jesus's mandate to Peter in John 21 fulfilled in this ministry of Peter in the earliest church.[11] It is true, but for Cullmann not particularly significant, that Peter was then the pastor of the entire flock of Christ, since in those first days that flock did not extend beyond the primal Jerusalem community. For Cullmann, this early ministry of Peter is also where the story ends. Jesus is indicating that Peter should lead the Church in its important and fragile first steps. But Cullmann vehemently denies that John 21 (or Luke 22) indicate any kind of ongoing office.[12] In fact, Peter himself, Cullmann argues, later handed over leadership of the Jerusalem community and of the wider church to James the brother of Jesus, so that Peter could devote himself to the larger mission to the Jews.[13]

---

shepherd the sheep on behalf of Jesus as David was to shepherd the sheep on behalf of YHWH. Because David is described as 'ruler' in Ezekiel, it would be natural to conclude that this was also the nature of the office given to Peter" (Urban C. von. Wahlde, *A Commentary on the Gospel and Letters of John. Vol. 2: Commentary on the Gospel of John* [Grand Rapids, MI: William B. Eerdmans Pub. Co., 2010], 902).

9. Cited in Raymond E. Brown, *The Gospel According to John*, The Anchor Bible (New York: Doubleday, 1966), no. 29-29A, 1105.

10. Attention should also be paid to the echo of John 21 in 1 Peter 5:2: "Tend [ποιμάνετε] the flock of God that is your charge." The echo does indicate that 'tend' is a command that applies to all pastoral ministry.

11. Oscar Cullmann, *Peter: Disciple, Apostle, Martyr: A Historical and Theological Study*, trans. Floyd V. Filson (Philadelphia: Westminster Press, 1953), 33-40, 64, 214.

12. Cullmann, *Peter*, 64, 208. Cullmann does grant that Mt 16:18, Peter as foundation of the Church, does imply an ongoing significance, but that significance resides in Peter's role as apostle and leader of the apostles. The apostolic mission and witness is foundational for the church throughout its entire history. Cullmann thus reads Mt 16:18 through the lens of Rev 21:14 and Eph 2:20 (pp. 209, 215, 221).

13. Cullmann, *Peter*, 40-55, 224.

If one attends only to the New Testament text, judging Cullmann's reading is difficult. For supporting evidence, he appeals to the presiding role of James, not Peter, at the meeting in Jerusalem depicted in Acts 15 and to Paul's claim in Galatians (2:12) that Peter feared those who "came from James."[14] While these two incidents constitute items to be explained by any advocate of a lifelong, church-wide leadership role for Peter, they are not insurmountable obstacles to such an understanding.

Cullman's larger argument that a succession in Peter's commission is impossible relies on his distinctive understanding of the time of Christ and the apostles as an unrepeatable midpoint. The Catholic reading is "connected with a failure to grasp the basic attitude of all New Testament thought. In opposition to Hellenism, it is characteristic of the thinking of Jesus as of all Biblical thinking that *what continues has its roots in the once-for-all unique event*... In this sense we must also regard all the apostolic action, including the loosing and binding promised to Peter, as *the basic event*. It belongs to what happened once for all; it belongs, one may say, to the incarnation of Christ."[15] In support of this claim Cullmann cites his study *Christ and Time*.[16] Cullmann's reconstruction of the understanding of time shared by "all Biblical thinking" is, at the very least, debatable and its application to the particular question of a succession in the role of Peter open to doubt. Catholic theology agrees Peter has no successor in his role as apostle. The distinction between the first generation and all later generations is not denied. The question is just what is the nature of that distinction.

Questions of this sort are not going to be settled by direct appeals to scripture.[17] Scripture plays an important role in the discussion of such questions, but the particular answers different persons find compelling will be shaped by a wide variety of other beliefs: beliefs about how God does and does not use the structured, visible church to achieve his ends; beliefs about the way grace does or does not elevate the human agent to participate in God's authoritative actions; beliefs about the relation between the communal, personal, and collegial aspects of ministry.[18] The path from a particular

---

14. Cullmann, *Peter*, 42f.

15. Cullmann, *Peter*, 211, emphasis in original.

16. Oscar Cullmann, *Christ And Time: The Primitive Christian Conception of Time and History*, trans. Floyd V. Filson (Philadelphia: Westminster Press, 1950).

17. For a recent Catholic survey of the background of papal primacy in the New Testament, conducted with ecumenical sensitivity, see Rudolf Pesch. *Die biblischen Grundlagen des Primats* (Freiburg: Herder, 2001).

18. Does that which is a church always have a pastor? If the universal church is a church, does it then rightly have a pastor? For a Lutheran argument along such lines, open to the possibility of some form of papal primacy, see Robert W. Jenson, *Systematic*

biblical passage to some large theological conclusion (such as "the bishop of Rome has a universal primacy") is mediated by wide range of other beliefs, in the light of which a particular reading of a particular passage will seem natural to one person and forced to another. Those beliefs are themselves shaped by the reading of the Bible, but the interaction of one's reading of a specific text and the set of beliefs one brings to the text from one's prior formation and reading is complex.[19] If two readers approach a text with a significantly different set of interpretively relevant beliefs, then they may read a text differently and no amount of direct exegesis of the text at hand will adjudicate the difference.

For this reason, I do not think a discussion that focuses directly on the interpretation of Jesus's command to Peter to "tend my sheep" will get very far. The most likely result will be a rehashing of confessional polemics. Far more useful, I believe, would be a discussion of how John 21 fits into larger patterns in John and in the Gospels as a whole. Over the last fifty years of ecumenical dialogues, significant progress has been made in laying out an ecumenically agreed picture of how the New Testament portrays Peter. Such a consensus is best summarized in the 1973 study *Peter in the New Testament*, commissioned by the US Catholic-Lutheran dialogue and involving Anglican, Catholic, Lutheran, and Reformed biblical scholars.[20] Shifting our focus from the controverted individual passages to these larger patterns may not immediately resolve differences, but it may raise a new set of more fruitful questions which, in the long ran, can change the background conditions for a discussion of the implications of such passages of John 21:15–17.

A preliminary comment needs to be made before I turn to two important patterns. I will simply assume in the following that the Bible is a text "inspired by God and profitable for teaching, for reproof, for correction, and for training in righteousness, that the man of God may be complete, equipped for every good work" (2 Tim 3:16–17). If that is so, then the reader should begin with an assumption that a passage under consideration is relevant, in some way, for the ongoing life of the Church. The difficulty, of course, is in determining in just what way some text is relevant. Patristic and medieval exegesis may have been too eager and inventive in their search for contemporary meaning, but their impulse was correct. If my assumption

---

Theology: The Works of God (New York: Oxford University Press, 1999), 234, 243.

19. See especially David H. Kelsey, *The Uses of Scripture in Recent Theology* (Philadelphia: Fortress Press, 1975); republished as David H. Kelsey, Proving Doctrine: The Uses Of Scripture In Modern Theology (Harrisburg, PA: Trinity Press International, 1999).

20. Raymond E. Brown, Karl P. Donfried, and John Reumann, eds. *Peter in the New Testament* (Minneapolis: Augsburg Pub. House, 1973).

is valid, then John 21 is not just providing us with historically interesting information about Peter and John in their relation to Jesus, but also saying something about the later church. In addition and in line with reading the text as inspired, I will read John, including chapter 21, as a finished whole[21] and as part of a canon which, while internally differentiated, is meant to be read as a whole.

Let me then turn to the way John 21 fits into two larger patterns, one spread across the Gospels and Acts and the other specific to John.

First, John 21, in both its subunits—the catch of fish and the dialogue between Peter and Jesus—is one of a series of texts that depict Peter, the most widely named and sharply depicted of the apostles. I have already noted the similarity of John 21 to the two other commissioning texts; Matthew 16 and Luke 22. The depiction of Peter in John 21 parallels aspects of these other texts.

First, Peter here plays a leadership role among the disciples. He says "I am going fishing" and the other disciples follow (v. 3). Such a leadership role is ascribed to Peter in all the Gospels and Acts, from early in Jesus's ministry (Mark 1:36; 3:16, and parallels; Luke 5:1-11; John 6:68) through the early days of the Jerusalem community (Acts 1:15; 2:14, 38; 3:6-7, 12, etc.).[22]

Second, as elsewhere, Peter here is impetuous. Just as in Matthew 14, where Peter is the one who steps out of the boat and walks toward Jesus on the water (14:28-30), so here Peter is the one who jumps out of the boat and rushes toward Jesus on the beach.

Third, and most importantly, Peter's fallibility is regularly portrayed in all four gospels. His fallibility can at times exist in close proximity to his role as confessor of the truth. It is Peter to whom "the Father who is in heaven" reveals that Jesus is "the Christ, the Son of Living God" (Matt 16 17), but Peter's confession is immediately followed by his, in Jesus's own words, satanic denial that Christ must suffer (Matt 16:23). In other passages, Peter's fallibility is intertwined with his impetuosity. Jesus's prophecy of Peter's threefold denial before the cock crows follows closely in all four gospels on Peter's insistence that he (and in Matthew and Mark, he alone) will follow Jesus come what may (Matt 26:33; Mark 14:29; Luke 22:34; John 13:36). In John

---

21. It is to be noted that, unlike the endings of Mark that follow Mark 16:8, we have no manuscript evidence that the Gospel ever circulated without chapter 21; Brown, *The Gospel according to John*, 1077. For a vigorous argument that John 21 belongs to the integral text on the basis of evidence internal to the Gospel, see John Breck, "John 21: Appendix, Epilogue or Conclusion?" *St Vladimir's Theological Quarterly* 36 (1992): 27-49.

22. For a summary of Peter as leader of the apostles in the Gospels and Acts, see Brown, Donfried, and Reumann, *Peter in the New Testament*, 159-62.

21, that Jesus asks Peter three times "Do you love me" has from the earliest commentaries[23] been recognized as a reminder of Peter's threefold denial. Peter's response perhaps shows how he has changed.[24] He does not impetuously proclaim his undying devotion, as he had earlier, but appeals to Jesus's own knowledge: "you know that I love you." He "grieves" that Jesus asks the question three times (v. 17), perhaps catching the reference to his threefold denial.[25] It cannot be accidental that all three of the Peterine commissioning passages lies in close juxtaposition to references to Peter's failings.[26]

The way the gospels consistently weave together Peter's leadership and his fallibility raise important questions, questions that should go beyond the standard argument over papal infallibility.

Each time Peter is commanded to shepherd the sheep, he is asked whether he loves Jesus. (Interestingly, the question is not whether he loves the sheep, but whether he loves Jesus). The obvious moral lesson is that all pastoral leadership must rest on a deep love of Christ. But we should press the question further. What happens when pastoral leaders fail in such love? Luther had an answer: "Therefore, the pope who neither loves nor is godly does not tend or keep Christ's word. Consequently, he is no pope either; he has neither power nor anything which is contained in the little word 'tending,' whatever it may be."[27] Scott Hendrix has argued that central to Luther's opposition to the papacy was a judgment that the papacy had radically failed in its pastoral task.[28] Catholic defensiveness is here pointless. There have been, and will again be, bad popes, popes who fail in various ways to "feed the sheep." The Anglican theologian Ephraim Radner has written a striking essay entitled "Bad Bishops," arguing that the test of a commitment to epis-

---

23. Augustine, *Jo, ev. trac.* 123.5 (Augustine, "Tractates on John," 445); Chrysostom, *Commentary on Saint John the Apostle and Evangelist: Homilies 48–88*, 471.

24. Chrysostom notes that Peter has become "a better and wiser man, now no longer boasting and contradicting' (Chrysostom, *Commentary on Saint John the Apostle and Evangelist: Homilies 48–88*, 471).

25. That Jesus initially asks "Do you love me more than these" may also be an echo of Peter's earlier implied insistence that he would stand out from the other disciples in following Jesus (Jn 13:37). A chastened Peter leaves the "more than these" phrase unanswered. In John, however, Peter does not explicitly claim "Even though they all fall away, I will not" (Mark 14:29; cp. Mt 26:33). A reading of the question that would have Jesus ask Peter "Do you love me more than you love these fishing implements" is grammatically possible, but makes little sense in context.

26. The denial that Jesus suffer in Mt 16:22–23; the prophecy that Peter would deny Christ three times in Luke 22:34; and the echo of the threefold denial in John 21: 15–17.

27. Luther, "On the Papacy in Rome, Against the Most Celebrated Romanist in Leipzig," 97.

28. Scott H. Hendrix, *Luther and the Papacy: Stages in a Reformation Conflict* (Philadelphia: Fortress Press, 1981), xii.

copal structure is how one follows even a bad bishop.[29] Catholics need to pursue an analogous line of thought about 'bad popes." The Catholic cannot accept Luther's argument. A pope who fails in love is still pope and still to be followed. But followed how? What sort of criticism comports with or is even required by such following? In what sense is suffering fallible leadership a part of our life in Christ?

The question can be widened. How does the Catholic understand the biblical intertwining of Peter's fallibility and Jesus's mandate, a mandate the Catholic understands as rightly implying the real, but limited, papal infallibility defined by Vatican I? An argument that Peter's fallibility is transformed by Jesus's death and resurrection may have some biblical basis,[30] but doesn't solve the problem, for the post-resurrection Peter can still fail in certain respects, as is clear in Galatians 2, the account of Paul's rebuke of Peter at Antioch. Attempts by some interpreters, most notably Jerome, to exonerate Peter of any failure at Antioch, have since Augustine generally been rejected.[31] Even if Peter's failure is understood as venial, as a failure of adequate consideration for the Gentiles in the community at Antioch,[32] it is still a failure. The Catholic theologian should take the recognition of this biblically attested fallibility not as an attack on Catholic teaching, but as an impetus to a more nuanced and complex picture of the authority of church leadership that is real, but remains a participation in Christ's care of the flock that is always his.

Such reflection can be aided by turning to the second Petrine pattern I wish to note, one unique to John's Gospel. Peter in John's Gospel is consistently shadowed by a second figure, "the disciple whom Jesus loved," the Beloved Disciple, usually taken to be John, the source of the Gospel. The two disciples are often contrasted. In his first named appearance, at the Last Supper, the Beloved Disciple "was lying close to the breast of Jesus," that is,

---

29. Ephraim Radner, "Bad Bishops: A Key to Anglican Ecclesiology," *Anglican Theological Review* 82 (2000): 321–41.

30. In Matthew, Jesus says that he will (future tense) build his church on this rock. In Luke 22, Peter is commanded to "strengthen your brethren" only after he has been sifted by Satan and has "turned again." The future reference is only missing in John 21, a post-resurrection text.

31. The argument between Jerome and Augustine on the interpretation of Galatians 2 can be traced in their exchange of letters; for both sides see letters 28, 40, 75, and 82 in Augustine. "Letters" in Nicene and Post-Nicene Fathers (Peabody, MA: Hendrickson, 1886), 1.7.209–593.

32. For a typical Catholic interpretation of Peter's failure as only venial and related to consideration for the effect of his action on the Gentiles, see the popular 19th-century commentary of John MacEvilly, Archbishop of Tuam, *An Exposition of the Epistles of St. Paul and of the Catholic Epistles*, Vol. 1, 3rd ed. (Dublin: W. B. Kelly, 1875), 362f.

he enjoys a privileged intimacy with Jesus (13:23). This intimacy is made clear when Peter asks the Beloved Disciple to find out from Jesus who is the disciple who will betray him (13:24). The Beloved Disciple, not Peter, is privy to Jesus's thoughts. Later, Peter and "another disciple," usually taken to be the Beloved Disciple, together follow Jesus after his arrest to the court of the high priest (18:15ff). It is the Beloved Disciple who gains admittance for Peter, although Peter, once inside, is challenged and denies Jesus three times (18:17, 25–27). At the foot of the cross, Peter is absent. Has he "scattered" with the other disciples, as Jesus said would happen?[33] The Beloved Disciple is present, however, and is entrusted with the care of Jesus's mother, being made a sort of foster son to her (19:26f).

The relation between Peter and the Beloved Disciple becomes more complex following the resurrection. When Mary Magdalene finds the tomb empty, she goes to "Simon Peter and the other disciple, the one whom Jesus loved" (20:2). The two disciples "run" to the tomb, but the Beloved Disciple "outruns" Peter and arrives first (20:4). Although he looks into the tomb and sees the grave clothes, he does not go in. Only after Peter arrives and goes in does the Beloved Disciple follow. Nevertheless, only of the Beloved Disciple, not of Peter, is it said that "he saw and believed" (20:8). Since the next verse immediately adds: "for as yet they did not know the scripture, that he must rise from the dead," the implication is that Peter did not yet believe.

John 21 is, as Hans Urs von Balthasar has noted, the climax of this fugue. When Jesus calls from the beach to the disciples in the boat, it is the Beloved Disciple, not Peter, who recognizes him and tells Peter: "It is the Lord" (21:7). As at the empty tomb, however, it is Peter who then presses forward, jumping from the boat to swim or wade ashore and Peter who later hauls the fish onshore (20:11).

The ensuing dialogue between Jesus and Peter, with its threefold question and mandate, can seem like a self-enclosed unit, without reference to the Beloved Disciple, but the earliest commentators already raised a difficult question: if Peter does love Jesus "more than these," then he would love Jesus more than the Beloved Disciple loves Jesus. Why then is the Beloved Disciple singled out as being especially loved by Jesus?

The end of the narrative is even more perplexing. After Jesus ends the dialogue with Peter by commanding: "Follow me [ακολούθει]," Peter notices that the Beloved Disciple is "following" [ἀκολουθοῦντα, 21:20; note, in Greek, simply 'following,'; not 'following them,' as some English translation add]. Is the Beloved Disciple simply walking behind Jesus and Peter, or is

---

33. "The hour is coming, indeed it has come, when you will be scattered, every man to his home, and will leave me alone" (16:32).

the Beloved Disciple already doing what Jesus just commanded Peter to do, i.e., follow? While Peter at the Last Supper gets the Beloved Disciple to ask a probing question to Jesus, as the reader here is explicitly reminded, Peter himself now questions Jesus about the future of the Beloved Disciple: "Lord, what about this man?" He receives what can only be taken as a rebuke: "What is that to you?" and is again commanded: "Follow me" (21:22).

What are we to make of this final example of the Peter-Beloved Disciple contrast that runs throughout the second half of John's Gospel and what might it imply about the commissioning of Peter that is embedded within it? Recent commentaries tend to explain the contrast in relation to conflicts within a posited distinct "Johannine community" which was struggling with how it would relate to the wider "Petrine" church. John 21 is then a kind of coded ecclesiastical reconciliation, perhaps appended after the completion of the rest of the Gospel, accepting the wider leadership of the church by a Petrine figure, but still asserting a privileged status for its own tradition, rooted in a real or merely symbolic Beloved Disciple.[34]

Such merely historical readings do not remove all theological relevance from the text but the implications of the text become strikingly thin: charismatic communities that rely on inspirations of the Spirit and are suspicious of hierarchy must finally accept a wider hierarchical leadership.[35] The sufficiently adventurous interpreter might, however, reject this reconciliation as a mistaken compromise with "Frühkatholizimus," clumsily pasted on to an already complete text and undermining its theological integrity.[36]

Earlier commentators, precisely because they assumed that John 21, like all of the Bible, is inspired for our edification, went looking for more in the text. The primary meaning of the Peter-Beloved Disciple contrast cannot be only an historical insight into the development of the community out of which the Gospel came, with some secondary significance for the later church. The Peter-Beloved Disciple contrast is about real individuals—that is taken for granted—but it also must directly be about something of immediate significance for the church and the Christian life as now lived.

---

34. "In the redactional chap. 21 we may have a more moderate voice persuading the Johannine Christians that the pastoral authority practiced in the Apostolic churches and in 'the church catholic' was instituted by Jesus and could be accepted without denigration of the specially favored place in history given by Jesus to the disciple(s) whom he loved most" (Raymond E. Brown, *The Community of the Beloved Disciple* [New York: Paulist, 1979], 162).

35. Raymond E. Brown, *The Churches the Apostles Left Behind* (New York: Paulist Press, 1984), 123.

36. Ernst Käsemann, "The Canon of the New Testament and the Unity of the Church" in *Essays on New Testament Themes* (Naperville, Ill.: Alec R. Allenson, 1964), 103.

The most thoroughgoing explanation of the contrast is found in Augustine's *Tractates* on John.[37] While some interpreters, such as Chrysotom and Cyril of Alexandria, focus on the differences of character between Peter and John, Augustine takes the difference as a sign of *duae vitae*, two sides of the Christian life that are both necessary for the church. Peter stands for faith, life in the temporal pilgrimage, life in the exile of this world, labor, bravery in the face of adversity, the restraint of the body, relief of need, pardoning sins so that one's own sins might be pardoned, enduring evils that so that one may not be elated by earthly goods. Johns stands for sight, life in the eternal mansion, repose, freedom from adversity, spiritual delight, the absence of need, the absence of anything to pardon and or to be pardoned for, freedom from all evil and adherence to the supreme good. "The one is good, but yet in misery; the other, better and blessed. This one was signified by the Apostle Peter, that other by John."[38]

The temptation is to read Augustine as referring to two "states of life," the active and the contemplative, so distinct that it can be said that one person leads the active life and another the contemplative life. Such a reading, however, ignores the details of Augustine's presentation and is explicitly rejected by him.[39] Every faithful Christian struggles with this age, both in the outer world and in his or her own self, enduring burdens that are painful, but salutary in the end. And every Christian is to some degree already in union with God, already lifted above need. Thus, every Christian is to some degree Peter and to some degree John. To put the words of Luther in Augustine's mouth, we are Peter *in re* and John *in spe*. Peter is the "not yet" of Augustine's eschatology; the Beloved Disciple is the "already."

Augustine does not stop here. Why does Peter love Jesus "more than these," but John is "the Beloved Disciple"? Because the Jesus who pardons and supports us in this life is a vivid presence, but we do not yet in the same way know or possess the Jesus with whom we will be one in contemplation. John's Jesus is further from us, and so we love him with less intensity. But

---

37. Chrysostom treats the contrast as merely psychological: Peter is "more ardent, ... more impulsive;" John is "more spiritual, ... more cautious." Thus, John first recognizes Jesus from the boat, but Peter jumps in the water to come to him more quickly (Chrysostom, *Commentary on Saint John the Apostle and Evangelist: Homilies 48–88*, 463). They are singled out because "they were about to take upon themselves the guardianship of the world" (Chrysostom, *Commentary on Saint John the Apostle and Evangelist: Homilies 48–88*, 474).

38. *Jo. ev. trac.* 124.5. English slightly altered from Augustine, "Tractates on John," 450. Latin at http://www.augustinus.it/latino/commento_vsg/index2.htm.

39. "Let no one, however, separate these distinguished apostles. In that which was signified by Peter, they were both alike; and in that which was signified by John, the will both be alike hereafter" *Jo. ev. trac.* 124.7; Augustine, "Tractates on John," 451.

Jesus loves us so that we might all be brought to a Johannine union with him. Thus John is paradigmatically the Beloved Disciple, he is the *telos* of Jesus's love.[40]

Why must Peter be crucified, but the Beloved Disciple remain or, more precisely, abide (μένειν, a loaded term in the Johannine vocabulary, as Augustine keenly observes even through the veil of his Latin translation)? Because the struggles of Peter are of this world alone, the "not yet" that defines Peter's role will pass away and that which forms the "not yet" as 'not yet' must be crucified. But the repose of the Beloved Disciple on the breast of Jesus will "remain" until he comes and then be perfected in glory. For Augustine, Jesus is saying: "Let perfected action, informed by the example of my passion, follow me; but let contemplation begun [*inchoata*] remain till I come, to be perfected when I come. For the godly plenitude of patience, reaching forward even unto death, follows Christ; but the fullness of knowledge remains until Christ comes, then to be manifested."[41] Peter, and not the Beloved Disciple, is made the shepherd who is called to lay down his life for the sheep, following his crucified Lord. But Peter is on pilgrimage toward the Johannine life and his ministry exists for the sake of the Johannine life.

The location of Peter's commissioning in this enigmatic, but profound climax of the Peter-Beloved Disciple interplay puts that commissioning in a context that is too often ignored. Two recent Catholic theologians, however, have reflected on this context.

In his 1937 work *Divided Christendom* [*Chrétiens Désunis*], Yves Congar developed a detailed analysis of two aspects or "planes" or "laws" of the church, the church "as being already the family of God and the community of those sharing the divine life, and as she is in this world, humanly conditioned and militant,"[42] the church as the mystical body of Christ and the church as institutional reality.[43] With explicit reference to Augustine's *Tractate* on John 21, he calls these the Johannine and the Petrine church.[44] These are not two churches, but two aspects of the one church, relating somewhat as soul and body. The analogy indicates a fundamental asymmetry; as the body is the instrument of the soul and exists for the sake of the soul and is dead without the soul, so the Petrine church exists for the sake of the Johannine church; it is its instrument and is dead without it, although the

---

40. *Jo. ev. trac.* 124.6; Augustine, "Tractates on John," 451.

41. *Jo. ev. trac.* 124.5; Augustine, "Tractates on John," 451.

42. Yves Congar, *Divided Christendom: A Catholic Study of the Problem of Reunion* (London: Geoffrey Bles, 1939), 76.

43. Congar, *Divided Christendom*, 216.

44. Congar, *Divided Christendom*, 79, nt 2.

soul cannot function in this life without a body.[45] Papal primacy (in fact, all ecclesiastical office) is strictly an institution of the Petrine church and is thus both subordinate and, eschatologically viewed, passing.[46]

A similar but more complex analysis is offered by Hans Urs von Balthasar in his *The Office of Peter and the Structure of the Church*.[47] Balthasar argues that our understanding of the church must be rooted in the "constellation" [*Konstellation*] of figures who surround Jesus: Mary, Peter (with the rest of the Twelve), John, Paul, James the brother of Jesus. The interaction of the figures in this constellation gives concretion to Jesus's engagement with humanity and so shapes the church.[48] Within this constellation, Peter and John relate as office and love. These cannot be separate, as is shown by Jesus's prefacing his commission in John 21 with his questions about Peter's love. John in a sense merges into Peter, as can be seen in the first chapters of Acts where John is always presented as Peter's silent companion (Acts 3:1, 3f, 11; 4:13, 19; 8:14).[49] Nevertheless, John will "remain," as Jesus explicitly says. He has his successors, as does Peter, but John's successors are not in an office, but are the saints, who are the true heart of the church, those who are entrusted with the care of Mary.[50] Peter cannot remain at the church's heart, for his ministry is "eccentric." He must go out to the edges to seek the lost sheep and haul in the fish. He must deal with disturbance, with Ananias and Sapphira, and sometimes must define the faith when it is undermined by dispute. His office will be his crucifixion.[51]

For Balthasar, the papal office is only rightly understood and practiced when Peter is related to John (and also to Mary, Paul, and James). As with Congar, the papacy has an authoritative place in the church, but that authority is to serve that which is more basic in the church, a reality manifest in John.

The two patterns I have noted in connection with John 21 will not directly alter conflicting opinions on just what is implied by Jesus's command

---

45. Congar, *Divided Christendom*, 80–87.

46. Congar, *Divided Christendom*, 78.

47. Hans Urs von Balthasar, *The Office of Peter and the Structure of the Church*, trans. Andrée Emery (San Francisco: Ignatius Press, 2007).

48. Balthasar, *Office of Peter*, 142–53.

49. "Peter needs the Johannine love to give the Lord the answer worthy of his office, and he also receives this love. Hence, from now on, Johannine love has its place in Peter, but missions given by Jesus do not cease. In the unfathomable mystery of Jesus' good pleasure, John retains his own mission, distinct from that of Peter." Balthasar, *Office of Peter*, 150.

50. Balthasar, *Office of Peter*, 242.

51. Balthasar, *Office of Peter*, 384f.

to Peter to "feed my sheep." What attention to them can do is give greater nuance to Catholic understandings of papal authority and embed that authority in a larger picture of the life of the church and what is essential to it.

On the one hand, such a wider context for discussion might in the long run open some new perspectives for ecumenical discussion of the sort of ministry God wills for his universal church. On the other hand, and more importantly, a more biblical, more widely focussed Catholic understanding of the Petrine ministry can enrich Catholic theology and practice, not just how the papacy is exercised, but also and especially the practice of how Catholics, including Catholic theologians, follow and sometimes suffer papal leadership.

The bishop of Rome is not the church, even if I would say, as a Catholic, that he holds a rightly authoritative place in that church. For the sake of that authoritative role as shepherd, a role I believe enjoined upon Peter and his successors by Jesus, attention to the nuances of the presentation in passages such as John 21 can only be helpful.

Response to Michael Root's John 21
Peter, John, and Jesus on the Beach

D. H. WILLIAMS (EVANGELICAL)

LET ME BEGIN BY saying it is an honor for me to participate in this conference, and that I'm especially glad to have this opportunity of responding to a thoughtful and carefully crafted paper as Michael Root has presented. I'm also impressed by the fact that he has wasted no time by jumping into the lion's den of papal primacy and the biblical exegesis that has supported that doctrine. Root makes it clear in the beginning that his concern was expounding the "essential background to the Catholic's approach" to John 21, which also entailed an examination of Matthew 16. Together they are said to demonstrate Peter's commission as the chief of the apostles. Undoubtedly, Peter is certainly a part of Jesus's inner circle and he is usually the one to say aloud what the rest of the disciples are thinking. By being a man of action—some may say impulsively—he invites attention to his role among the disciples. He is the one who confesses Jesus's Sonship and then is called Satan for rejecting the Son's purpose. And he is the one taught that loving God is the first step of feeding the Lord's sheep.

Nonetheless, Root understands that Catholic exegesis about Peter's primacy in calling could all be quite valid, but that does not inexorably lead to the theological conclusions articulated by Vatican I concerning the Roman bishop's primacy in the Christian world. I certainly agree. Much has to be mediated to move from the Scripture of Matthew 16 to a doctrine about papal primacy—a point that is of course true of all church doctrines which are said to be derived from the Bible. And I think Root's statement in this regard is worth hearing again: "The way the gospels consistently weave together Peter's leadership and his fallibility raise important questions, questions that should go beyond the standard argument over papal infallibility." Root wants to hear the text without the encumbrance of the later doctrines—to the degree that that's possible.

First I want to look at the earliest written responses to John 21 and Matthew 16. For Root to claim that Peter as the unique shepherd of the church is "the most common reading of John 21 in the patristic and medieval periods" was just too tempting for me not to test further such a broad remark.

With special regard to the patristic evidence, two things should be noticed when it comes to Matthew 16 or John 21: 1) We need to be careful about lumping together a rather amorphous body of commentaries and sermons as if they present a monolithic view. I have no doubt Root is aware of this. 2) Having just warned against making sweeping generalizations, I will now make one about Matthew 16; namely, that a common feature of early church exegesis about Peter's confession is the way in which it was less interested in what the passage says about Peter than it says about the Church and Christ's identity.

To be sure, Peter's bold confession put him in a special position when it came to the revelation of salvation history. Leo of Rome plainly states it occurred "by the very Spirit of the Father operating in his believing heart."[1] And Augustine once referred to Peter as the "first and chief in the ranks of the apostles."[2] Yet, there is more going on in Matthew 16 that transcends Peter's role. Peter is only the rock because Christ is. In his commentary on Matthew that survives, Origen "the *Gates of Hades will not prevail over it.* "But what is "it"? Origen asks. Is it the rock upon which Christ builds the church? Or is it the church? It is an ambiguous expression after all. Or are the church and the rock one and the same? But the church, as a building of Christ, who built it wisely as "a house upon the rock" (7:24), is invulnerable to *the gates of Hades*...which have no power over the church.[3]

Augustine follows a similar line of reasoning "There are many places in Scripture where Peter can stand for or represent the Church, and above all in this particular passage Matthew 16 says Augustine, because not just Peter, but Paul and the other apostles rec'd the Keys to the Kingdom"[4] It's no surprise that Cyprian considered Matthew 16 is demonstrative of the church is founded on the bishops, nor Peter did not understand that he was being given the primacy.[5] Some patristic writers argue that Peter was

---

1. Leo of Rome, Sermon 62.2.
2. Ibid., Sermon 76.4
3. Origen, *Commentary on Matthew* 12.11, 15
4. Augustine, Sermon 149.7.
5. Cyprian, Ep. 70.

too unstable to be regarded as a "rock," a point proven very poignantly in John 21. On these grounds, Philoxenus of Hierapolis asserted that Martha's profession in John 11 is "more sound and exact than that Simon's" and thereby more blessed.[6]

Root does an excellent job is portraying the way in which Peter is both stable and faithful and other times just the reverse. Peter suggests making three tabernacles for Moses, Elijah and Jesus, but he is rebuked by God for not understanding the only Son of God. He seems to function as the typical human response—good and bad—to the unfolding of divine events. This way of interpreting Peter's role in the gospels is to see him as representing the "everyman," who has moments of great courage and belief and still also falls into doubt and sometimes paralyzed to follow the way of faith. Origen declares that we ourselves can become what Peter also became, that is, blessed. The grounds for the blessing applicable to Peter are also applicable to us, because flesh and blood did not reveal to us that Jesus was the Christ, the Son of the living God.[7] Augustine too states that "Peter . . . symbolizes us all."[8] A literary analogy suggests itself. In the Adventures of Sherlock Holmes, the character of Watson is the fallible, often baffled, fully human counterpart to Holmes's brilliance and inhuman ability for connecting the varied trails of evidence. With amazement, Watson and the reader watch Holmes make sense out chaotic events to solve the case. In both Matthew 16 and John 21, Peter is Watson to Jesus's Sherlock; Peter exemplifies every believer who has moments of great perception as well as a tendency toward self-centeredness and loss of divine understanding.

Such a portrait of Peter has had tremendous attraction for evangelicals and conservative Protestants who want to be bold for God in acts of witness or possess insight that shows an open heart to the Spirit. Wherein much emphasis is placed on relationship as an unmistakable mark of authenticity, Peter's shining and bumbling acts with Jesus offers a hopeful template for the Christian who wants to believe but needs help in doing so. Whether Matthew 16 or John 21, the alternating moments of courage and confusion speak not about bishops, but of "every believer" who is growing in the Lord. Jesus's question to Peter, "Do you love me?" is the quintessential inquiry that God makes to every disciple.

A third element of Root's paper which would greatly interest Free Church communions is his candid discussion about bad popes. Again, there are questions about that the way the gospels weave together Peter's

---

6. Philoxenus of Hierapolis, *Fragment 27*, CSCO 392:26–8.
7. Origen, *Commentary on Matthew* 12.9–10, GCS 40:80–86.
8. Augustine, Sermon 76.4.

leadership and fallibility that "should go beyond the standard argument over papal infallibility." When it comes to John 21, Peter is asked three times whether he loves Jesus, from which is his love for the sheep is gauged. But, asks Root, what happens when pastoral leaders fail in such love? "There have been and will again be, bad popes, popes who fail in various ways to 'feed the sheep'" Who can ever forget Doré's depiction of Pope Nicholas III (Canto 19) upside down in the mire with only his legs and feet extending upwards? Dante asks

> Pray tell me now. Just what amount of treasure
> Our Lord required in payment from St. Peter
> Before he gave the keys into his hands?
> Forsooth, he only demanded, 'Follow me.'

At first Nicholas mistakes Dante for another pope, Boniface VIII, who was also accused of simony and whom Dante expected to take Nicholas's place. At present, I find it easier to discuss the subject of "bad bishops" when it comes, for instance, to the Episcopalians in the United States. Radner's essay, which Root cites, seeks to determine what is the "essence" of the episcopacy, so that "bad" bishops can help us clarify what is needed for a good one. Radner begins by acknowledging the episcopal essence has been in the past identified in terms of doctrinal integrity, personal moral integrity,[9] but he goes on to claim, rather thinly if not questionably, that these are *ideals* of the essence; not the essence. Given what has happened to the Episcopal church in the United States over the last twenty years, one would have thought Radner would wanted to take the "high ground." But he doesn't. Although he admits "No doubt there *are* doctrinal truths or moral conditions that the Church and her people are led to struggle for and guard," "[o]ur vocation, rather, is to suffer in unity, around our bishops, for the sake of embodying the shape of Jesus Christ in flesh and blood."[10] Bad popes or bishops, despite their disruptive and corruptive influence, "can never subvert the possibility of the Church's service, and can, in cases of extraordinary challenge, even heighten it."[11] I take this to means that the episcopal essence, then, whether Anglican or Roman Catholic is its own structure, and survives good and bad shepherds, and even the bad may stimulate and better the church toward doctrinal or moral truths. This principle sounds something like Tertullian's quip that the Church needs heretics for orthodoxy to be formulated.

---

9. As with the early church. More specifically, I would argue for the canons of Serdica as an excellent example of what a "good" bishop was expected to be.

10. Radner, "Bad Bishops," 340.

11. Ibid., 329.

The question here for Evangelicals and Free Church Christians is how bad is "bad" when it comes to tolerating the church's shepherds. What constitutes an unacceptable "bad" wherein deposement is in order? Denying the Trinity? Disavowing the OT as part of the Bible? Defending homosexual marriage?[12] Of course this these important point of contention for all church communions whether they have bishops or not. But it is safe to say that almost all non-episcopally structured Churches would not accept that the "essence" of pastoral ministry (ordained or not) is found in its office. The nature of Peter's failings in John 21 or Acts never brings his moral character into question. I suspect the apostolic leadership would have look differently if it had. In any case, Peter's failings were always followed by his repentance; the lack of which makes a "bad" pope or bishop very bad indeed.

For historical Protestantism the problem with the sixteenth and seventeenth century Reformation is that too much baby was thrown out with the water, and this may apply to the episcopal system. I am of the mind that it does. Even the Free-ist of Free churches have always had their papal-like leaders: Ted Hagaard, Jimmy Swaggert, Joel Osteen, where the term "pastor" comes hazardously close to what I suspect Prof. Root and I would agree is a "bad" kind of pope (so to speak). Nonetheless, an episcopal system is conjoined with the concept of hand-cuffing a congregation into tolerating a "bad" shepherd, or worse, a magisterium giving direction to a congregation from a distance that does not abide with the will of the congregation. Again, a non-episcopal system has not saved evangelical/Free churches from the abuses they fear. Ecclesial monarchs come in all forms.

Having said this, let me finally observe that evangelical/Free church Churches would not favor Radner's formula that a bad bishop can enable a congregation to suffer through its shepherd's unfaithfulness or moral fall. Such churches follow after an "essence" of purity or holiness when it comes to its leaders, lay or clerical. They endorse that view which interprets the church always in need of restoration or better known as *ecclesia reformata sed semper reformanda*. Such a principle, however, is not the antithesis of an episcopal structure and hopefully not a magisterium.

In the end I must admit that the tension between a purist impulse and an established episcopacy is built into the church's fabric. It is noteworthy that the early church never solved its constant conflicts between bishop governance and the sorts of holiness movements that emerged such as Montanism, Novatianism and Donatism. One could chart the manifestations of the purist impulse in every church age unto the present. Let me quickly add,

---

12. Former Bishop of the Episcopalian Church USA, William Griswold insisted in a pastoral letter that the issues surrounding the episcopal ordination of an avowed homosexual should not be church dividing; Williams, "Diffusive Disintegration" 389–93.

I am not trying to resurrect the *Trail of Blood*! Rather, the question of the church's structure in relation to the purity of its leaders has always been the basis of good and necessary, if unwelcome, contention. And so, a Free Church Protestant will always ask about a church leader, "how bad is bad?"

Giving Honor to Whom Honor Is Due
A Reply to Michael Root

DAVID BRADSHAW (ORTHODOX)

PROFESSOR ROOT'S PAPER REMINDS us that the ecclesiological question of the proper role of the Papacy cannot be separated from the exegetical question of how we are to understand the figure of Peter in the New Testament. It also reminds us that the latter question is important in its own right, for it is in essence the question of how we are to give due honor to one of the greatest saints of the Church. Although this question is of importance for Protestants as well as Catholics and Orthodox, for the latter two it carries particular gravity because of the prominent role of the saints within our faith. For Orthodox as well as for Catholics, St. Peter is the "head of the honored apostles and rock of the Faith."[1] Professor Root's paper is helpful in focusing our attention on some of the complexities surrounding the question of how to give St. Peter his due.

With this common goal in mind, I will begin by offering some observations about how St. Peter has traditionally been venerated in the Orthodox Church. This will lead me to some mildly polemical remarks regarding the patristic exegesis of the passage before us and its relevance to the Roman Catholic view of the Papacy. I will end by explaining why I find the typological reading of the figures of Saints Peter and John offered by Professor Root, although stimulating, ultimately unsatisfactory.

---

1. Nassar, *Divine Prayers and Services of the Catholic Orthodox Church of Christ*, 552.

From ancient times St. Peter has been commemorated in the East, as in the West, primarily on June 29, the Feast of Saints Peter and Paul.[2] This feast is given special gravity by being preceded by a fast, a distinction it shares in the Orthodox calendar with only Pascha, Christmas, and the feast of the Dormition of the Theotokos. (The fast is of variable length depending on the date of Pascha, but typically lasts for a couple of weeks.) The icon of the feast of Sts. Peter and Paul is a familiar one. It depicts the two saints embracing or, in some versions, standing in front of a church or holding a miniature church building between them.[3] The icon emphasizes the mutual love and respect of the two great apostles, perhaps in a deliberate corrective to the impression of tension that one might take away from reading Galatians 2. The hymns of the feast similarly emphasize the equality of the two saints and their shared labors for the Faith. Here, for example, is one of the initial hymns during Vespers:

> With what delightful songs of praise shall we extol Peter and Paul, those two wings of divine knowledge, flying to the four quarters of the earth and ascending to heaven, those two hands of the gospel of grace, those two feet of the preaching of truth, those two rivers of wisdom, those two horns of the Cross through which Christ, who possesses the Great Mercy, did demolish the haughtiness of demons?[4]

A later hymn refers to St. Peter's being blessed with the keys of the kingdom of heaven, but not in a way that elevates him over St. Paul:

> Let us extol Peter and Paul, the two great luminaries of the Church; for they did shine forth in the firmament of faith, transcending the sun in brilliance, and by the rays of their preaching led forth the Gentiles from ignorance to divine knowledge. Wherefore one of them was nailed upon the Cross, making his way to heaven where he received the keys of the kingdom from Christ himself; and the other was beheaded with the sword and carried to the Savior, being blessed as is meet. . . . By their prayers, therefore, O Christ our God, demolish our enemies and establish the Orthodox Faith, for thou art the lover of mankind.[5]

---

2. There is also feast of the chains of St. Peter (commemorating the chains which fell from him in prison, Acts 12:7), celebrated in the East on January 16 and in the West on August 1.

3. A variety of such images can be found by doing a computer search on "icon saint Peter and Paul."

4. Nassar, *Divine Prayers*, 548, slightly modified.

5. Ibid., 549–50.

This hymn gently suggests that the gift of the keys does not make Peter superior to Paul, for just as the two were equal in their martyrdom, so they were (presumably) equally blessed afterward. A later hymn is more explicit on this point, stating that the two are "co-enthroned in grace" (τῆς χάριτος σύνθρονοι).[6]

Of particular note for our purposes is a hymn that alludes directly to John 21. In light of its liturgical prominence, this hymn constitutes the most authoritative interpretation of our passage within the Orthodox tradition.

> Christ, by enquiring three times, Peter, lovest thou me? did make right the three denials. Wherefore, Simon cried unto the Lord who knows all secrets, saying, Thou knowest all things; thou knowest that I love thee. After this the Savior said to him: Feed my sheep, feed my ewes, feed my sheep which I have fashioned for salvation with my own blood. Beseech thou him, therefore, O Apostle blessed of God, to grant us the Great Mercy.[7]

It is important to note here both what is said and what is not said. What is said is that Christ by his three questions "made right the three denials." That is, the hymn finds in our passage not just "a reminder of Peter's threefold denial" (as acknowledged by Professor Root), but an action taken by Christ to *correct and restore* the damage done by that denial. The hymn thus seems to agree with the view, cited by Professor Root as belonging to Calvin, that Peter by his denial in some sense forfeited his apostleship and had to be restored by Christ.

Such a view in fact long antedates Calvin. One of its classic sources is the *Commentary on John* of St. Cyril of Alexandria. Cyril comments:

> Seized with pure fear, the divine Peter thrice denied the Lord. [Christ now] heals the one who has suffered evil, and elicits by various questions his thrice-repeated confession, putting forth this one as a remedy for that, and furnishing his correction as a counterweight to his sins. For a transgression that was verbal, and only in mere words supplied ground of accusation against him, could surely be wiped out in the same fashion as it was committed.... Therefore, by his thrice-repeated confession the thrice-repeated denial of the blessed Peter was done away, and by the saying of our Lord, "Feed my lambs," we must understand a renewal as it were of the apostleship already given to him, washing away the disgrace of the fall that had come between,

---

6. Ibid., 551 (where this phrase is translated "equal in grace and rank"). For the Greek see *Megas kai Hieros Sunekdimos Orthodoxou Christianou*, 754.

7. Nassar, *Divine Prayers*, 548.

and obliterating the faint-heartedness that arose from human infirmity.[8]

Cyril's contemporary, Theodore of Mopsuestia, similarly understands our passage as depicting "the remedy of a triple confession [applied] to the triple wound of denial," whereby Christ "removed from Peter's soul those three struggles in which Satan tempted" him.[9] Nor was such a view confined to the East. St. Ambrose writes that "by feeding well the flock of Christ with the food of faith, he [Peter] effaced the sin of his former fall. For this reason is he thrice admonished to feed the flock; thrice is he asked whether he loves the Lord, in order that he may thrice confess him, whom he had thrice denied before his crucifixion."[10]

Perhaps most interestingly, such an interpretation is developed in some detail by St. Augustine. Augustine writes in his *Homilies* that "the Lord questioned him [Peter] three times, so that a threefold confession might cancel the threefold denial."[11] Returning to the subject later, he repeats that the Lord "obliges him [Peter] three times to confess his love, because three times he had denied him through fear."[12] In a final homily dealing with our passage, Augustine even imagines himself addressing Peter:

> Do not feel hurt, apostle. Answer once, answer again, answer a third time. Let confession conquer three times with love, because self-assurance was conquered three times by fear. What you had bound three times must be loosed three times. Loose through love what you had bound through fear.[13]

This last homily of St. Augustine is particularly significant for the Orthodox tradition because it has been incorporated into some versions of the *Synaxarion*, the book of saints' lives appointed to be read in church, as the reading for June 29. In the *Synaxarion* version, the passage last quoted reads: "That one [Peter], to whom were given the keys of the kingdom and the right to bind and to loose, bound himself thrice by fear and cowardice, and the Lord thrice loosens him by His appeal and by his [Peter's] confession of strong

---

8. Cyril of Alexandria, *Commentary on John*, Book XII.

9. Theodore of Mopsuestia, *Theodore of Mopsuestia*, 167.

10. Ambrose, *On the Christian Faith* 5, Prologue sect. 2 (284). I owe this reference along with some of those that follow to Edward Siecienski, who generously shared with me the chapter of his work in progress, *The Papacy and the Christian East: A History*, dealing with patristic exegesis relating to St. Peter.

11. Augustine, Sermon 229P.2 (328).

12. Augustine, Sermon 229N.1 (320).

13. Augustine, Sermon 295.4 (199).

love."[14] The Greek version of the *Synaxarion* does not incorporate this homily by Augustine and so does not include a direct parallel. However, it comments on our passage in a somewhat similar way, observing: "Peter, offsetting his triple denial with the triple confession of love, was restored to his place as leader of the apostolic choir by the divine power of repentance, and was confided by the Lord with the pastoral responsibility for His Church."[15]

In honesty, it should be noted that not all patristic exegetes interpret Peter's three-fold denial and three-fold confession in this way. St. Cyril of Jerusalem sees Peter's recovery as accomplished at the moment of his weeping: "weeping shows the repentance of the heart, and therefore he [Peter] not only received forgiveness for his denial, but also held his apostolic dignity unforfeited."[16] St. John Chrysostom similarly sees Peter's recovery as brought about through his tears: Peter "performed a second baptism with the tears from his eyes. By crying bitterly, he wiped away his sin; thereafter, he was entrusted with the keys of the heavens."[17] No doubt this difference is due in part to pastoral concerns, for Cyril and Chrysostom are writing in contexts where they naturally seek to emphasize the efficacy of a tearful repentance. The other exegetes seem to be reading our episode primarily in its context within St. John's Gospel. Significantly, John is alone among the evangelists in not mentioning Peter's tears, as he is also the only one to describe Peter's later threefold confession.[18] Surely these two facts are not unconnected; it would seem that he omits Peter's weeping precisely in order to highlight the contrast between the apostle's denial and his later confession.

Despite appearances, I do not think that there is here any real contradiction. In order to reconcile the Synoptic and Johannine accounts (as interpreted by their respective exegetes), one need only suppose that Peter was in fact forgiven at the moment of his repentance, but that an open act of reconciliation was still required to fully heal the breach his action had made. After all, the same is true, according to traditional Catholic and Orthodox teaching, of anyone who has truly repented but has yet to undergo sacramental confession. Along the same lines, we may suppose that Peter's apostolic office was still his in the eyes of God, but because of his public denial it required a public seal and reaffirmation.

---

14. See more online: http://oca.org/saints/lives/2014/06/29/101840-the-holy-glorious-and-all-praised-leaders-of-the-apostles-peter.

15. Hieromonk Makarios of Simonos Petra, *The Synaxarion: The Lives of the Saints of the Orthodox Church*, vol. 5, 656.

16. Cyril of Jerusalem, *Catechetical Lectures* II.19 (13).

17. John Chrysostom, "Concerning Almsgiving and the Ten Virgins," sect. 20 (40).

18. See Matt 26:75, Mark 14:72, Luke 22:62, John 18:27.

All of this pertains to the first point made in the hymn, that Christ by his three questions "made right the three denials." Let us now turn to what the hymn does *not* say. It makes no mention of the idea that (to quote Professor Root) "Peter is here made the unique shepherd of the flock." Admittedly, the hymn hardly aims to give a complete exegesis. But the patristic exegetes of John's Gospel mentioned earlier—Cyril of Alexandria, Theodore of Mopsuestia, and Augustine—do so, and they too do not find here the bestowal of any office or responsibility different from that of the other apostles.[19] The fullest discussion is that of Augustine in the third of the homilies already cited. Augustine first affirms that the rock upon which Christ promises to build his Church is not Peter as an individual, but Peter's confession of faith: "Upon what you [Peter] have just said, *You are the Christ, the Son of the living God*, I [Christ] will build my Church."[20] In light of his confession, "Peter . . . was given the privilege of representing the whole Church," so that "it is not just one man that received these keys, but the Church in its unity."[21] Augustine goes on to buttress his point by citing the passage in John 20 where the power to remit or retain sins is given to all the apostles, and that in Matthew 18 where "whatever you bind on earth shall be bound in heaven" is said to all the disciples. This view of Peter as emblematic of the Church, and of the keys as given to the Church as a whole, is one that Augustine frequently affirms elsewhere.[22]

Significantly, both of the points I have noted in the hymn—the restoration of Peter to the apostleship, and the absence of any special commission—were affirmed formally by the bishops of the synods of Constantinople, Antioch, and Jerusalem in their response to the "Epistle to the Easterns" of Pope Pius IX in May 1848. They write: "Our divine Fathers, with one accord, teach that the sense of the thrice-repeated command, *Feed my sheep*, implied no prerogative in St. Peter over the other Apostles, least of all in his successors. It was a simple restoration to his Apostleship, from which he had fallen by his thrice-repeated denial."[23]

---

19. Professor Root cites at this point Augustine's *Tractates on the Gospel of John* 124.5 (n. 5). It is true that Augustine refers there to Peter as the "first apostle" and speaks of "the primacy of his apostleship," but his primacy is presented as an already settled fact, not something newly created or enhanced in this episode. Of course much turns on what is *meant* by such primacy, and for that question Augustine's *Homilies* are the most revealing source.

20. Augustine, Sermon 295.1 (197).

21. Ibid., Sermon 295.2 (197-98).

22. E.g., ibid., Sermon 76.1-4, 149.5-6, *Tractates on the Gospel of John* 124.5; cf. la Bonnardière, "Tu es Petrus," 451-99.

23. "Encyclical of the Eastern Patriarchs, 1848: A Reply to the Epistle of Pope Pius IX, 'to the Easterns,'" section 12.

To the extent that there is an official Orthodox interpretation of our passage, then, that is it. In light of such a view, one might wonder what it means to refer to St. Peter—as the hymns of June 29 *also* refer to him—as the "head of the honored apostles and rock of the Faith." Professor Root rightly cites St. John Chrysostom as offering a more robust view of Peter's authority than the texts I have so far mentioned. In the last of his *Homilies on St. John*, Chrysostom states twice that in this episode Christ "entrusted to Peter the primacy over his brethren."[24] Chrysostom evidently sees this event as bringing about a real change in Peter's status, for he says that because of his new primacy, Peter "not only did not depend on the other disciple [John] to act as intermediary for him [as he had at the Last Supper, John 13:24], but he even sought for information himself from the Master, on behalf of the other. And it was John who remained silent, while he was the one who spoke to Christ."[25]

That, at least, is how the relevant passage reads in the most commonly used English translation. The term here rendered "primacy" is *prostasia*. Lampe's *Patristic Greek Lexicon* offers two translations for this term: (1) support, protection, patronage; (2) charge, government, leadership. The former meaning is familiar to Orthodox from the Kontakion to the Theotokos sung at the Little Entrance, *Prostasia tōn Christianōn*, "Protection of Christians." This hymn addresses the Theotokos, not as one who has authority over Christians, but as their patroness and intercessor. Interestingly, Lampe places the passage we are discussing from Chrysostom under this meaning; that is, he takes it that, according to Chrysostom, Peter has been entrusted with the patronage and protection of the brethren. This seems to me at least as plausible a reading as that which sees him as being granted primacy in the sense of an authority to command. It is consistent with Chrysostom's remark that Peter now directly addresses the Master to ask about John, for that is more nearly the act of a patron and intercessor than an exercise of command. Furthermore, Chrysostom goes on to say that Peter and John *together* "were about to take upon themselves the guardianship of the world," so it seems that he does not wish to indicate a sharp difference between them as regards government or leadership.[26]

---

24. Chrysostom, *Saint John Chrysostom*, 470, 473. For the Greek see PG 59, col. 478, 480.

25. Ibid., 473.

26. Ibid., 474. Note also earlier in the same work, where Chrysostom describes St. John as "the pillar of the churches in the world, . . . [who] possesses the keys of heaven" (Homily 1.2). Elsewhere he remarks casually that "to me John seems to be greater, not only than the others, but even than his brother [i.e., James]," *Homilies on the Gospel of St. Matthew* 32.5 (213). In discussing the Transfiguration he states simply that Peter,

It is also important to note that a belief in the equal dignity and honor of the apostles was a commonplace in the patristic era, and was no doubt assumed by Chrysostom as understood among his hearers. St. Cyprian of Carthage, for example, although recognizing a special role for Peter as embodying the unity of the Church, observes that "the rest of the apostles were also the same as was Peter, endowed with a like partnership both of honor and power."[27] St. Ambrose states, in relation to Matt 16:15–16, that Peter's primacy was "the primacy of confession, not of honor; the primacy of belief, not of rank."[28] St. Cyril of Alexandria, in his controversy with Nestorius, uses the equality in honor of Peter and John as a stock example of how equality of honor does not imply unity of nature.[29] And we have already observed the testimony on this point of Augustine. Such statements are hardly surprising, for in the only passage in the Gospels where Christ explicitly addresses the question of rank among the apostles, he says merely that they will sit together upon thrones judging the twelve tribes of Israel.[30] He does not so much as hint that Peter is to be given precedency over the others.

Thus the passage in Chrysostom is, at best, rather ambiguous regarding the exact nature of Peter's authority. I draw attention to this ambiguity, not only to neutralize an apparently countervailing piece of evidence, but as emblematic of a larger ambiguity in the concept of authority itself. Authority can take many forms, ranging from the right to issue commands to the sort of authority (if that is the right word) possessed by a patron and protector. Somewhere within this spectrum there is what we may call collegial leadership. Anyone who has ever served as a department chairman will be only too aware that to serve as a spokesman who is in some sense responsible for the welfare of a collegial body by no means entails the right to command the members of that body. On the contrary, it may consist largely in the duty to ensure that collegial deliberations take place properly and in other ways to serve one's fellows so as to help them to attain their own proper voice. Although space forbids a full discussion, it seems to me that

---

James, and John were leaders of the apostles, without attempting to posit any ranking among them (Ibid., 56.2).

27. Cyprian of Carthage, *On the Unity of the Church* 4 (422).

28. Ambrose of Milan, *The Sacrament of the Incarnation of Our Lord* 4.32 (230). See also *On the Holy Spirit* II.158 ("Neither was Paul inferior to Peter, although the latter was the foundation of the Church [152]).

29. "For the equality honor does not unite the natures, and indeed Peter and John were equal in honor to each other, insofar as they were both disciples and holy apostles, except that the two were not one"; Cyril of Alexandria, Epistle 17.10 (84); cf. idem, *Against Nestorius* II.1.

30. Luke 22:24–30; cf. similar episodes (but with a different outcome) at Mark 10:35–45 and Matt 20:20–28, as well as Matt 19:27–28.

this is roughly the kind of leadership that Peter exercises among the apostles in Acts and in the episodes recorded elsewhere, such as Galatians 2. There is thus no inconsistency in insisting, as does the service of the Feast of Sts. Peter and Paul, that these two great apostles were "co-enthroned in grace," and allowing (as does the Greek *Synaxarion*) that Peter "was confided by the Lord with the pastoral responsibility for His Church." Equality of rank is entirely consistent with different spheres of authority when that authority is collegial.

Finally, lest there be any doubt, let us note the most direct evidence we have of how Peter understood his own place within the Church, the two Petrine epistles.[31] Both begin with the simple affirmation, "Peter, an apostle [or in 2 Peter, a servant and an apostle] of Jesus Christ." In 1 Peter, Peter goes on to address the elders simply as a "fellow elder" (συμπρεσβύτερος, 5:1). His instruction to them seems deliberately to echo the charge he had received from Christ, even using the same verb, *poimainein*: "feed (ποιμάνατε) the flock of God which is among you" (5:2). There surely could be no clearer indication that we are not to understand *poimaine* in John 21 as bestowing a unique right of command, for Peter's own usage applies it to the ministry shared by all the elders.[32] The same understated modesty is evident in II Peter. Referring to his experience as an eyewitness of the glory of Christ at the Transfiguration, Peter does no more than group himself among the other apostles: "this voice which came from heaven we heard, when we were with him on the mount" (1:18). He makes no claim that his experience bestowed upon him any special authority.

In light of such considerations, it seems to me quite unwarranted to say, as does *Pastor Aeternus*, that "Peter alone in preference to the other apostles, either singly or as a group, was endowed by Christ with the true and proper primacy of jurisdiction."[33] Nor do I think that recognizing such a primacy is the appropriate way to honor him. Although it is true that the Orthodox Church lauds Peter as the "head of the honored apostles and rock of the Faith," 'head' here has the sense of collegial leadership, not that of—to again quote *Pastor Aeternus*—"the full and supreme power of jurisdiction over the whole Church."[34] For similar reasons, the assertions of *Lumen Gentium* that

---

31. Like Professor Root, I shall assume a canonical reading of Scripture, including, in the present case, that these epistles are indeed by St. Peter.

32. Note also the similar admonition of St. Paul to the elders of the church of Ephesus, "Take heed therefore unto yourselves, and to all the flock, over the which the Holy Ghost hath made you overseers, to feed (ποιμαίνειν) the church of God, which he hath purchased with his own blood" (Acts 20:28).

33. *Pastor Aeternus* 1:3054 (611).

34. Ibid., 3:3064 (613–14).

Christ "placed blessed Peter over the other apostles" and that he "formed [the apostles] after the manner of a college or a stable group, over which he placed Peter" seem to me equally unwarranted.[35] Peter's place is not *over* the other apostles, but *among* them, as their spokesman and leader, but not as their governor.

Finally I will comment briefly upon Professor Root's very interesting explication of the contrast between the roles of Peter and the Beloved Disciple in John's Gospel. There is much here that I find helpful. I would agree that Augustine's reading of Peter as representing the Christian life *in via* and the Beloved Disciple as representing eternal beatitude is an illuminating way to think about this contrast. (That is not to say that it is the only possible way, of course, for the contrast is rich and can bear multiple interpretations.) However, I would see a larger gap than does Professor Root between Augustine's interpretation and those of Yves Congar and Hans Urs von Balthasar. The latter authors are not merely explicating a theme in the Gospel of John, but offering a global interpretation of opposing aspects or elements within the Church. For Congar these are the Church militant and the Church in glory, which he labels, respectively, as Petrine and Johannine; for Balthasar they are the elements of "office," represented by Peter, and that of love, represented by John.

What troubles me about these readings is that they tend to diminish St. Peter at the expense of St. John, making him emblematic of something that is "subordinate" and "passing." For Balthasar, Peter, as representing office, "cannot remain at the church's heart . . . [but] must go out to the edges to seek the lost sheep and haul in the fish"; for Congar, the Petrine Church is like the body in relation to the Johannine Church, which is the soul. Surely there is little evidence for such a contrast between the actual figures of Peter and John in the Gospels, much less in the New Testament as a whole. One has only to read the Johannine epistles to see that John too exercises authority and is burdened by the care of his flock. Peter, for his part, is in his own way just as much of a mystagogue and intimate of the Lord as is John.[36] There are differences between them, to be sure, but the differences reflect their characters and temperament, not a painful sacrificial mission that is given to one (Peter) but not to the other.

---

35. *Lumen Gentium* 3:4142–43 (877).

36. Byzantine exegetes sometimes developed the view of Peter as mystagogue in interesting and surprising ways. For examples, see the homilies on the Transfiguration translated in Daley, *Light on the Mountain*, especially those of an anonymous author of the seventh to eighth centuries and of St. Anastasius of Sinai (both inspired by the exclamation of Peter in Matt 17:4, "Lord, it is good for us to be here"); Gregory Palamas, *Triads* III.1.36 (on Peter at Pentecost as a model of one filled with the divine energies).

In fact, even leaving aside the figures of Peter and John, I would question the very terms in which these contrasts are presented. To contrast office and love as different elements in the Church, as does Balthasar, seems to me, if not positively mistaken, at least a case of misplaced emphasis. The love of the apostles was manifested precisely *in and through the exercise of their office*, as their words and deeds abundantly testify. The Pauline metaphor of the Church as the body of Christ offers a profound meditation upon the unity of love and authority in the Church, even when that authority may be misused.[37] More generally, to love others fully often means precisely to take up responsibility for them. Cain when he asked "am I my brother's keeper?" was simultaneously refusing both love and responsibility. To dichotomize love and office by assigning them to separate paradigmatic figures, whoever those figures may be, thus seems to me to obscure more than it illuminates.

I would also question the terms in which Congar contrasts the Church as an "institutional reality" and the Church as "the mystical body of Christ." There is no such contrast in Scripture. On the contrary, as I have mentioned, St. Paul seems to understand the exercise of authority in the Church precisely as a manifestation of the Church's mystical unity:

> And his gifts were that some should be apostles, some prophets, some evangelists, some pastors and teachers, to equip the saints for the work of ministry, for building up the body of Christ, until we all attain to the unity of the faith and to the knowledge of the Son of God, to mature manhood, to the measure of the stature of the fullness of Christ. (Eph 4:11–13, R.S.V.)

God ordains authority in the Church so as to lead us *collectively* to "the measure of the stature of the fullness of Christ." As with every divine action, there is much here that can only be pondered in a mystery. But surely in doing so it is of little help to separate sharply the institutional and the mystical, assigning them to different paradigmatic figures. Our task is not to further separate things that already, at first glance, seem so different; it is to perceive their inner unity.

In closing, I must express my regret that I am not able to agree with the Roman Catholic reading of the passage before us. To read John 21 as bestowing upon one apostle a unique primacy of jurisdiction would offer a straightforward pattern for church government that could do much to bring order where order has often been badly needed. It is surely no accident that the passage was read in this way (from the time of Pope St. Leo) primarily in the Roman church, for it was always the genius of the Romans to establish clear lines of command and straightforward, rational procedures

---

37. See Rom 12:4–8, 1 Cor 12:12–31, Eph 1:22–23, 4:4–16, 5:23, 29–30.

for resolving disagreement. This genius was one of God's gifts to the ancient Church, and the Orthodox have suffered much over the years by its loss. Let us pray that, out of the many grievous mistakes that have led us to this point, God will yet bring something of a beauty that is worthy of his great love for the Church.

Root Final Response

SOMETIMES IT IS HARD to get off the playground without getting into a fight. One can keep one's hands in one's pockets and avoid heated language, but some disputes may be unavoidable. In my presentation on John 21, I tried to avoid the traditional fights over whether and how the text does and does not imply this or that understanding of the leadership of the Bishop of Rome. Any full ecumenical engagement of the papacy must take up the task of the biblical roots of Catholic teaching and practice, but without sufficient space and time to set up an adequate context for the discussion the chance of avoiding the usual stalemate seem to me small. Thus, I took a more oblique approach, seeking to attend to details in the text and bring out some patterns often neglected by modern exegetes, patterns which might prove fruitful in the long run not just for a more fruitful ecumenical discussion, but also for a more nuanced Catholic understanding of papal primacy.

I much appreciate the responses by Professors Williams and Bradshaw, from both of which I learned new things. My response will have three parts. First, I will deal with some exegetical questions. Second, I will address some differences over the reading of the Fathers. Finally, I will take up some larger questions.

Exegetically, my presentation was limited quite consciously to a consideration of John 21. In doing so, I noted the larger pattern of Petrine texts in the New Testament of which John 21 forms a part. As noted, three of the four gospels have something that looks like a commissioning of Peter by Jesus. The interpretation of the individual passages needs to pay some attention to the larger pattern (e.g., that in each case, there is a closely linked allusion to Peter's fallibility). Nevertheless, I did not take up the interpretation of Matt 16:18 or Luke 22:32 in any detail. The "rock" passage in Matt 16:18 is notoriously open to various readings, as Professor Williams rightly notes. Peter's fallibility certainly does link him to all Christians, but that Peter is being presented in Matthew 16 or in the other passages simply as an "everyman" seems implausible. Whether the "rock" in Matthew 16 is Peter, Peter's faith, or Jesus himself, some connection between that rock and the specific individual Peter is implied by the word-play involved in Peter's new name. Otherwise, including the name-change in the passage becomes pointless. Matthew 16 does not tell us just what is that relation to the "rock" specific to Peter, but Peter is clearly being singled out in some way; he is more than "everyman."

In relation to the reading of John 21, two closely interrelated differences arose: on the one hand, does the text describe only Peter's rehabilitation after his denial of Christ or does it also depict some sort of commissioning, and on the other hand, did the Fathers tend to one or the other of these readings?

The allusion to Peter's threefold denial would seem to imply that John 21 is depicting some aspect of Peter's full recovery from his denial of Christ. But much militates against seeing that as the only or even primary point of the passage. In John 20:1–10, Peter seems already back in some sort of leadership position. When Mary Magdalene finds the tomb empty, she goes to Peter and the Beloved Disciple (v. 2) and the two go together to the tomb (v. 4). If Peter was still in such need of public rehabilitation, then why is he still the one to whom Mary Magdalene goes with the news and why is he still closely associated with the Beloved Disciple? How is he still playing a leadership role among the disciples just prior to the appearance of Jesus on the beach (21:3)? In addition, a reading of the passage as exclusively concerned with Peter's rehabilitation and involving no specific commissioning of Peter must address why Peter (and Peter alone) is told to "feed" and "tend" the sheep. Those commands can only be part of a rehabilitation without a special commissioning if his rehabilitation is part of his restoration to an apostolic office shared with the other disciples which involved then all in the same activities of tending and feeding (as Calvin reads the text). But does the Gospel of John understand the disciples as holding such an office? Apart perhaps from John 20:23 on binding and loosing sins, there is no indication in John's Gospel of such a shared, pastoral apostolic office. As far as I can tell, most recent commentators on this passage find in it some sort of commissioning of Peter.

I must again emphasize that I am not here arguing that a developed understanding of Petrine primacy can be directly read out of John 21 or, for that matter, from the New Testament as a whole. I am arguing only that, across diverse stands of the New Testament, Peter is depicted as receiving some sort of shepherd-like leadership role directly from Jesus. As I noted, this conclusion has been generally agreed in the most detailed recent ecumenical discussions, especially the Catholic-Lutheran study *Peter in the*

New Testament. To say this much is not to settle the question of the nature of papal primacy; it is merely to raise it. It does, however, form a useful point of departure for further discussion.

In my presentation, I said: "That Peter is here made the unique shepherd of the flock is the most common reading of the text in the patristic and medieval periods, both East and West." I gave references to Augustine, Chrysostom, and Gregory the Great. For medievals in the West, one could add Bonaventure and Aquinas. "Most common" does not mean "all" and there are definite exceptions, the most important, as Professor Bradshaw notes, being Cyril of Alexandria.

I should have been clearer that I was not denying that the Fathers found other things going on in John 21, including some aspect of Peter's rehabilitation. As Professor Bradshaw rightly notes, this rehabilitation does play a prominent role in patristic discussions. In a sermon, focus on Peter's penitence would be a natural lesson to be drawn from the text, of more relevance to the hearers than Peter's leadership role. Rehabilitation and commissioning can both be found and many Fathers found both. Professor Bradshaw notes Theodore of Mopsuestia's emphasis on Peter's rehabilitation, but Theodore could also say: "It is Peter, *chosen by the Lord himself to feed his flock*, who merits three times to hear the words 'Feed my little lambs; feed my lambs; feed my sheep.' And so, by feeding well the flock of Christ with the food of faith, he effaced the sin of his former fall." Here both some sort of commissioning by Jesus and Peter's rehabilitation are combined.

Very little of my presentation depends on whether such a reading of John 21 is merely "common" in the patristic and medieval periods (which seems to me beyond dispute) or "most common." Again, I am here making no argument that such interpreters generally found a "right to command" (Professor Bradshaw's phrase) in John 21, merely that they found in this passage some sort of commissioning of Peter.

My primary interest in the presentation was in the complex ways John 21 (and the other Petrine texts with which it forms a pattern) contextualize Peter, both by juxtaposing his commissioning with reminders of his fallibility and by contrasting him with the Beloved Disciple. On both these points, interesting questions were raised by the respondents.

Professor Williams asks a reasonable question: how bad is bad? The point of the question, I take it, is just how bad must leadership be before one deserts such leadership. The Catholic believes that the primacy of the Bishop of Rome is not a human creation we can desert when it fails in this way or that, but a divine gift and mandate to which the Church is bound. Of course, the Catholic also believes that, by the assistance of the Holy Spirit, the teaching of the Bishop of Rome will not fundamentally mislead. The

Truth will be found in such teaching—perhaps badly put, with a heavy hand, without nuance, but there to be found. Because of that divine institution and assurance, the Catholic has the blessing of never having to consider leaving, of being free to commit to the specific, historically constituted "love of the brothers and sisters which is the communion of Church."

That blessing brings with it a peculiar ecumenical challenge: to show, even when papal leadership leaves something to be desired (which is to be expected, to some degree), that commitment to such leadership enhances and deepens Christian life, thought, and holiness. Popes may need to be respectfully challenged in certain ways; such may be the way the Holy Spirit assists the Pope. Some popes may be the cross we bear. Nevertheless, we are to bear them, joyfully, as a gift of God and do so as a witness to Catholic communion. Such a witness will, I think, be just as ecumenically important as detailed exegetical arguments about Matthew 16, Luke 22, and John 21.

Professor Bradshaw's question is about the figural reading of the Peter-Beloved Disciple relation developed by Augustine, Congar, and Balthasar. In particular, he is concerned with a possible opposition between an institutional and a spiritual Church. This worry is quite reasonable, especially in the shortened version I had to give of Congar and Balthasar. But these are distinctions, not separations. As I noted, Balthasar in particular emphasizes that John "merges" with Peter following John 21 and Jesus's question to Peter "Do you love me?"

I introduced this figural reading because I believe it is ecumenically important. Catholics need to show that hierarchy, the "Petrine church," the structures that serve the mediation of salvation, exists for something more fundamental, the Johannine church, the life of unity with the Trinity and thus with all the saints. In heaven, the structures of the Petrine church will be left behind (there is no temple in the New Jerusalem, Rev 21:22); the communion that is the Johannine church will be eschatologically permanent.

The details of this figural reading can certainly be questioned, but I do think it gets at an important point the Gospel of John is making with its contrast of Peter and the Beloved Disciple. Catholics (and, in their own way, Orthodox) need to show in their communal lives that this subordination of the Petrine to the Johannine, of hierarchy to that which hierarchy serves, life in union with Christ and the Spirit, is real. Too often, others do not see this subordination and arguments about papacy and episcopacy then fall on deaf ears.

The Second Vatican Council emphasized that renewal of one's own tradition is an important ecumenical task (*Unitatis redintegratio*, §7). Ecumenical encounters should move all of us to greater fidelity to Christ and renewal should make our forms of life more attractive and open to others.

Catholics need to consider how we understand and live out Christ's commission to Peter. Attention to the biblical texts where we find that commission is a necessary step in that process.

Bibliography

Aagaard, Anna Marie, and Peter Bouteneff. *Beyond the East-West Divide: The World Council of Churches and The Orthodox Problem.* Geneva: World Council of Churches, 2001.

Aland, Kurt, ed. *Kurzgefaßte Liste der griechischen Handschri en des Neuen Testaments.* Berlin: De Gruyter, 1994.

Ambrose. *On the Christian Faith.* In vol. 10 of *The Nicene and Post-Nicene Fathers,* Series 2. Edited by Henry Wace. Translated by E. Romestin. Peabody, MA: Hendrickson, 1996.

———. *On the Holy Spirit.* In vol. 10 of *The Nicene and Post-Nicene Fathers,* Series 2. Edited by Henry Wace. Translated by E. Romestin. Peabody, MA: Hendrickson, 1996.

Ashton, John. *Understanding the Fourth Gospel.* Oxford: Oxford University Press, 2007.

Augustine. "Adulterous Marriages." In *St. Augustine Treatises on Marriage and Other Subjects.* Vol. 27 of *Fathers of the Church Patristic Series.* New York: Fathers of the Church, 1955.

———. *Homilies on the First Epistle of John.* In vol. 1 of *The Works of Saint Augustine.* Edited by Daniel E. Doyle and Thomas Martin. Translated by Boniface Ramsey. Hyde Park, NY: New City, 2008.

———."Letters." In *Nicene and Post-Nicene Fathers, Vol. 1 (First Series),* 209-593. Repr., Peabody, MA: Hendrickson, 1886.

———. *The Literal Meaning Genesis.* In vol. 41 of *Ancient Christian Writers.* Mahwah, NJ: Paulist, 1982.

———. "Sermon 229." In *The Works of Saint Augustine.* Vol III, *Essential Sermons,* edited by Boniface Ramsey and translated by Edmund Hill, 283-85. New Rochelle, NY: New City, 1993.

———. *Tractates on the Gospel of John.* Vol. 7 of *A Select Library of the Nicene and Post Nicene Fathers of the Christian Church,* edited by Philip Schaff. Peabody, MA: Hendrickson, 1994.

Balthasar, Hans Urs von. *The Office of Peter and the Structure of the Church.* 2nd ed. Translated by Andrée Emery. San Francisco: Ignatius, 2007.

Barnes, Corey. *Christ's Two Wills in Scholastic Thought: The Christology of Aquinas and Its Historical Contexts.* Toronto: PIMS, 2012.

Barrett, C. K. "The Dialectical Theology of St. John." In *New Testament Essays.* London: SPCK, 1972.

Bartsch, Hans Werner, ed. *Kerygma and Myth: A Theological Debate.* New York: Harper & Row, 1961.
Basil. *St. Basil the Great on the Holy Spirit.* Translated by Dave Anderson. Crestwood, NY: St. Vladimir's Seminary, 1980.
Bathrellos, Demetrios. *The Byzantine Christ: Person, Nature and Will in the Christology of Saint Maximus the Confessor.* Oxford: Oxford University Press, 2004.
Bauckham, Richard. *The Testimony of the Beloved Disciple: Narrative, History and Theology in the Gospel of John.* Grand Rapids: Baker, 2007.
Behr, John. *Irenaeus of Lyons: Identifying Christianity.* Oxford: Oxford University Press, 2015.
———. "Reading the Fathers Today." In *A Celebration of Living Theology: A Festschrift in Honour of Andrew Louth,* edited by Justin Mihoc and Leonard Aldea, 7–19. New York: Bloomsbury, 2014.
Bernard of Clairvaux. *On Loving God: De Diligendo Deo.* Surrey, BC: Eremitical, 2010.
Betz, John R. "After Barth: A New Introduction to Przywara's Analogia Entis." In *The Analogy of Being: Invention of the Antichrist or the Wisdom of God?,* edited by T. J. White, 35–86. Grand Rapids: Eerdmans, 2011.
Beza, Theodore. *Jesu Christi Domini Nostri Novum Testamentum sive Novum Foedus. . . Ejusdem Theod. Bezae.* Cantabrigiae: Danielis, 1642.
Boersma, Hans. *Heavenly Participation: The Weaving of a Sacramental Tapestry.* Grand Rapids: Eerdmans, 2011.
Boethius. *Consolation of Philosophy.* Translated by David R. Slavitt. Cambridge, MA: Harvard University Press, 2010.
Bondi, Roberta C. *Three Monophysite Christologies: Severus of Antioch, Philoxenus of Mabbug and Jacob of Sarug.* London: Oxford University Press, 1976.
Bonhoeffer, Dietrich. *Letters and Papers from Prison.* Vol. 8 of *Dietrich Bonhoeffer Works.* Edited by John W. de Gruchy. Translated by Isabel Best, Lisa E. Dahill, Reinhard Kraus, and Nancy Lukens. Minneapolis, MN: Fortress, 2010.
Breck, John. "John 21: Appendix, Epilogue or Conclusion?" *St Vladimir's Theological Quarterly* 36.1 (1992) 27–49.
———. *The Power of the Word: In the Worshiping Church.* Crestwood, NY: St. Vladimir's Seminary, 1986.
Brown, Raymond E. *The Churches the Apostles Left Behind.* New York: Paulist, 1984.
———. *The Community of the Beloved Disciple: The Life, Loves, and Hates of an Individual Church in New Testament Times.* New York: Paulist Press, 1979.
———. *The Epistles of John.* New York: Doubleday, 1982.
———. *The Gospel According to John.* In vol. 29 of *The Anchor Bible,* edited by William Foxwell Albright and David Noel Freedman. New York: Doubleday, 1966.
Brown, Raymond E., Karl P. Donfried, and John Reumann. *Peter in the New Testament: A Collaborative Assessment by Protestant and Roman Catholic Scholars.* Minneapolis: Augsburg, 1973.
Bruner, Frederick Dale. *The Gospel of John: A Commentary.* Grand Rapids: Eerdmans, 2012.
Burgess, Joseph. *In Search of Christian Unity: Basic Consensus/Basic Differences.* Minneapolis: Fortress, 1991.
Caird, G. B. *A Commentary on the Revelation of St. John the Divine.* New York: Harper & Row, 1966.

Calvin, John. *The Gospel According to St. John 11-21 and The First Epistle of John*. Translated by T. H. L. Parker. Grand Rapids: Eerdmans, 1961.

———. *A Harmony of the Gospels: Matthew, Mark, and Luke*. In vol. 2 of *Calvin's New Testament Commentaries*. Edited by David W. Torrance and Thomas F. Torrance. Translated by T. H. L. Parker. Grand Rapids: Eerdmans, 1979.

———. *Institutes of the Christian Religion*, Vol. 2. Edited by John T. McNeill. Translated by Ford Lewis Battles. Philadelphia: Westminster, 1960.

Carson, D. A. *The Gospel According to John*. PNTC. Grand Rapids: Eerdmans, 1990.

Casey, Maurice, *Is John's Gospel True?* London: Routledge, 1996.

Chrysostom, John. *Commentary on Saint John the Apostle and Evangelist: Homilies 48-88*. Translated by Sister Thomas Aquinas Goggin. The Fathers of the Church, vol. 41. New York: Fathers of the Church, 1960.

———. "Concerning Almsgiving and the Ten Virgins." In *On Repentance and Almsgiving*, translated by Gus George Christo. *Fathers of the Church*, vol. 96. Washington, DC: The Catholic University of America Press, 1998.

Congar, Yves. *Divided Christendom: A Catholic Study of the Problem of Reunion*. London: Geoffrey Bles, 1939.

———. *Tradition and Traditions: An Historical and a Theological Essay*. London: Burns and Oates, 1967.

Cornelius À Lapide. *The Great Commentary of Cornelius À Lapide: The Holy Gospel According to St. John*. Translated by Thomas Wimberley Mossman. Edited by Michael J. Miller. Fitzwilliam, NH: Loreto, 2008.

Coupler-Ross, Elizabeth. *On Death and Dying*. New York: Scribner, 1969.

Cyril of Alexandria. *Commentary on the Gospel of John*. In vol. 1 of *A Library of the Fathers of the Holy Catholic Church Anterior to the Division of the East and the West*. London: James Parker, 1874.

Cullmann, Oscar. *Christ And Time: The Primitive Christian Conception of Time and History*. Translated by Floyd V. Filson. Philadelphia: Westminster, 1950.

———. *Peter: Disciple, Apostle, Martyr: A Historical and Theological Study*. Translated by Floyd V. Filson. Philadelphia: Westminster, 1953.

Custer, Jack. *The Holy Gospel: A Byzantine Perspective*. Woodland Park, NJ: God With Us, 2004.

Daloz, Lucien. *Nous avons vu sa gloire: Une lecture spirituelle de Jean*. Paris: Desclée de Brouwer, 1989.

Denzinger, Heinrich, and Peter Hünermann, eds. *Enchiridion Symbolorum Definitionum et Declarationum de Rebus Fidei et Morum*. 43rd ed. San Francisco: Ignatius, 2012.

Derrett, J. Duncan M. "Law in the New Testament: The Story of the Woman Taken in Adultery." *New Testament Studies* 10 (1963) 1-26.

Desjeux, Xavier. *Voir l'invisible: l'Évangile de Jean, un chemin de contemplation*. Nouan-le-Fuzelier: Éditions des Béatitudes, 2001.

Ephrem. *Commentary on Tatian's Diatessaron*. In *Saint Ephrem's Commentary on Tatian's Diatessaron: An English Translation of Chester Beatty Syriac MS 709*. Edited and translated by C. McCarthy. Oxford: Oxford University Press, 1993.

Esler, Philip Francis, and Ronald A. Piper. *Lazarus, Mary and Martha: Social-scientific Approaches to the Gospel of John*. Minneapolis, MN: Fortress, 2006.

Evagrius of Pontus. "On Prayer." In *The Philokalia*, vol. 1, edited by G. E. H. Palmer, Philip Sherrard, and Kallistos Ware. London: Faber and Faber, 1979.

Fee, Gordon. "Codex Sinaiticus in the Gospel of John: A Contribution to Methodology in Establishing Textual Relationships." *New Testament Studies* 15 (1968) 23-44.

Fowl, Stephen E., ed. *Theological Interpretation of Scripture*. Malden, MA: Blackwell, 1997.

Frank, S. L., ed. *A Solovyov Anthology* (with introduction by Hans Urs von Balthasar). London: Saint Austin, 2001.

Funk, F. X., ed. *Didascalica et Constitutiones Apostolorum*. Paderbornae, 1905.

Gargano, Guido-Innocenzo. *Lectio divina su il Vangelo di Giovanni*, vol. 1. Bologna: Edizioni Dehoniane, 1992.

Garrigues, Jean-Miguel. *Le Saint-Esprit sceau de la Trinité: Le Filioque de l'originalité trinitaire de l'Esprit dans sa personne et sa mission*. Paris: Cerf, 2011.

Gavrilyuk, Paul L. Review of "Beyond the East-West Divide: The World Council of Churches and the Orthodox Problem" by Aagaard & Bouteneff. *Occasional Papers on Religion in Eastern Europe* 24.2 (2004) 36-40.

Gregory, Caspar René. *Textkritik des Neuen Testamentes*. Leipzig: J. C. Hinrichs, 1900-1909.

Gregory the Great. *Forty Gospel Homilies*. Translated by Dom David Hurst. Cistercian Studies Series. Kalamazoo, MI: Cistercian, 1990.

Hart, David Bentley. *The Beauty of the Infinite: The Aesthetics of Christian Truth*. Grand Rapids: Eerdmans, 2004.

———. "No Shadow of Turning: On Divine Impassibility." *Pro Ecclesia* (2002) 184-92.

Hays, Richard B. *Reading Backwards: Figural Christology and the Fourfold Gospel Witness*. Waco: Baylor University Press, 2014.

Hendrix, Scott H. *Luther and the Papacy: Stages in a Reformation Conflict*. Philadelphia: Fortress, 1981.

Hengel, Martin. *The Johannine Question*. London: SCM Press, 1989.

Hennecke, Edgar. *New Testament Apocrypha*. Philadelphia: Westminster, 1963.

Henry, Matthew. *Matthew Henry's Commentary on the Whole Bible: Vol. 5, Matthew To John*. London: n.p., 1714.

Hermann von Soden. *Die Schri en des Neuen Testaments*. 4 vols. Berlin: Glaue, 1902-1910.

Hill, Charles E. *The Johannine Corpus in the Early Church*. Oxford: Oxford University Press, 2006.

Hills, Edward F. *The King James Version Defended*. 4th ed. Des Moines, IA: Christian Research, 1984.

Hodges, Zane C. "The Woman Taken in Adultery (John 7:53-8:11): the Text." *Bibliotheca Sacra* 136 (1977) 318-32.

Holmes, Michael W. *The Apostolic Fathers: Greek Texts and English Translations*. 3rd ed. Grand Rapids: Baker Academic, 2007.

Jean-Philippe, Kaefer. Review of "Les Personnages dans l'évangile de Jean: Miroire pour une Christologie Narrative" by Alain Marchadour. *Revue Théologique de Louvain*: 36.2 (2005) 239-40.

Jeffrey, David Lyle. "False Witness and the Just Use of Evidence in the Wycliff Pistel of Swete Susan." In *The Judgment of Susannah: Authority and Witness*, edited by Ellen Spolsky, 57-71. Atlanta: Scholars, 1996.

Jenson, Robert W. *Systematic Theology. The Works of God*. Vol. 2. Oxford: Oxford University Press, 2001.

John Cassian. *John Cassian: Conferences*. Edited by Colm Luibhéid. Translated by Eugène Pichery. *The Classics of Western Spirituality*, vol. 7. New York: Paulist, 1985.

Johnson, Alan F. "A Stylistic Trait of the Fourth Gospel in the *Pericope Adulterae*." *Bulletin of the Evangelical Theological Society* 9 (1966) 92.

Jüngel, Eberhard. *God as the Mystery of the World: On the Foundation of the Theology of the Crucified One; in the Dispute between Theism and Atheism*. Grand Rapids: Eerdmans, 1983.

Käsemann, Ernst. "The Canon of the New Testament and the Unity of the Church." In *Essays on New Testament Themes*, 95–107. Naperville, IL: Alec R. Allenson, 1964.

———. *The Testament of Jesus*. Philadelphia: Fortress, 1968.

Kasper, Walter. *That They All Might Be One: The Call to Unity Today*. London: Continuum, 2008.

Keating, Daniel. "Supersessionism in Cyril of Alexandria." *Studia Patristica* 68 (2013) 119–24.

Keith, Chris. *The Pericope Adulterae: The Gospel of John, and the Literacy of Jesus*. Leiden: Brill, 2009.

———. "Recent and Previous Research on the Pericope Adulterae (John 7.53 8.11)." *Currents in Biblical Research* 6 (2008) 377–404.

Kelly, Anthony, and Francis J Moloney. *Experiencing God in the Gospel of John*. New York: Paulist, 2003.

Kelsey, David H. *Proving Doctrine: The Uses of Scripture in Modern Theology*. Harrisburg, PA: Trinity Press International, 1999.

———. *The Uses of Scripture in Recent Theology*. Philadelphia: Fortress, 1975.

Kik, J. Marcellus. *Ecumenism and the Evangelical*. Philadelphia: Presbyterian and Reformed, 1958.

Law, Timothy Michael. *When God Spoke Greek: The Septuagint and the Making of the Christian Bible*. Oxford: Oxford University Press, 2013.

Lester, J. Cappon, ed. *The Adams-Jefferson Letters: The Complete Correspondence Between Thomas Jefferson and Abigail and John Adams*. Williamsburg, VA: University of North Carolina Press, 1959.

Levering, Matthew. *Participatory Biblical Exegesis: A Theology of Biblical Interpretation*. Notre Dame, IN: University of Notre Dame Press, 2008.

Lewis, C. S. Introduction to *On the Incarnation*, by Athanasius. Translated by John Behr. Crestwood, NY: St. Vladimir's Seminary, 2012.

———. *Mere Christianity*. New York: Harper Collins, 2009.

Lincoln, Andrew. *Truth on Trial: The Lawsuit Motif in the Fourth Gospel*. Grand Rapids: Baker Academic, 2001.

Lindars, Barnabas. "Rebuking the Spirit: A New Analysis of the Lazarus Story of John 11." *New Testament Studies* 38 (1992) 89–104.

Lossky, Vladimir. *In the Image and Likeness of God*. Crestwood, NY: St. Vladimir's Seminary, 2001.

Luther, Martin. "On the Papacy in Rome, Against the Most Celebrated Romanist in Leipzig." In *Church and Ministry I*. Luther's Works 39, 49–104. Philadelphia: Fortress, 1970.

MacEvilly, John. *An Exposition of the Epistles of St. Paul and of the Catholic Epistles, Vol. 1*. 3rd ed. Dublin: W. B. Kelly, 1875.

Mathewes-Green, Frederica. *First Fruits of Prayer: A Forty-day Journey through the Canon of St. Andrew*. Brewster, MA: Paraclete, 2006.

McGrath, Alister. "Evangelical Anglicanism: A Contradiction in Terms?" In *Evangelical Anglicans: Their Role and Influence in the Church Today*, edited by R. T. France and A. E. McGrath, 10–21. London: SPCK, 1993.
Melodus, Romanus. "Kontakion on the woman of Samaria." Translated by Marjorie Carpenter. *Kontakia of Romanos, Byzantine Melodist*, vol. 1. Columbia: University of Missouri Press, 1970.
Metzger, Bruce. *A Textual Commentary on the Greek New Testament*. New York: United Bible Societies, 1971.
———. *The Text of the New Testament*. Oxford: Oxford University Press, 1964.
Meyer, Harding. "Fundamental Difference—Fundamental Consensus." *Mid-Stream* 25 (1986) 247–59.
Mitchell, Margaret. *Paul, the Corinthians and the Birth of Christian Hermeneuetics*. Cambridge: Cambridge University Press, 2010.
Moberly, Walter. *The Bible, Theology, and Faith: A Study of Abraham and Jesus*. Cambridge: Cambridge University Press, 2000.
Moltmann, Jurgen. *The Crucified God: The Cross of Christ as the Foundation and Criticism of Christian Theology*. San Francisco: Harper and Row, 1974.
Morard, Martin. "Thomas D'Aquin Lecteur Des Conciles." *Archivum Franciscanum Historicum* 98 (2005) 211–365.
———. "Une source de saint Thomas d'Aquin: le deuxième concile de Constantinople." *Revue des Sciences Philosophiques et Théologiques* 81 (1997) 21–56.
Morris, Leon. *The Gospel According to John*. Grand Rapids: Eerdmans, 1971.
Mother Mary, and Kallistos Ware, trans. *The Lenten Triodion*. London: Faber and Faber, 1978.
Müller, Mogens. *The First Bible of the Church: A Plea for the Septuagint*. Sheffield: Sheffield Academic, 1996.
Murray, Paul, ed. *Receptive Ecumenism and the Call to Catholic Learning: Exploring a Way for Contemporary Ecumenism*. Oxford: Oxford University Press, 2008.
Nassar, Seraphim. *Divine Prayers and Services of the Catholic Orthodox Church of Christ*. Englewood, NJ: Antiochian Orthodox Christian Archdiocese of America, 1979.
Neuhaus, Richard John. "Salvation is from the Jews." *First Things*, November 2001. Online: http://www.firstthings.com/article/2001/11/8220salvation-is-from-the-jews.
Newman, John Henry. *An Essay on the Development of Christian Doctrine*. Notre Dame: University of Notre Dame Press, 1989.
Origen. *Commentary on the Gospel of John, Books 13–32*, translated by Ronald E. Heine. Vol. 89 of *The Fathers of the Church*. Washington, DC: The Catholic University of America Press, 1993.
Painter, John. *1, 2 and 3 John*. Sacra Pagina, vol. 18. Collegeville, MN: Liturgical, 2002.
Papadopoulos, Gerasimos. *The Gospel of St. John: A Commentary*. Translated by Peter A. Chamberas. Brookline, MA: Holy Cross Orthodox Press, 2010.
Parsenios, George L. *Rhetoric and Drama in the Johannine Lawsuit Motif*. Tübingen: Mohr Siebeck, 2010.
Pentiuc, Eugen J. *The Old Testament in Eastern Orthodox Tradition*. Oxford: Oxford University Press, 2014.
Pesch, Rudolf. *Die biblischen Grundlagen des Primats*. Freiburg: Herder, 2001.

Petra, Hieromonk Makarios of Simonos. *The Synaxarion: The Lives of the Saints of the Orthodox Church*. Translated by Maria Rule, and Joanna Burton. Vol. 5. Ormylia, Greece: Holy Convent of the Annunciation of Our Lady, 2005.

Poole, Matthew. *Annotations upon the Holy Bible, being a Continuation of Mr. Pool's Work by Certain Judicious and Learned Divines*. London: n.p., 1685.

Potterie, Ignace de la. *The Hour of Jesus*. Staten Island, NY: Alba, 1990.

Radner, Ephraim. "Bad Bishops: A Key to Anglican Ecclesiology." *Anglican Theological Review* 82 (2000) 321.

Raith, Charles, II. *Aquinas & Calvin on Romans: God's Justification and Our Participation*. Oxford: Oxford University Press, 2014.

Renan, Ernest. *Vie de Jésus*. Paris: Gallimard/Folio, 1974.

Ridderbos, Herman. *The Gospel According to John: A Theological Commentary*. Grand Rapids: Eerdmans, 1997.

Robinson, Maurice A. "Preliminary Observations Regarding the *Pericope Adulterae* Based upon Fresh Collation of Nearly All Continuous-text Manuscripts and over One Hundred Lectionaries." *Filologia Neotestamentaria* 13 (2000) 35–59.

Salvation Army. "From the Heart of Jesus Flowing." In *The Song Book of the Salvation Army*. 3rd ed. London: Salvationist, 1970.

Shilling, Frederick A. "The Story of Jesus and the Adulteress." *Anglican Theological Review* 37 (1955) 91–106.

Schnackenburg, Rudolf. *Commentary on the Gospel of John*. Translated by Kevin Smith. New York: Seabury, 1980.

Schönborn, Christoph von. *Sophrone de Jerusalem: vie Monastique et Confession Dogmatique*. Paris: Beauchesne, 1972.

Simonetti, Manlio. *Biblical Interpretation in the Early Church: An Historical Introduction to Patristic Exegesis*. Translated by J. A. Hughes. Edinburgh: Bloomsbury T. & T. Clark, 2002.

Smith, D. Moody. *The Theology of John*. Cambridge: Cambridge University Press, 1995.

Solovyov, Vladimir Sergeyevich. *A Solovyov Anthology*. Edited by S. L. Frank. Introduction by Hans Urs von Balthasar. New York: Saint Austin, 2001.

Spolsky, Ellen. *The Judgment of Susannah: Authority and Witness*. Society of Biblical Literature: Early Judaism and its Literature. Atlanta: Scholars Press, 1996.

Stump, Eleonore, and Norman Kretzman. "Eternity." *Journal of Philosophy* 8 (1981) 429–58.

Tanner, Norman, trans. *Decrees of the Ecumenical Councils*, vol. 1. Washington, DC: Georgetown University Press, 1990.

Theodore of Mopsuestia, *Commentary on the Gospel of John*. Ancient Christian Texts. Translated by Marco Conti. Downers Grove, IL: IVP Academic, 2010.

Thomas Aquinas. *Commentary on the Gospel of John*. Translated by James A. Weisheipl and Fabian Larcher. Washington DC: Catholic University of America Press.

Thompson, Marianne Meye. *The God of the Gospel of John*. Grand Rapids: Eerdmans, 2001.

———. *The Humanity of Jesus in the Fourth Gospel*. Philadelphia: Fortress, 1988.

Trites, Allison, *The New Testament Concept of Witness*. Society for New Testament Monograph Series, vol. 31. Cambridge: Cambridge University Press, 1977.

———. "The Woman Taken in Adultery." *Bibliotheca Sacra* 131.522 (1974) 139–46.

Tyrrell, George. *Christianity at the Crossroads*. London: Longmans, Green, 1913.

von Schönborn, Christoph. *Sophrone de Jerusalem: vie monastique et confession dogmatique.* Théologie historique 20. Paris: Beauchesne, 1972.

Wahlde, Urban C. von. *A Commentary on the Gospel and Letters of John. Vol. 2: Commentary on the Gospel of John.* Grand Rapids: Eerdmans, 2010.

Weigel, George. *Evangelical Catholicism: Deep Reform in the 21st-Century Church.* New York: Basic Books, 2014.

Whitacre, Rodney A. *John.* Downers Grove, IL: InterVarsity, 1999.

White, Thomas Joseph. *The Incarnate Lord: A Thomistic Study in Christology.* Washington, DC: The Catholic University of America Press, 2015.

———. "Kenoticism and the Divinity of Christ Crucified." *The Thomist* 75 (2011) 1–41.

———. "The Voluntary Action of the Earthly Christ and the Necessity of the Beatific Vision." *The Thomist* 69 (2005) 497–534.

Williams, D. H. "The Diffusive Disintegration of Catholicity." *Pro Ecclesia* 23 (2003) 389–93.

Wren, Brian A. *Poems of Grace: Texts of The Hymnal 1982.* New York: Church Publishing, 2000.

Wright, N. T. *Surprised by Scripture: Engaging Contemporary Issues.* San Francisco: HarperOne, 2015.

Yeago, David. "The Spirit, the Church, and the Scriptures: Biblical Interpretation and Interpretation Revisited." In *Knowing the Triune God*, edited by James J. Buckley and David S. Yeago. Grand Rapids: Eerdmans, 2001.

Young, Frances M. *Biblical Exegesis and the Formation of Christian Culture.* Cambridge: Cambridge University Press, 1997.

Yule, G. Udnv. *The Statistical Study of Literary Vocabulary.* Nottingham: Shoestring, 1968.

Zevini, Giorgio S. D. B. *Commentaire spirituel de l'Évangile de Jean.* Translated by Madeleine Rayer. Paris: Médiaspaul, 1995.

www.ingramcontent.com/pod-product-compliance
Lightning Source LLC
Chambersburg PA
CBHW030614230426
43661CB00053B/1984